AF560088

PEASANTS BETRAYED

Peasants Betrayed

Essays in India's Colonial History

KAPIL KUMAR

MANOHAR
2011

First published 2011

ISBN 978-81-7304-919-4

Published by
Ajay Kumar Jain *for*
Manohar Publishers & Distributors
4753/23 Ansari Road, Daryaganj
New Delhi 110 002

Typeset by
Kohli Print
Delhi 110 051

Printed at
Salasar Imaging Systems
Delhi 110 035

To all those peasants
who were the victims of
'forced suicides' and thus
lost their lives in today's
modern India

Contents

PART 3: COMMUNALISM?

Preface

The present work is a collection of my research papers that were published between 1982–9. I also includes two unpublished papers. The purpose is to make these writings which discuss the peasants' issues *vis-à-vis* nationalism and colonialism during the 1920s, 1930s and 1940s available to the students and scholars at one place. Most of the research on these papers was carried out during the late 1970s and 1980s—particularly between 1982 and 1985 during my post-doctoral fellowship at Nehru Memorial Museum & Library, New Delhi. I could not devote much time to research after joining my present institution as the concentration was more on conceptualizing and developing multi-media History course materials for the students. 1992 onwards I switched over to applied history and as a result conceptualized, coordinated and edited the tourism programmes. However, in the last three years, along with the tourism studies, I have been again concentrating on historical research. My colleagues in the History faculty in IGNOU had all been insisting that I should return to History writing and this insistence has been very inspiring. For this, I am grateful to them, particularly Profs. Swaraj Basu and Abha Singh.

I would like to acknowledge all scholars and friends who have been a source of inspiration and discussions with whom stimulated my thought process. I owe a lot to Dr. S.K. Mittal (former Head of History Department, Meerut College, Meerut and my Ph.D. Supervisor) whose motivation and guidance shaped my career.

I can never forget the generosity and guidance of Late Prof. Ravinder Kumar (former Director, Nehru Memorial Museum & Library, New Delhi) in his encouragement for making a place for myself in Delhi for I was educated in a small town like Meerut and started my teaching career from Ghaziabad.

During the initial phase of my research in the mid-1970s I had some interesting experiences of the academic life in Delhi. There were scholars like Prof. Sumit Sarkar and Prof. K.N. Panikkar who encouraged scholars like us coming from small places like Meerut and I am greatful to them for their encouragement and guidance. At the same time one encountered the 'elite' who found it difficult to accept youngesters like us as researchers.

Discussions with Smita Tiwari Jassal, Sujata Patel, Gyanesh Kudasiya, A. Murali, Asad Zaidi, Biswamoy Pati, Suneet Chopra, Vinay Behal and others helped me sharpen my ideas. Late Prof. A.N. Pandeya (IIT, Delhi) was a great intellectual inspiration who often showed me the path towards understanding Gramsci's writings, the Ramcharitmanas and Vedic interpretations. Kumkum Sangari, Sudesh Vaid and Tanika Sarkar's intellectual inputs helped me in developing a perspective on gender issues in History.

I am also grateful to friends like Profs. Y. Vaikuntham, Dilbagh Singh, Bhagwan Josh, S. Irfan Habib, Ranjan Chakrabarty, Sajal Nag and my colleagues Profs. A.R. Khan, Ravinder Kumar, A.S. Narang, Pradeep Sahni, E. Vayunandan and Darvesh Gopal for constantly encouraging me in my academic endeavours. I am extremely grateful to my parents, wife and son, who even in spite of my repeated negligence of responsibilities towards them always remained a strong source of inspiration. I can't end without thanking Parag Gupta, Senior Assistant at IGNOU who took all the pains and provided all assistance in the preparation of this book.

New Delhi
30 April 2011

KAPIL KUMAR

Introduction

Why study the peasants? What is the relevance of such historical research in the contemporary context? Why talk of peasants' betrayal? These are questions one may ask before picking up this collection of research papers. As per my understanding, with the exception of India being an independent democratic nation and in spite of the development that has taken over the last sixty-three years, the peasants are still confronted with the issues, problems and to a large extent exploitation of the same magnitude that they faced and fought against during the colonial era. The intentional marginalization and side-tracking of their issues for the sake of fighting the Bigger Zamindar, i.e. the British, with an assurance by the leadership to take up and solve them in independent India have proved to be fallacious as demonstrated in contemporary society. And today, I feel ashamed when in spite of all tall claims made by the central government and the parties in power in the states, one sees the dead body of a peasant who has committed suicide on the TV screen, and mind it, its not just an isolated case from Vidarbha but the numbers are increasing every day even in Punjab or many other so-called prosperous states. How should one feel when one sees poor children replacing bullocks to plough the farms of a politician? One can only praise the news channel for telecasting it and then witness some political shouting over the issue and soon something else will be there to relegate this issue into the background and a few days later it fades from our memory also. On the one hand, the urban and semi-urban consumers are fed up with soaring agricultural prices and on the other hand, the producers are famished. How does one react to not one but many Nandigrams? Doesn't the acquisition of peasants' land by the state for handing them out to large estate developers and multi-nationals remind one of the snatching of peasants' fields by the taluqdars and the zamindars during the colonial period? The landless keep on wandering for their livelihood and we have a parliament with more than three hundred members who are multi-billionaires. This showcases India as an extremely rich country with a large poor populace; that the rich and upper middle classes flourish in independent India at the cost of the poor.

No doubt, we have excelled in information technology, our satellites have landed on the moon, the stock markets are soaring, and there are great foreign currency reserves, higher literacy, more schools, colleges and universities, a much better infrastructure, a rising middle class, etc. One can go on adding to the list of achievements of independent India in many glorious ways, be it the globalization or the domination of market economy where we have even put education on sale as a commodity rather than imparting it. In spite of this multi-fold progress and development how long can one keep the curtain on ground realities? They have to be accounted for or else in which direction would this nation go? There are diverse directions pulling the country often in collaboration with one or the other as per the suitability of the interests. Caste ghettos are strengthened. Parochial regional sentiments dominate in all states—the voices raised in Maharashtra are no exception. Criminalization of politics, stoking communalism through instigation or appeasement, rampant corruption at all levels in life and so on are the characteristics of Indian political life. Perhaps, these are the aspects that lead our leaders to declare with pride that India is still a nation in the making. How different are the present policies in terms of dividing the society or appeasing some than those adopted under the British rule? How come you become a refugee in your own country? Can there be a more sick society where the living are sometimes declared dead to grab their belongings or pensions? Can one understand the agony and pain of these elder citizens who have formed the Jivit Mritak Sangh (Association of the Living Dead), while the state and its organs remain mute spectators. One can go listing many other issues like the resurgence of the khaps and killing of youth which the rulers conveniently describe as 'honour killings' and talk of special legislation rather than treating them as direct murders or the peasants going back to medieval forms of protest with the modern political system having failed to deliver the basics. In every election campaign that I have experienced since the 1970s, a span of forty years, I am amazed to find that even in the most prosperous regions of western Uttar Pradesh the prime demand of the rural dwellers is to get water, electricity and a metalled road. Issues like education, employment and health are all secondary.

The peasant leadership during the freedom struggle consistently pointed out that the peasant issues have to be a part of the struggle. This was ignored on the pretext of first ousting the British, what some historians also describe as the primary contradiction. Today, the same is being rehearsed in the name of first making India a superpower, a developed nation and an IT society. Hence, one should not raise uncomfortable questions as regards development for whom or whose development? etc.

II

History is not just a study of the past or of the dead. In fact, it is a critical evaluation of all the aspects of past that had a bearing on human and societal development in order to make the present generations knowledgeable about their evolution so that by analysing both, i.e. the past and the present, they can plan for a better future. Many discard this third aspect by keeping history alive as a study of the dead only, not realising that by doing so they are making it a dead subject.

History is a vibrant and dynamic discipline and has to keep pace with new researches and developments. It has multiple levels of uses for social development. Does the historian have a social responsibility? Is there any future for history as a discipline? The role of a historian should not and cannot be confined to historical research and teaching. The historian has a major role in societal development—particularly in multi-cultural and multi-ethnic developing societies. The past four decades in India have shown interesting and very often contradictory trends in the teaching and practising of history along with the kind of uses and abuses this subject has been put to. As far as research is concerned it has emerged as the most lively and volatile discipline among the social sciences. For example, the emergence of Subaltern and the 'Subaltern to Subaltern' in the early 1980s ushered freshness in the discipline with lively debates on many themes that had been intentionally ignored by the dominant streams of thought among the historians and many younger-ones producing excellent research other than the traditional ideological approaches of Imperialist, Nationalist and Marxist historiography. This period also witnessed the sharpening of the swords amongst historians not only belonging to the rival factions but also intimidation of fellow travellers, nepotism, groupism, creation of ghettos and suppression of independent thinking in the garb of one ideology or the other. By now, in fact, most of the historians who had researched agrarian relations or feudalism, having fully understood their characteristics, had established their own feudal academic empires and the history departments as their personal fiefdoms.

On the contrary, I strongly argue that the crucial role for the historian is to contribute towards understanding the contemporary social realities in the historical context to determine what went wrong? Which were the alternatives that were left out? Are those alternatives still viable or do they require certain modifications to meet the present or future requirements? This can be accomplished by encouraging comparative studies. Such comparative studies are vital for future development and they also reinforce the relevance of historical research and history teaching in contemporary society. I emphasize on this role of the historian for I consider him/her as the most conscious human having studied/researched the various aspects of societal evolution and development and there by acquainted with the merits or demerits of the past that need to be taken care of in present or futuristic policy formation and planning. I am not advocating that the historian should become an astrologer, but definitely one who can point out critically the pros and cons by applying and using the information and knowledge that historical investigation enriches us with. There is a strong need for a paradigm shift in historical research to make it more meaningful for developmental purposes.

III

I started teaching in 1976 and my first paper was published in 1978 on 'Baba Ram Chandra and Peasants' Upsurge in Oudh', jointly authored with my supervisor Dr. S.K. Mittal to whom I owe a lot. In 1979, I submitted my thesis where I cited Gramsci and discussed the Subaltern in relation to the peasant struggles. From 1982 onwards Ranajit Guha's brilliant work on Elementary Aspects of Peasant Insurgency and his edited *Subaltern Studies* volumes enriched the discipline of history with the Subaltern Historiography emerging as a major historical discourse that initiated a fresh debate. Since then I have preferred to describe myself as a 'subaltern to subaltern'. Most of the papers in this collection were published earlier in different scholarly publications and their relevance may not have been lost in today's age of market economy where the peasantry continues to be the biggest sufferer. Hence, I decided to publish them as a collection in three thematic parts.

In the first part (Peasant Mobilization) are the papers that revolve around Baba Ram Chandra, an astonishing example of rural leadership in the history of Modern India.

The first paper is an account of the Oudh peasants' movement under the leadership of Baba Ram Chandra of a period when the young Jawaharlal Nehru made his entry into the freedom struggle. It is also a narrative of the peasants' exploitation, mobilization and their betrayal by the urban Congress leaders in spite of the former supporting them.

The next three papers analyse the role Baba Ram Chandra played in the life of the Oudh peasantry—politically, intellectually and socially. The papers on 'Using the *Ramcharitmanas*. . .' and on the use of Vedic literature for mobilization should be eye-openers in present-day politics and a lesson to be learnt from history where the religious literature united the communities in the countryside in the struggle against the landlords and the British rather than dividing them or fanning communal hatred. They also demonstrate that the religious texts are not the monopoly of any community or the dominant castes but repositories of vast knowledge that is relevant in contemporary society depending on what you derive out of them in understanding and explaining the reality.

The next one on the rural women demonstrates that the women issues were very much a part of the struggles of the peasantry in the countryside having been taken up in the 1920s and 1930s by the women themselves. These issues are still alive in most parts of rural India. The solutions offered at that time were amazing and in many cases even relevant today. I have yet to come across the existence of an all women peasant organization—Kisanin Sabha, and its contribution to both, gender issues as well as political participation in other parts of the country during the freedom struggle in the countryside as was the case in Oudh.

I could have merged the next four papers on Congress-Peasant relations that are included in Part 2 (The Peasants of Congress) into a separate book but decided against it for each one of them was written in a specific context and in spite of some duplication in the narrative I preferred to maintain their originality. The first paper in this part on Gandhi, attempts at understanding him from the peasant's point of view and the way that was transformed into political action—looking at Gandhi from below. As an appendix to this paper I have added my review of Shahid Amin's paper on the Mahatma published in *Subaltern Studies-3*. Though, I may differ with him on certain issues, his scholarly contributions on peasant history go a long way.

The next paper was presented at a seminar on 'Economy, Society and Polity in Modern India' organized by the Nehru Memorial Museum & Library, New Delhi. It deals with the Congress–peasant relationship at the national level and at the same time draws examples from the local levels for the 1930s. The paper that follows, while touching on the issues mentioned above brings in some more evidences and also describes the various categories of peasant leadership from 1917 onwards.

The paper on Ideology and Congress was an attempt to enrich the debate on Prof. Bipan Chandra's formulation of the 'Long Term Dynamics' of the Congress. It questions the hypothesis presented by Prof. Chandra on the basis of documentary evidences in relation to the Congress attitude towards the peasants and their struggles. The last paper in this part, presented in a seminar at the Indian Institute of Management, Ahmedabad, is on Big Business and Peasantry. It attempts to bring at one place how the capitalists in India looked upon the peasant movements and manoeuvred to suppress them. At the same time all these papers deal with issues like introduction of caste as a factor in selecting Congress candidates for elections; introduction of booth capturing and bogus voters in elections for Congress delegates for the first time; and the reasons for the peasants standing behind the Congress in the freedom struggle in spite of being sidetracked or betrayed by the leadership. I hope the readers will bear with me for some overlapping in these papers.

In Part 3 (Communalism?), the last paper in this collection, is in a way linked to the theme for it was the peasantry that bore the brunt of partition in spite of the unity and harmony between Hindus and Muslims during the peasant movements. This paper argues for a paradigm shift in understanding, researching and teaching inter-community relations. All shades of historians who conduct post-mortems on the Partition of India and the creation of Pakistan by using different ideological tools have highlighted and stressed upon its causes, genocide and violence, barbarianism and so on what I consider as the negative and dark aspects of human history. The impact has been one of hatred, increasing communal feelings and riots as generations of students have been fed with this information. Agreed, such events did take place and are history. But alongside these events something else also happened in history though howsoever meagre it might have been. In the midst of Partition violence there were also cases where the neighbours belonging to one community saved the lives or gave shelter to those of the other community. Do the history books contain such cases? Hardly any! Is it not the job of the historian to transmit such history to the next generation and of course with a judgement that this was humanism? This was rationality, this was peace and this was a brotherhood that needs to be practised in the modern world. Can't the historian play a role in bridging the gap between hostile communities? Unfortunately, the historian has added to this to run his or her own shop where as the writers and the media have done a much better job. If peace is the need of the day then the history of peace has to be researched and taught—you can't establish a peaceful world by teaching the history of violence, hatred and genocides. It is keeping these aspects in view that I have added this paper which was presented at a conference organized by the University of South Australia in 2008 under the aegis of UNESCO for betterment of inter-community relations.

I would also like to emphasize here that historical research can go a long way to enrich the knowledge and information for all disciplines, provided the historians have clarity about the developmental role and the relevance of its contribution in building a knowledge society. I am one of the strong advocates of Applied History —a theme whose relevance and utility I shall be emphasizing upon in my forthcoming collection on Tourism Studies.

I hope that the collection will be of some use for scholars and students.

PART 1

PEASANT MOBILIZATION

CHAPTER 1

Baba Ram Chandra and Peasant Upsurge in Oudh, 1920–1921*

New trends in historical research have brought 'the peasant' and their 'struggles' into some prominence. Of late a new assessment of peasant struggles in India has come to occupy considerable space in the pages of Western literature.[1] Some Indian writers have also attempted to shed light on one or the other aspect of the struggles of the Indian peasantry.[2] Peasants themselves are no longer treated as the 'object of history' and a non-contributing class to historical and political change. They are seen to have often played a crucial, and at times decisive, role in accelerating the pace of national liberation and transformation. Jawaharlal Nehru has noted how the peasantry, 'turned to the Congress and gave it its real strength'.[3] Unfortunately, the Congress, because of the class-interests of its leadership, failed to harness this strength for a broad-based,

*This paper was published in joint authorship with Dr. S.K. Mittal in *Social Scientist*, Vol. 6, No. 11, June 1978.

[1] W.F. Crawley, 'Kisan Sabhas and Agrarian Revolt in the United Provinces 1920 to 1921', *Modern Asian Studies*, Vol. 5, 1971. D.N. Dhanagare, 'Peasant Protest and Politics: The Tebhaga Movement in Bengal (India), 1946-47', *The Journal of Peasant Studies*, Vol. 3, No. 3, April 1976. Kathleen Gough, 'Peasant Resistance and Revolt in South India', *Pacific Affairs*, Vol. XLI, No. 4, Winter 1968-69.

[2] M.H. Siddiqi 'Peasant Movement in Partapgarh', *Indian Economic and Social History Review*, September 1972; S.K. Mittal and Krishan Dutt, 'Raj Kumar Sukul and Peasant Upsurge in Champaran', *Social Scientist*, Vol. 4, No. 9, April 1976; K.K.N. Kurup, 'The Peasant Movement in Kasargod Taluk 1935-1942', *Journal of Kerala Studies*, Vol. 2, March 1975, Part I; Sukh Bir Chaudhury, *Peasants and Workers Movement in India*, New Delhi, 1971.

[3] Jawaharlal Nehru, *An Autobiography*, New Delhi, 1962, p. 52.

revolutionary transformation. The object of this chapter is to highlight some aspects of the peasant struggle of Oudh, and the role played by Baba Ram Chandra, a forgotten hero of the movement, in it.

THE AGRARIAN SITUATION IN OUDH

The exploitation of and the tyranny practised against the Oudh peasantry by the rapacious landlords and their minions are a known reality in the annals of peasant history. After the uprising of 1857, the British created and buttressed a small class of taluqdars in Oudh to help them in their colonial domination of this part of India. These feudal barons and their 'kinsmen' led luxurious, Westernized lives, and the burden of their high living fell on the poor peasantry. They heaped numerous indignities on the peasantry to realize their extortionate demands. *Nazarana* (gift payments), *bedakhli* (eviction), *rasad* (compulsory supplies) and *begar* (forced labour) were not the only weapons in their hands. They would also impose cesses like *hathiana*, *moturana*[4] and so on to meet their extravagance. The taluqdars wielded the sword of eviction to pressurize the tenantry into paying higher cesses, as owing to increases in population there was a growing demand for more and more holdings. *Nazarana* had become such an evil that some peasants were painfully forced to commit the most heinous sin of *katya vikraya* (sale of daughters) to raise *nazarana* money.[5] Forced labour on a wage ranging between 2 to 8 paise per day was a common practice. Even these wages were generally not paid.[6] Further, the peasantry had to provide rasad and *begar* to the touring government officials, failing which they were exposed to the wrath of their landlords.

The outbreak of the First World War resulted in scarcity and

[4] *Hathiana* was imposed as a cess on the peasantry if the taluqdar had to purchase an elephant and if a car was to be purchased *moturana* tax was levied on the peasantry.

[5] Mehta Report, No. 753/1920, Revenue, UP State Archives (hereafter UPSA).

[6] *Independent*, 24 September 1920.

high prices, adding to the existing problems of poverty, unemployment and under-employment. In Oudh, the loyal supporters of the Empire—the taluqdars—squeezed the peasantry dry by forcibly raising war loans and recruits to aid their masters, leading to increased discontent. On the national scene, the Rowlatt Bill agitation, the Punjab wrongs, and the Khilafat question had put a severe strain on the patience of the people. These came as an anti-climax soon after the exhilaration and enthusiasm generated by Wilsonian sentiments, the declarations of the Allied leaders and the successful accomplishment of a socialist revolution in Russia.

The British government was well aware of dire conditions prevailing in the Oudh areas. But any step taken to improve the peasants' lot was bound to annoy the taluqdars, which the government could not afford as they were the upholders of the empire against 'seditious' opposition. J.S. Meston, the Lieutenant-Governor of the United Provinces, wrote in 1916, regarding an amendment to the Tenancy laws, that:

> The landlord, may become a bulwark against the disintegrating forces of *swaraj* agitation. We should certainly do nothing that will add to or perpetuate any grievance which may tend to throw them into the arms of the advanced and irresponsible politician. . . . At the moment however any radical changes of this nature would only provoke intense controversy and set the landlords as a body against us, which is the last thing we wish.[7]

This was the sole reason that the amendment of the Oudh Rent Act, which might have averted the agrarian crisis, was kept pending. According to this Act of 1886 the peasants were given seven year leases on land but they had no hereditary rights or even life tenancies. The peasants of Oudh were ready to take to any means to achieve redressal of their grievances. They formed a peasant organ-

[7]Nos. 588/1916 Revenue UPSA. Even after the disturbances when the Oudh Rent Act was being amended the government had the same considerations. 'It is a great thing particularly in these days to have so loyal and important a body, as the taluqdars are, on the side of the Government instead of having them unanimously arrayed amidst us.' Viceroy Reading to Harcourt Butler, 5 July 1921, Butler Collection, Reel No. 12, Nehru Memorial Museum & Library (hereafter NMML), New Delhi.

ization, the Kisan Sabha, at Rure in Partapgarh district—under the homegrown leadership of poor peasants like Jhinguri Singh and Sahdev Singh, who set up small sabhas which were not able to extract the desired concessions from the taluqdars and their protectors—the British government. They however, sought out people of greater education than themselves, like Baba Ram Chandra, who agreed to take up the cause of the oppressed peasantry.

THE EARLY YEARS

Baba Ram Chandra, whose real name was Shridhar Balwant Jodhpurka, was a Maharashtrian Brahmin. He was born in the year 1864 in a small village of Gwalior Estate.[8] He left for Fiji as an indentured labourer in 1904[9] and there he changed his name to Ram Chandra Rao in order to conceal his identity, as the Maharashtrian Brahmins were suspect in the eyes of the British.[10] It is difficult to concur with the view of Panigrahi that he changed his name 'to add to his person some religious and moral colour'.[11] He stayed in Fiji for thirteen years (1905–17) and took active part in the movement to emancipate the lot of the indentured labourers. He has been referred to in the official literature as 'a successful agitator in Fiji'.[12] He came in contact with Manilal Gandhi, a com-

[8]Ram Chandra's Manuscript Diary (hereafter RMD) (F). Our sincere thanks to Shrimati Jaggi, the widow of Baba Ram Chandra, of village Daudpur, tahsil Patti, district Partapgarh, for providing to us his papers. These papers along with many others collected during a field trip have been deposited in the NMML, New Delhi. At the time of writing this paper they had not been classified, hence file Nos. are not mentioned.

[9]RMD (F). Also RMD, No. 1, M.H. Siddiqi mentions that Ram Chandra returned from Fiji in 1904 (see 'Peasant Movement in the United Provinces 1918–22', unpublished thesis, Jawaharlal Nehru University, New Delhi, 1974, p. 134).

[10]RMD(1).

[11]D.N. Panigrahi 'Peasant Leadership', in B.N. Pandey (ed.), *Leadership in South Asia,* New Delhi, 1977, p. 94. He mentions that he had changed his name to Ram Chandra after his return from Fiji.

[12]Mehta Report.

panion of C.F. Andrews, who took keen interest in social and emancipatory movements in Fiji.[13] Ram Chandra often used religion to organize the people. He was responsible for the staging of 'Ram Lila' (a traditional and very popular stage drama displaying the life of the Hindu God Rama) in Fiji which helped in creating a sense of solidarity among the coolies of Indian origin. He also ensured the dismissal of an official who rode roughshod over the religious sentiments of the coolies. He led popular demonstrations in Fiji, to focus on the grievances of indentured labourers.[14] He smuggled into India an article on the deplorable and inhuman conditions of indentured labourers, which was published in *Bharat Mitra*, a newspaper from Calcutta.[15] The Fiji government was alarmed by this article and was on the lookout for its writer. The articles created such a furore that Ram Chandra was advised by his friends to leave Fiji before the authorities were able to lay their hands on him.[16]

Ram Chandra returned to India in 1917 because he wished to carry on the battle on behalf of the indentured labourers in India itself.[17] Further, a letter from Bal Gangadhar Tilak advised him to come to India and carry on the struggle.[18] In India he started giving discourses on religion which endeared him to the simple and religious peasantry of Oudh who flocked in ever greater numbers to listen to him. The change from social to religious questions was attributed by him to some divine visions he had while asleep.[19]

FORMATION OF THE KISAN SABHA

Ram Chandra was persuaded by Jhinguri Singh and Sahdev Singh to throw in his weight with them to ameliorate the lot of the

[13] Ram Chandra and Dr. Manilal Gandhi had developed good understanding which later on resulted in Manilal's arrival in Oudh to study the peasants' problems.

[14] RMD (F).

[15] Ibid.

[16] Ibid.

[17] Ibid.

[18] Ram Chandra's Writings.

[19] Ibid.

peasantry through the Kisan Sabha which was already functioning with its headquarters at Rure. The formation of a Kisan Sabha at Rure, it has been contended by Siddiqi, had no direct connection with the peasants' grievances. The place was chosen, he argued, because it was 'sanctified by a myth close to the heart of the peasants'.[20] His contention is based on the Mehta Report in which the lines of Tulsidas's popular epic *Ramcharitmanas* have been cited, *Raj samaj virajat Rure* (In the assembly of kings the two brothers shone like two moons in the galaxy of stars). The word *rure* means beautiful and it was construed to mean the Rure village. Hence he opined that the formation of a kisan organization there was due to the religious susceptibilities and superstitious beliefs of the people. The people of Rure had no grievances and were suffering from no disabilities. Panigrahi writes that 'By formally inaugurating the Kisan Sabha from this village. Ram Chandra was, in terms of sociological analysis, using symbols which were intelligible to the simple peasant families.'[21] In fact, the Kisan Sabha at Rure was not inaugurated by Ram Chandra but by Jhinguri Singh and Sahdev Singh, much before the entry of Ram Chandra into the movement. 'The Kisan Sabha', wrote Ram Chandra, 'had started functioning before I came to Rure in 1919.'[22] In our view, Rure was chosen after considerable deliberation and not merely due to religious propensity as Siddiqi and Panigrahi tend to suggest. It was an underproprietary village, and hence, out of the reach of taluqdari oppression. The fear of the taluqdars was so pervasive that the leaders considered it more convenient to operate from Rure, comparatively a safe place to carry on their pro-peasant activities.

RAM CHANDRA'S AGRARIAN PROGRAMME

Soon Ram Chandra won the admiration of the peasantry which came to look on him as their deliverer. He heard their unending tales of misery and at first contacted the taluqdars and sought

[20] Siddiqi, op. cit., p. 73.

[21] Panigrahi, op. cit.

[22] Ram Chandra's Writings. Also interview with Ram Bahadur Singh (nephew of Jhinguri Singh) of village Rure, tahsil Patti, district Partapgarh. He gives 1917 as the year of the formation of the Kisan Sabha. This Sabha still exists in Rure.

their help to bring succour to the afflicted peasantry. They, naturally, were found to be unwilling to do away with their tyrannical practices.[23] Rebuffed by the taluqdars, he now turned to the district authorities to enlist their cooperation in his mission, but nothing tangible emerged. He then made a direct appeal to the peasantry and urged the *kisans* to stand on their own feet. He exhorted them to withhold all kinds of cesses, *nazarana*, *begar*, and pay only the normal rent. He held up the example of *Dankani Bandobast* prevalent in Jaunpur district, under which their counterparts, only a few miles away, were far happier than they. His was not the mere clap-trap of oratory, for he also enunciated an eightfold programme for the upliftment of the peasantry: (1) Payment of rent in advance of the fixed time; (2) Reservation of jungle tracts for the grazing of cattle; (2) Sinking of wells and digging of tankers; (4) Planting of orchards; (5) Half area to be sown with grain crops and half with cotton, and opening of three cotton mills, one in each tahsil, to employ people as labourers, spinners and weavers; (6) Establishment of seed or grain depots at every three *kos*; (7) Acceleration of female education by the itinerant *updeshikas* (teachers); and (8) Creation of a union among the zamindar, kisan and *mazdur* (labourer).[24] The Deputy Commissioner of Partapgarh commented that Ram Chandra became 'a magnet of attraction' who supplied 'some mental pabulum to a people usually intellectually starved in these out of the way places'. The people, he added, 'attended his meetings and many fraternized with him'.[25]

BEGINNINGS OF THE MOVEMENT

The peasantry of Oudh was stirred to action in May 1920 under the leadership of Ram Chandra. The local administration, fearing a breach of law and order, directed Ram Chandra to stop his poisonous propaganda calculated to incite class hatred and ill-will. The Deputy Commissioner of Partapgarh asked Ram Chandra to forward the complaints of the peasants to him.[26] Ram Chandra

[23] G.P. Sinha to Butler, 12 September, 1920. F. No. 358/1920, Police UPSA.
[24] Mehta Report.
[25] Ibid.
[26] Ibid.

instructed Jhinguri Singh and Sahdev Singh to file written complaints with the Deputy Commissioner. They marched with one thousand men and women to the office of the Deputy Commissioner to lay their complaints before him. Rure became a centre for receiving the complaints of the peasantry. By this time, the peasantry had shed its fear and its consciousness was growing rapidly. The peasant movement increased its strength because of the cohesion of the Kurmis and low caste peasants, who formed the bulk of the peasantry. They were subjected to extreme, ruthless oppression in comparison with the limited oppression experienced by the less numerous high caste peasants.

What made Ram Chandra the leader of the mass of peasantry? Undoubtedly, the peculiar socio-economic circumstances provided the basis for such an event. The taluqdars and zamindars were not only unrelenting in their oppression but increased it over time. The number of evictions increased in Partapgarh from 1,655 during 1918–19 to 2,593 during 1919–20.[27] The landowners missed no opportunity to inflate rents on their holdings. The term *murdafaroshi* (literally meaning the practice of selling corpses) brings out the cruelty involved in the fresh letting out of land at higher rents soon after the death of a tenant. Even the charge under the head *nazarana* increased out of all proportions in the period preceding 1920.[28] The dispossessed and disgruntled peasantry sought shelter under the Kisan Sabha's umbrella.

UNITY WITH THE FREEDOM STRUGGLE

Ram Chandra wished to broaden the movement and therefore decided to bring in Mahatma Gandhi and other educated, urban leaders into the movement. He gave the example of Champaran where the tenants were said to have secured their release from the planters' tyranny due to Mahatma Gandhi's intervention.[29] With this aim in view Ram Chandra organized a march of five hundred peasants

[27] Ibid., Exhibit 'I'.

[28] Ibid.

[29] Ibid. Also RMD. See also *Leader*, 23 September 1920.

on foot from Patti to Allahabad, a tract stretching over 75 kilometres.[30] It was the first march on foot and must thus occupy a place of honour in the annals of peasant struggles. Curiously enough, Jawaharlal wrote somewhat disparagingly of the march and its leadership:

> He (Ram Chandra) had no programme of any kind and when he had brought them (peasants) to a pitch of excitement he tried to shift the responsibility to others. This led him to bring a number of peasants to Allahabad to interest people there in the movement.[31]

Ram Chandra had hoped to meet Gandhi at Allahabad as he was scheduled to be there on his way back from Benares where he had gone to attend a meeting of the AICC. Throughout the day the marchers spoke of their difficulties in the city. In the evening, a meeting held at 'Balua Ghat', was attended by Jawaharlal Nehru. The UP Kisan Sabha arranged for the stay of the marchers.[32] Ram Chandra was anxious to link the peasant movement with the freedom movement. The bourgeois' nationalist leadership, it appears, was not enthusiastic and was somewhat reluctant to take up the cause of the peasantry. As Raj Kumar Sukul had tugged at the sleeves of Gandhi and forced him to come to Champaran,[33] so Ram Chandra and the marchers clung on to the bourgeois nationalist politicians and would not return from Allahabad without concrete assurances of help. Jawaharlal wrote: 'They would accept no denial

[30]The figure of the numbers of marchers varies. Mehta places it at 500; Jawaharlal Nehru is also of the same view. M.H. Siddiqi gives it as 200. According to S.P. Sen (ed.), *Dictionary of National Biography* (hereafter *DNB*), VIII M-R Calcutta, 1974, p. 432 the figure is 15,000 of marchers. We have taken the official figure as officers are in the habit of giving conservative figures. The March took place in early June 1920.

[31]Nehru, op. cit., p. 53.

[32]The UP Kisan Sabha had been formed in 1917 by the Malviya group and since then it had been voicing peasants' grievances. Krishan Kant Malviya, P.D. Tandon, Inder Narain Diwedi and Gauri Shanker Mishra were its prominent leaders.

[33]See Mittal and Dutt, op. cit.

and literally clung on to us. At last I promised to visit them two days or so later.'[34]

VACILLATIONS OF THE NATIONALIST LEADERSHIP

The nationalist politicians found an enthusiastic peasantry greeting them at every village they visited in the district of Partapgarh. Jawaharlal Nehru was amazed to see the organizing capacity of the illiterate peasants.[35] It was thus that the first Prime Minister of independent India had his first direct contact with the peasantry, and was emotionally moved to see the 'naked, starving and crushed picture of India'.[36] Rural India felt elated at the support extended by the citybred politicians. Their frequent visits created a deep impression on the rural folk. They also ventilated the grievances of the peasantry through the press and from the platform.[37] The Rure based Kisan Sabha stepped up its activities under the impact of these forces.[38] However, while on the one hand the bourgeois nationalist leadership exhorted the peasants to stand united, on the other, it sought for a compromise between the oppressors, and the oppressed.[39] It did not go beyond this nor did it place before the peasantry any concrete programme of action by which the peasantry would secure its release from feudal oppression.

Baba Ram Chandra intensified the struggle and asked the peasantry to stop payment of illegal cesses and the cultivation of *sir* lands (lands under the direct control of the taluqdars). He also appealed to the peasantry not to accept those lands for cultivation from which their fellow peasants had been evicted.[40] The peasantry, by and large, obeyed the exhortation. The very few tenants who

[34] Nehru, op. cit., p. 51.

[35] Ibid.

[36] Ibid., p. 52.

[37] *Independent*, 3 July 1920; *Abhyudaya*, 24 July 1920.

[38] Mehta Report.

[39] *Abhyudaya*, 24 July 1920; Mehta Report.

[40] Hailey to Keane, 5 September 1920. 358/1920 Police UPSA. Also see Ram Chandra Papers.

were lured by the zamindars to occupy such lands were intimidated into following the example of their numerous counterparts. The local Kisan Sabha, under the impetus of Ram Chandra, advised the peasantry to take up 'direct action'.[41] The spirit of defiance and rebellion had permeated the peasantry of Oudh. The menacing situation and the increasing incidents of breach of peace brought the peacemakers (the urban bourgeois politicians) on the scene. Consequently several conferences were held to restore peace in the troubled locality. The local Kisan Sabha adopted a tough line while the bourgeois nationalist politicians urged reasonableness and compromise. V.N. Mehta, the Deputy Commissioner of Partapgarh, laid the blame for the disturbances at the doors of the peasant leadership. He perceptively remarked, 'I think the local sabha had got a bit tired by the patient tactics of the Allahabad Kisan Sabha. It could not afford to wait for the law to alter after taking its own time.'[42] This reveals the difference in attitude between the bourgeois-led and the peasant-led organizations of the peasants. The bourgeois nationalist leadership was more interested in exploiting peasant discontent to further its own political and party ends. The elder Nehru's letter to the younger Nehru was not without significance. He wrote:

> If one or two visits like this to other parts of the Partapgarh district can be arranged there will be some chance for a pure nationalist getting into the council inspite of the Raja Bahadur of Partapgarh.[43]

Despite conferences and peace efforts, peace did not return to the area. The taluqdars opposed tooth and nail the bestowal of any concession on the peasantry as it would lower their prestige and lead to a loss of 'face'.[44] The situation grew from bad to worse and while Jawaharlal Nehru and P.D. Tandon condemned the acts of high handedness by the peasants, they also urged the authorities

[41] Mehta Report.

[42] Ibid.

[43] Motilal to Jawaharlal, 14 June 1920. Jawaharlal Nehru Papers, Correspondence, Vol. 65, No. 3836, NMML.

[44] *Abhyudava*, 24 July 1920.

to withdraw the cases arguing that these might aggravate the situation further. The Allahabad leadership made it clear to the peasantry that if it persisted with such action, it would be deprived of bourgeois-nationalist support.[45] The disturbances continued unabated. Within the short period of a week about eight cases of high handedness were reported and criminal prosecution followed. Almost in every case Ram Chandra and his lieutenants were involved, not as actual participants but as instigators.[46]

RAM CHANDRA'S ARREST AND PEASANT REACTION

Ram Chandra had wielded an enormous moral authority over the Oudh peasants and had made himself one of them. His organizing capacity and his indigenous, semi-religious methods of propaganda in a backward area without any modern means of transportation and communication, enhanced his stature as a rural leader. He devised an indigenous method of addressing the vast congregation of peasants. He would suspend a cot horizontally with ropes between trees and use it as a pulpit, and address the gatherings of thousands without any loud speaker.[47] He would write with his neat hand hundreds of pamphlets for distribution. The last sentence of these handbills always was, 'Please pass it on after reading'. He *characterized* himself as the *Oudh kisan sewak* (a server of Oudh peasantry).[48]

To the taluqdars and the guardians of law and order Ram Chandra had become a source of danger. They smelt Bolshevism in his activities and foresaw a mutiny much more dangerous than the one in 1857.[49] The government moved against Ram Chandra

[45] Mehta Report.

[46] *Leader*, 5 September 1920.

[47] *Swatantrata Sangram Ke Sainik*, Vol. 26, district Fyzabad, UP, Lucknow, 1972, p. (Chai) and Vol. 13, District Partapgarh, p. (Khai).

[48] Several such pamphlets and handbills are in the possession of the authors which were collected during the fieldwork.

[49] Ram Gopal Singh to Viceroy, 11 September 1920. 358/1920 Police, UPSA.

and his associates on very flimsy grounds on 28 August 1920.[50] They were charged under Sections 107 of the Criminal Procedure Code and 379 of the Indian Penal Code. They were refused bail and were lodged in Partapgarh jail despite clear instructions to the contrary by V.N. Mehta who at that time was on leave. He had contended that an imprisonment would make Ram Chandra a 'greater hero'.[51] Their messiah had been sent to the gallows and this was more than what the peasants could swallow. A throng of about four to five thousand peasants assembled on 1 September, in the compound of the court where he was to be tried to have a glimpse of their hero. The authorities thought it wise to try Ram Chandra and his friends in the jail compound itself. The CID officials have described the mood of the masses as being such that they were 'ready to die for their leaders'.[52] The irate mob of peasants rushed to the jail gates around 5 p.m., but ultimately dispersed without taking recourse to any serious action.

The authorities were at a loss as to what should be done with the arrested leaders. The hearing of the case had to be postponed. Meanwhile the peasants resolved to secure the release of their leaders. Handwritten leaflets in Hindi and Urdu were circulated, calling upon the peasantry to reach the city for that purpose. The Allahabad bourgeoisie rushed to the scene. Jawaharlal Nehru and Gauri Shanker Mishra briefly addressed the peasants in Patti area urging them to go *en masse* to the *Sadr* (Magistrate) and demand the release of Ram Chandra, or get themselves placed in jail.[53] The Acting Deputy Commissioner wanted to proceed against Jawaharlal and Mishra but was prevented by the Commissioner.[54] The Deputy

[50] The charge against Ram Chandra was the 'abetment of theft, of a log of wood and in another case it was that a landlord's servant was assaulted by some men and then taken to Ram Chandra'. DIG III Range to IG, 12 September 1920 and Hailey to Keane. F. No. 358/1920 Police, UPSA.

[51] V.N. Mehta to Butler, 15 September 1920. 358/1920 Police UPSA. Mehta went on leave on 19 August and Brijlal was the Acting Deputy Commissioner at that time.

[52] CID Report on Partapgarh disturbances, 358/1920. Police UPSA. Also *Independent*, 12 September 1920.

[53] Hailey to Keane, 8 September 1920. 359/1920 Police, UPSA.

[54] Ibid.

Commissioner convened a meeting of the local Zamindari Association and appealed to the peasants to remain calm. The zamindars were evasive about the illegal exactions and the petty harassment of the peasants.[55] The taluqdars pressurized the administration into dealing harshly with the troublemaker Ram Chandra, but were reticent in promising to do away with their illegal, oppressive practices. Inevitably, the situation did not alter.

The restive peasantry surged round the Partapgarh jail on 10 September, in a fresh bid to secure their leader's release.[56] Rumours were afloat that Gandhi would also be visiting Partapgarh to plead with the government on behalf of Ram Chandra.[57] The police was kept on its toes[58] but fearing appalling casualties owing to the 'density and proximity' of the crowd, decided to take the first rush on the bayonets.[59] The authorities pleaded with the mob to disperse but all in vain. Finally the local pleaders, Matabadal Pande in particular, assured the crowd that Ram Chandra would be released the next day.[60] The peasants were somewhat pacified, but they decided to camp on the outskirts of the town only to reassemble in greater numbers the next morning. Mahatma Gandhi was also telegraphically requested to reach the spot immediately.[61] The Acting Deputy Commissioner, the Jail Superintendent, Matabadal Pande and Parmeshwar Dayal went to Ram Chandra's cell to enlist his cooperation in dispersing the crowd. Ram Chandra demanded the release of all his companions and a payment to the peasantry as compensation for the expenditure incurred in coming to Partapgarh.[62]

[55] Confidential fortnightly report of the Commissioner Fyzabad for the first half of September 1920. 358/1920 Police, UPSA.

[56] The number varies. Ram Chandra himself places it at 40,000–50,000; *Leader* gives it 20,000; *Independent* 20,000 and the authorities place it between 10,000 to 40,000. The date 20 November is not correct.

[57] *Leader*, 23 September 1920.

[58] Brijlal to Hailey, 12 September 1920. 358/1920 Police, UPSA.

[59] DIG O'Conner to IG Kaye, 12 September 1920. 358/1920 Police, UPSA.

[60] *Leader*, 23 September 1920. Also see Siddiqi's article op. cit.

[61] *Independent*, 14 September 1920.

[62] Ram Chandra's notes.

RETREAT OF THE AUTHORITIES

The authorities and the peacemakers were tense. The authorities, after some semblance of a hurried trial as a sort of face saving device, decided to release him on a personal bond of Rs. 500 along with three securities each of the same amount. Then Ram Chandra 'was taken in a car and left in a sugar cane field'.[63] Had the authorities not released him, the surging crowd, which outnumbered the police, would have secured his release by ransacking the jail. The mood of the determined crowd forced the imperial power into capitulation. The bold peasantry won the day, though during the thirty-eight hour long confrontation the Allahabad bourgeoisie had kept themselves at a 'safe distance'.[64]

The local authorities withdrew all the cases on instructions from the Commissioner, as the grounds were flimsy and at best would have resulted in small punishments adding further to the prestige of the accused.[65] Jhinguri Singh wanted to sue the taluqdars of Ramganj and Amargarh estates, but 'Ram Chandra prevented him from doing so as all energies had to be harnessed for the impending struggle.[66] Ram Chandra promised to work with V.N. Mehta, who by now had rejoined the services as Deputy Commissioner, provided he pursued the peasants' grievances vigorously with the government. The Commissioner wrote to the Lieutenant-Governor that Ram Chandra be 'treated as the mouthpiece of the tenants' for it would 'flatter him and please the kisans'.[67] Mehta himself suggested the appointment of Ram Chandra and Jhinguri Singh as officials to mediate between the taluqdars and the peasantry but the proposal could not materialize.[68] The government realized that unless something was done to remove the grievances of the peasantry, the situation might become explosive. It asked the Deputy Commissioner, Mehta, to enquire into the causes of the agrarian disturb-

[63] Ibid.

[64] Brijlal to Hailey, 12 September 1920. 358/1920 Police, UPSA.

[65] Hailey to Butler, 12 September 1920. 358/1920 Police, UPSA.

[66] Ram Chandra's notes.

[67] Hailey to Butler, 12 September 1920. 358/1920 Police, UPSA.

[68] Ram Chandra's papers. Also see Siddiqi op. cit.

ances and the grievances of the tenants.[69] The peasantry won its second victory when it forced the government to conduct an enquiry into their conditions. The resultant Mehta Report unmasked the tyranny of the taluqdars. The Lieutenant-Governor, nicknamed as Taluqdar Butler, was irked to see his taluqdar friends exposed. He did not allow the report to be printed in its entirety. He fulminated, 'Mehta perhaps knew nothing of the controversies of tenant right and it was out of the question to print all the stuff'.[70]

THE MOVEMENT GAINS MOMENTUM

The events of August-September brought Ram Chandra such fame that the peasantry of Oudh looked to him as their liberator. Matabadal Koyari invited him to Kalkaliapur, a village in Rasulpur estate of Rai Bareilly in October. He launched a Kisan Sabha organization on 28 October.[71] He made very frequent visits to several villages of Rai Bareilly, organized the units of the Kisan Sabha and galvanized the masses of the peasantry. The landlords were alarmed. He addressed large gatherings and emphasized Swadeshi, Hindu-Muslim unity and the need to educate the masses. He advocated complete abstention from the forthcoming polls and worked to upset the chances of taluqdari candidates.[72] He proclaimed 20 December as kisan day and exhorted the Oudh peasantry to assemble in the largest possible numbers at Ajodhya on that day.

Meanwhile, the movement had assumed new dimensions and a more revolutionary outlook. The yoke of the taluqdars was shaken. Thakurdin,[73] an ex-servant of the Raja of Parhat, founded a sabha

[69] Mehta Report.

[70] 753/1920 Revenue, UPSA.

[71] 50/1921 General, UPSA, 57, 61.

[72] Ibid. Also Commissioner, Lucknow to Chief Secretary to UP Govt., 11 November 1920. 358/1920 Police, UPSA.

[73] Thakurdin has been described by Siddiqi (vide his article, op. cit., p. 323) as an exploiter who robbed Paul in order to rob Peter soon. In our view he was animated by anti-landlord feelings. Although he was not a member of the Ram Chandra led Kisan Sabha, Ram Chandra held a high opinion of him. RMD (1).

on the borders of Partapgarh and Jaunpur districts which treated with contempt the zamindari servants who conveyed ejectment orders; seized the grain of the *mahajans* (moneylenders) and ensured its distribution among the peasants. The taluqdars had announced cash awards for his arrest.[74] The uprising led by Thakurdin became so formidable that the police, all along assisted by the landlords, had to be deployed in the disturbed localities. The landlords, with the help of the police, let loose a reign of terror. Villages were plundered and women molested.[75] Thakurdin was arrested but the movement could not be crushed; rather it gained in momentum.[76]

The Ajodhya meeting was approaching and Ram Chandra had encamped there a few days before. He contacted local leaders of Fyzabad like Lalanji, an advocate, and Kedarnath to help him make the kisan rally a success. They would not believe that the peasants would assemble in such numbers defying the wintry weather. To their surprise the peasants poured into Ajodhya from all directions. Jhinguri Singh led the contingent from Partapgarh, Amol Sharma[77] and Matabadal Koyari headed the Rai Bareilly troop. The marchers carried banners demanding the end of taluqdari oppression and rent the sky with slogans. The priests opened the temple doors to the peasants, offering them a place to stay, and Hindus and Muslims stayed together.[78] On 20 December, Gauri Shanker Mishra presided over this meeting of the Oudh Kisan Sabha. Ram Chandra occupied the stage dressed like a prisoner bound with ropes. He described the peasantry as tied like himself with ropes of bondage-bondage to the government, taluqdars and the capitalists.[79] He would untie the ropes only when the peasantry assured him of unity to bring to an end the triple bondage. After loud assurances from the audience Gauri Shanker untied the ropes.[80] Satya Devi, speaking on

[74] RMD (1).

[75] Ibid. Also *Abhyudaya*, 11 December 1920.

[76] RMD (1).

[77] Amol Sharma was the person who was held responsible for Chandaria riot which ultimately led to the Munshiganj firing on 7 January 1921.

[78] RMD(1).

[79] Ram Chandra's notes, point 8.

[80] Report on Ajodhya meeting, 358/1920 Police, UPSA. Also RMD (1).

behalf of women, assured the participation of women in the movement.[81] It was decided to send two representatives to the Nagpur Congress to represent the cause of the peasantry.[82] It was announced that the next meeting would be held on 15 January, 1921 at Unchahar in Rai Bareilly district where the message of the Nagpur Congress would be made known. The massive rally of peasants, estimates of their numbers varying from fifty thousand to one lakh, was a unique spectacle in the annals of the peasant movement in India. J.A. Farron wrote to the Deputy Commissioner of Rai Bareilly about the new awakening. The Ajodhya conference and the activities of Ram Chandra infused new life into the meek frame of the Oudh peasantry. He commented:

> . . . they returned (from the Ajodhya conference) more than ever filled with a sense of real and fancied wrongs. They fell to discussing these in local panchayats which have since been formed in every village, for the first time in history they had begun to realize the power of an united peasantry. . . . If they stood together, *nazarana, begari* and other oppressive taxes would automatically cease. The political education . . . was progressing. They were learning the value of concerted action.[83]

Ram Chandra now moved to Bara Banki on the invitation of Kashi Parsad who had attended the kisan rally at Ajodhya. The peasantry of this district was seething with discontent due to zamindari oppression and the levy of illegal cesses. On reaching Bara Banki, Ram Chandra was accorded a hero's welcome; he was taken in a huge procession throughout the city and was welcomed with slogans hailing him.[84] The frightened taluqdars, recognizing discretion to be the better part of valour, befriended Ram Chandra. The zamindars of Bhayara attended their meeting on 26 December and decided to relinquish all zamindari dues beyond rent. Chaudhuri Mohamed Ali, an influential zamindar, announced his intention to stop eviction, *nazarana* and *begar* in his estate.[85] The taluqdars

[81] *Leader*, 23 December 1920.
[82] Jawaharlal Nehru to Editor, *Independent*, 21 January 1921. Also RMD (1).
[83] J.A. Farron to the Deputy Commissioner, Bareilly. 50/1921, General UPSA.
[84] RMD(1).
[85] *Independent*, January 1921.

of Gadia, Shahpur and Baqar Hosain estates invited Ram Chandra, the *bete noire* of the Partapgarh taluqdars, to visit their estates.[86] With better landlord-peasant relations and with the taluqdars behind him at Bara Banki, Ram Chandra tried to channellize the peasant movement for the implementation of the Congress programme. He told the audience at Rudauli (a village in Bara Banki district) on 29 December not to tolerate the *zulum* (tyranny) of the district authorities and the police. He exhorted them to take to swadeshi and hand spun cloth.[87] His speeches preached disaffection against the government. He even asked the British to quit the country as it did not belong to them. He declared that the 'Government is treacherous, tyrannical and dishonest and I will not rest until I have driven it out'.[88] He instituted a district Kisan Sabha with Pandit Sarju Parsad as its *sarpanch* (president). It was devised to ensure that the zamindars of Bara Banki kept up their promises and illegal cesses were not realized from the peasantry.

THE NAGPUR CONGRESS

Ram Chandra's fortnight-long tour of Bara Banki coincided with the session of the Nagpur Congress (December 1920) which endorsed the programme of Non-Cooperation and triple boycott, that is, boycott of the legislature, the courts and the schools. On the positive side, the Congress emphasized Hindu-Muslim unity, opening of national schools, removal of untouchability, *swadeshi* and so on-demands which came to be known as the 'constructive programme'. Bara Banki witnessed not only complete Hindu–Muslim fraternization but the Muslims outnumbered their Hindu compatriots in showering praises on Ram Chandra. The Baba made strenuous efforts to raise Rs. 10,000 for the construction of a national school.[89] The movement of the Oudh peasants against taluqdari oppression thus got intertwined with the national movement.

[86] Ibid., 9 January 1921.
[87] Ibid., 1 January 1921.
[88] Ibid., 10 and 25 March 1921.
[89] Ibid., 13 January and 10 March 1921.

The new year began with the revolt of the Oudh peasantry in the Rai Bareilly district where large crowds moved from one estate to another destroying the crops of taluqdars.[90] The tyrannical yoke of the landed aristocracy had become unbearable. Ram Chandra was at Bara Banki. The urban bourgeois nationalist leadership was busy with the Congress programme. The kisan organizations were at cross purposes with each other. The desperate peasantry took to violence on a large scale. The movement assumed the dimensions of a class wall which climaxed in bloodshed on 7 January 1921 at Munshiganj. The perpetrators of the Munshiganj massacre—a miniature Jallianwala[91]—were congratulated by Sir Harcourt Butler, the Lieutenant-Governor of the United Provinces.[92] The Munshiganj firing brought to the fore the old, accumulated grievances of the Oudh peasantry. It evoked such an emotive reaction that the national press and leaders were unanimous in condemning the brutal incident and demanding an enquiry.[93] However it is an episode which requires separate treatment, and is not within the scope of this paper.

NATIONALIST BETRAYAL

Ignorant of the events at Rai Bareilly, Baba Ram Chandra went to Lucknow at the summons of Maulana Abdul Bari, a Khilafat leader.[94] There he came to know of the Munshiganj tragedy but he was virtually a prisoner of Maulana Bari. Ram Chandra wrote: 'I felt annoyed and whenever attempted to leave the place, the soldiers (Bari's men) would restrict me. . . . I even wept and wrung my hands in despair but none bothered. I was at a loss to know why I

[90] Home Political Nos. 195-216/1921, February-B, NAI. Also 'Agrarian Disturbances in Rai Bareilly', 50/1921 General, UPSA.

[91] *Daily Pratap*, 13 January 1921. NNR of UP, NMML.

[92] 5/1921General, UPSA.

[93] Almost every newspaper demanded it. N.H. Kunzru demanded disciplinary action against men guilty of firing at Munshiganj in the Legislative Council, Legislative Council Proceedings of UP. Vol. 1.

[94] RMD (1).

was treated so.'[95] With Ram Chandra in his custody, Abdul Bari telegraphed Mohamed Ali that he should inform Mahatma Gandhi about Ram Chandra's whereabouts and seek Gandhi's instructions as to what was to be done with Ram Chandra, for he (Bari) apprehended a grave situation in case Ram Chandra was allowed to proceed to Rai Bareilly. Bari added in his telegram that if Ram Chandra was stopped from proceeding no further disturbances need be apprehended.[96] Shaukat Ali telegraphed back that Gandhi desired Ram Chandra to pacify the peasantry in accordance with his creed of non-violence.[97] Gandhi's confirmation of Shaukat Ali's telegram followed soon after.[98] The perplexed Ram Chandra was told by Abdul Bari on the strength of the above telegrams that he would not let Ram Chandra go anywhere as it was the wish of the leaders.[99] The day of the announced meeting at Unchahar had come but Ram Chandra was helpless and failed to reach there. The meeting was declared illegal under the Seditious Meetings Act by the government. In order to minimize attendance at the meeting, trains were diverted to other routes on 15 January and at some places the peasants were forcibly restricted from boarding the trains.[100] The meeting was scheduled to decide on the crucial question of withholding the payment of rent.[101] It would be recalled that the Congress had not considered the issue of non-payment of rent as part of the Non-Cooperation programme. Abdul Bari and Jangilal Chaurasiya discouraged the peasants who had collected at

[95] RMD (1), Ram Chandra learnt of the Munshiganj incident at Lucknow where he was detained, and not at Bara Banki as mentioned by M.H. Siddiqi, unpublished thesis, op. cit., p. 251.

[96] Abdul Bari to Mohamed Ali, 13 January 1921. F. No. 50-3/1921 General, UPSA.

[97] Shaukat Ali to Abdul Bari, 14 January 1921, ibid.

[98] Gandhi to Abdul Bari, 15 January 1921. Bombay Secret Abstracts 1921. *Collected Works of Mahatma Gandhi*, Vol. XIX (*1920–21*), Ahmedabad, 1965.

[99] RMD (1), p. 39. Also Ram Chandra's notes.

[100] RMD (1), p. 40. *Independent*, 18 January 1921.

[101] Commissioner Fyzabad to Chief Secretary to UP Govt., 14 January 1921, 50/1921 General, UPSA.

Lucknow from going to Unchahar.[102] Jawaharlal, Madan Mohan Malviya and Gauri Shanker Mishra persuaded the peasants who had already assembled at Unchahar to disperse and return to their homes.[103] The determined peasantry dispersed for want of proper guidance and leadership. The whole episode makes curious reading and forces home the conclusion that the bourgeois nationalist leadership betrayed the peasants and their movement. Motilal Nehru in a letter to his son, realistically contrasted the methods of the kisans and the Congress intelligentsia as far back as December 1918:

> The Secretary and some members of the Kisan Sabha came to see me this evening . . . the work they have done and are doing is admirable and affords a striking contrast to the methods of the so called 'intelligentsia'; the latter talk a great deal and spend the rest of the time in dreaming, but the kisans are practical men and once they are convinced that they have to do something they do it.[104]

Motilal Nehru wrote to Abdul Bari to send Ram Chandra to Anand Bhawan[105] in complete secrecy. Escorted by two armed servants of Abdul Bari and dressed in a Muslim woman's apparel (*burqa*) Ram Chandra proceeded to Allahabad. He was told that all this was being done to avoid police detection.[106] At Allahabad he was taken straight to the residence of the Nehrus only to be detained for the second time by the 'loyal' nationalists.[107] In his presence a new UP Kisan Sabha was launched with Motilal as its president in opposition to the Malviya led Kisan Sabha.[108] The former Kisan Sabha wished to bring the peasantry into the Non-

[102] Ram Chandra's notes.

[103] *Independent*, 19 January 1921.

[104] Motilal to Jawaharlal, 13 December 1918. Jawaharlal Nehru Papers, Part I, Correspondence, Vol. 63, No. 3732, NMML.

[105] Nehru's residence at Allahabad.

[106] Ram Chandra's notes.

[107] Ram Chandra's Writings (a note written by him on 28 September 1941 during his imprisonment at Lucknow).

[108] The UP Kisan Sabha under Madan Mohan Malviya's influence was opposed to non-cooperation and in this way Motilal Nehru could embarrass Malaviya. See Crawley, op. cit.

Cooperation movement while the latter opposed the move. The grievances of the peasantry were lost in the petty squabbles of the two kisan sabhas. Jhinguri Singh, Matabadal Koyari and others on learning of Ram Chandra's detention at Allahabad, reached there and ensured his release.[109]

The small party left on foot for Partapgarh and enroute Ram Chandra told the peasantry:

> . . . now we shall have to fight for our honour. Lives will have to be sacrificed, lands and houses will have to be given up. It may well become difficult to dwell even under the trees. These rich and honourable persons (urban intelligentsia and politicians) will clash among themselves on the strength of your support. It will take another fifteen to twenty years for the redressal of your real grievances as parties professing faith in legal battles have sprung up.[110]

The non-cooperators, particularly Jawaharlal and Gauri Shanker Mishra, toured the areas which were the scenes of the recent agrarian disturbances urging the peasants to cast their lot with the Non-Cooperation movement. They proclaimed that all their grievances would be liquidated on the attainment of *swaraj*.[111] They were joined by Ram Chandra on certain occasions, but the latter's concern was more with the liquidation of the peasants' grievances.

NEW TRENDS IN THE PEASANT MOVEMENT

The peasant movement in Oudh was no longer under the control of its chief architect, Baba Ram Chandra. In January 1921, the peasantry had acted independently of its leadership. Ram Chandra's name inspired such confidence among the Oudh peasants that several spurious Ram Chandras appeared on the scene.[112] In Fyzabad and Sultanpur districts one Suraj Parsad alias Ram Chandra,

[109] Ram Chandra's notes.

[110] Ram Chandra's Writings cited in fn. 107.

[111] *Leader*, 28 January 1921.

[112] 'Ram Chandra is himself somewhat a multiple personality nowadays as all small men call themselves by his name'. Hailey to Lambert, 10 January 1921, 60/1921, Gen UPSA.

whom W.F. Crawley confused with Baba Ram Chandra,[113] established a sabha and declared himself the ruler of a tract. The proclaimed tract was delimited and bedecked with flags. He denounced the entry of the police and arrested those who were on patrol duty. He decreed the non-payment of rent and abolished all zamindari rights.[114] The government and zamindari servants such as *patwaris, chowkidars* and *karinda* were made to pay money as fine.[115] The government deployed seventy armed *sowars* to effect his arrest on 29 January near Goshiaganj. He was sent to Fyzabad jail by a special train.[116] The word about his arrest was whispered around the fields, hearths and houses of the neighbouring peasantry. A big mob of peasants, the ranks of which continued to swell, assembled at the Goshiaganj railway station. They squatted on the railway track to prevent the train from moving. Finally the police had to resort to firing to disperse the crowd and several people were injured.[117]

ARREST AT KASHI VIDYAPITH

The government was divided over the issue of Baba Ram Chandra's arrest. The Commissioner of Fyzabad opined that his arrest would 'most certainly exasperate' the peasantry, and would lead to reprisals.[118] The Commissioner suggested relief measures to calm down frayed tempers instead of arresting the peasant leaders. The question of arrest was placed before the Lieutenant-Governor who after consulting his cabinet gave the green signal.[119] Ram Chandra was arrested on 10 February at Benares under Sections 124A (sedition) and 133A (promoting enemity between classes) for his inflammatory speeches at Bara Banki in early January.

The style of arrest adopted by the government was typical of an

[113] Crawley, op. cit.

[114] 'A note on spurious Ram Chandra', 50/1921 Gen UPSA.

[115] Ludvic Porter to Butler, 15 February 1921, ibid.

[116] Hailey to Lambert, 29 January 1921. 50-2/1921. Gen UPSA.

[117] Home Political, Nos. 195-216 1921 February-B, NAI, p. 21. Legislative Council Proceedings of UP, Vol. I, 1921.

[118] Hailey to G.B. Muir, 14 January 1921. 50/1921. Gen UPSA.

[119] 'Let it proceed, the cabinet agreed', Butler, 29 January 1921, ibid.

imperialist power. He was arrested before a crowd of 80,000 people soon after the opening ceremony of Kashi Vidyapith where he had gone at the invitation of Gauri Shanker Mishra. His arrest caused a great flutter and the Nehrus had to appeal to the crowd to remain peaceful.[120] After his arrest he was seated in Gandhi's room[121] from where he was taken to Benares Central Jail, and was locked in a cell meant for mad dogs.[122] Kapil Dev Malviya's contention was not without foundation that the government purposely selected the occasion to effect the arrest for had it resulted in disturbances it would have discredited Gandhi and his gospel of non-violence.[123] Jawaharlal Nehru held the same opinion.[124] K.D. Malviya further opined that the government was afraid to arrest so popular a leader anywhere except under the protection and indirect help of Gandhi.[125]

The news of his arrest spread like wild fire. In Bara Banki complete *hartal* was observed, and people assembled at the local jail to have a glimpse of him under the impression that he was locked up there.[126] The district authorities refused to try him at Bara Banki. The Deputy Commissioner of Bara Banki wrote: 'It is my firm belief that if Ram Chandra is tried in this district dangerous riots will take place both in Bara Banki and in Fyzabad and Rai Bareilly. These riots will undoubtedly require a strong military force to quell.'[127] He was, therefore, taken to Lucknow from Benares under the strictest surveillance. Even the station staff was not allowed to come to the platform until the special train had left.[128]

[120] *Independent*, 12 February 1921. Also Ram Chandra's notes.

[121] Gandhi's speech at Fyzabad, 10 February 1921. Home Political, No. 87/1921, NAI.

[122] Ram Chandra's notes.

[123] *Independent*, 12 February 1921.

[124] Ibid., 16 February 1921.

[125] Ibid., 12 February 1921.

[126] Ibid., 16 February 1921. Also Intelligence Bureau Records (hereafter IBR) relating to Kisan Sabha movement in the possession of Nehru Memorial Fund, New Delhi.

[127] Papers relating to Ram Chandra's trial, Motilal Nehru Papers (Legal) 1929-21, F. No. 44, NMML. Also *Independent*, 23 February 1921.

[128] *Independent*, 13 February 1921.

The Oudh peasantry was agitated by the arrest of their beloved leader. The non-cooperators and the Congress leadership were worried about the mood of the peasantry. Gandhi promptly declared his arrest as a sacred event and urged upon the peasantry not to demand his release as it would displease Ram Chandra.[129] Motilal Nehru sent Shah Saghir as his messenger to assuage the hurt feelings of the people of Bara Banki. Leaflets bearing the names of Motilal, Jawaharlal and Gauri Shanker, were distributed requesting the peasantry neither to agitate to secure his release nor to assemble to have his *darshan*.[130]

THE CONGRESS AND THE PEASANTRY OF OUDH

Ram Chandra who had an uncanny gift of sensing the mood of the peasantry, harped more on the theme of ending the taluqdars' tyranny. His removal from the scene left the peasants leaderless. The non-cooperators now had a monopoly in the field and the credulous peasantry was led to believe that the Congress stood for the immediate redressal of their grievances. Acharya Narendra Dev lamented: 'The Congress was not then willing to fight for the economic demands of the kisans though in its struggle the Congress assuredly desired the cooperation of the kisans.'[131] Mahatma Gandhi avoided all direct contacts with leaders of the Oudh kisan movement during his visit to these areas.[132] With no faith in class war Gandhi wished the leadership of the peasants to remain with the Nehrus:

> You should bear a little if the zamindar torments you. We do not wish to fight with the zamindars. We are fighting a big zamindar . . . zamindars are also slaves

[129] Gandhi's speech at Fyzabad, op. cit.

[130] IBR, op. cit. Moreover, the text of this leaflet issued by the Congress after his arrest does contain the curious formula that 'We must not be unhappy over this (his arrest) and must not even try to get him released'.

[131] Acharya Narendra Dev, *Socialism and the National Revolution*, Bombay, 1946, p. 60.

[132] No. 1/1921, Home Political Deposit, NAI.

and we do not want to trouble them. . . . If the zamindars harass them I would ask my kisan brethren not to fight with them but adopt a conciliatory attitude. They can go to Pandit Motilal Nehru and Jawaharlal Nehru who are sacrificing men and the kisan should act according to their decisions.[133]

He considered the peasants' movement as being 'anterior to and independent of' the Non-Cooperation movement.[134] Baba Ram Chandra, somewhat bitterly but significantly, commented:

Pandit Motilal ji, an advocate of the taluqdars, must have told Mahatma ji (Gandhi) that the Non-Cooperation movement or the movement for attaining *swaraj* could not proceed unless the Kisan movement is disrupted, because Baba Ram Chandra is a person in whose presence no other leader could influence the peasants. After his arrest only shall I (Motilal) be able to bring the peasants into 50 the Non-Cooperation movement. This was not an assumption on my part but a firm belief.[135]

Though Motilal Nehru might not have been instrumental in bringing about his arrest, it was in the interest of the Congress to suppress the rural leadership.[136] Ram Chandra's trial was held at Lucknow. He faced the trial boldly but was disappointed to see that Gandhi and Motilal Nehru had turned indifferent after he had been arrested.[137] He refused the services of Shaukat Ali and argued his case himself.[138] He was sentenced to two years' rigorous

[133] Gandhi's speech at Fyzabad, op. cit., Also see *Young India, Instruction to UP Peasants,* 9 March 1921; *Collected Works of Mahatma Gandhi,* Vol. XIX (*1920–21*), Ahmedabad, 1965.

[134] *Young India,* 18 May 1921; *Collected Works of Mahatma Gandhi,* Vol. XX, 1921, p. 1061. Also see P.D. Reeves, 'Politics of Order' *The Journal of Asian Studies,* Vol. XXV, No. 2 February 1966.

[135] RMD No. 5.

[136] See Crawley, op. cit., p. 95. Unfortunately the file of Ram Chandra's arrest has not been transferred to the National Archives of India which might have thrown some light on the issue.

[137] Advance copy of a para to appear in UP Secret Abstracts, 12 March 1921, 50/1921. Gen UPSA.

[138] *Independent,* 10 March 1921 (Perhaps he could not forget the treatment meted out to him at Abdul Bari's place and refused Shaukat Ali's services).

imprisonment and a fine of Rs. 2,000 or further imprisonment for six months.[139]

Thus the strong organization of the Oudh peasantry was shattered and Ram Chandra attributed it to the acts of the advocates and high class people, the bourgeois nationalist leaders.[140] It was he who had brought these leaders close to the peasantry, but was so frustrated by their betrayal that he went to the extent of writing that:

> . . . the literate persons may either have *swaraj* or they may beg, their profession is only theft and dacoity as they use the peasants for their own interests. To appease the peasants they would scold the zamindars or government officials and after being entertained by them they will leave in cars, having sown the seeds of ill will.[141]

Ram Chandra had never opposed the Congress programme, but the Congress leaders, though eager to bring the countryside into the national struggle, were not prepared to accept peasant leadership which stood not only for political liberty but also for economic emancipation.

LATER YEARS

After his release in 1923, Ram Chandra, learning from the experience he had gained during the movement of 1920–1, supported the Kisan Sabha movement in opposition to the Congress.[142] Throughout his life he worked for the emancipation of the peasantry and even thought of uniting the peasants of the world.[143] But he also supported the Congress demands for the freedom of the country and took active part in all the Congress sponsored movements. He was imprisoned in 1930, 1941 and again in 1942 for anti-government activities. He respected the leadership of Gandhi and Nehru

[139] *Independent*, 19 March 1921.
[140] Ram Chandra to G.B. Pant, April 1949, Baba Ram Chandra Papers.
[141] Ram Chandra's Writings.
[142] UP Secret Abstracts 1924, Intelligence Office, Lucknow.
[143] Baba Ram Chandra Papers.

but was displeased on seeing that the Congress was influenced by the capitalists and the taluqdars.[144] He was frustrated to see that the taluqdars had infiltrated into the Congress organization after the independence of the country, but thought himself to be too old to organize the peasants once again for liberating them from the clutches of their oppressors.[145] During his last days Ram Chandra led a miserable life. He died in 1950. Before his death he wrote: 'Had I been their (Congress leaders') yes man, I too would have lived in big bungalows and enjoyed all the comforts of life.'[146]

[144] Ibid.
[145] Ibid.
[146] Ibid.

CHAPTER 2

The *Ramcharitmanas* as a Radical Text: Baba Ram Chandra in Oudh, 1920–1950*

The peasantry[1] has been one of the most deprived social classes in Indian society. Yet, it has played a vital role in the struggle against imperialism and its allies and still continues its struggle against oppressive social forces. In certain cases, and particularly in Oudh, the radical rural intelligentsia represented by *babas, fakirs, sadhus* and *sannyasis*[2] attempted an 'innovative transformation' of the peasants to create a stage of 'cleavage'[3] or class consciousness. Belonging to peasant families, they played the role, in Gramscian terms, of 'organic intellectuals'[4] in the countryside. They were not revolutionaries of any accepted description belonging to any defined social class; nor did they conform to the behaviour pattern or articulation style

*The paper was earlier published in Sudhir Chandra (ed.), *Social Transformation and Creative Imagination*, Delhi, 1984 (an NMML publication). I am thankful to Profs. A.N. Pandeya and Sudhir Chandra for their valuable suggestions.

[1] By peasantry we mean all those peasants who actually work on the fields and this includes agricultural labourers. For a detailed discussion on the categories of rich, middle and poor tenant-peasants and agricultural labourers in Oudh see Kapil Kumar, *Peasants in Revolt: Tenants, Landlords, Congress and the Raj in Oudh, 1886–1922*, Delhi, 1984.

[2] During the 1920-2 peasants' movement a number of such characters played a radical role. Besides Baba Ram Chandra, some of the others were, Baba Janki Das, Faqir Faruq Ahmed, Rahamat Ali Shah, Shah Nairn Ata, and Sadhu Suraj Prasad. Madari Pasi made use of *Gita, Ramayan, Katha Sat Narain, Qur'an* and *Milad Sharif* to mobilize peasants.

[3] Antonio Gramsci, *Selections From The Prison Notebooks*, London, 1971, p. 52.

[4] Ibid., p. 3.

of the recognized leadership. Unlike the urban leaders, they did not indulge in sophisticated oratory or political propaganda for the purpose of mobilization. Their exercise rested on a deep understanding of the situation and a critical diagnosis of contemporary social reality. Aware of social contradictions, they directed the ideas and aspirations of the peasants by identifying themselves with the interests of the latter, and by working out and making coherent 'the principles and problems raised by the masses in their practical activity, thus constituting a cultural and social block'.[5] These leaders employed in pithy and telling ways the religious, cultural and traditional symbols of their society, in order to expose its existing exploitative structure and to foster anti-imperialist and anti-feudal sentiments among the peasants.

The transformation which the radical rural intelligentsia aspired for during the colonial era did not occur in an organized manner at an all India level. The peasants' initiatives to overthrow the hegemony of the colonial state and of the dominant social groups in colonial India remained sporadic in temporal as well as geographical terms. These fragmentary initiatives were not only crushed by the more effective actions of the dominant social groups, but they were also successfully utilized by the latter to overthrow the colonial hegemony, as Gramsci puts it, 'in order to conserve the assent of the subaltern groups and to maintain control over them'.[6]

According to Gramsci, 'over a certain period of history in certain specific historical conditions religion has been and continues to be a 'necessity', a necessary form taken by the will of the popular masses and a specific way of rationalizing the world and real life, which provided the general framework for real practical activity'.[7] Religion had and has its *reactionary* as well as *rational* aspects in the social life of the peasantry and religious literature is used as an instrument to uphold and sustain these two *contradictory aspects*. It has always been used by the ruling classes and oppressive social forces as a device to maintain their hegemony over the oppressed masses; to teach the toiling poor to resign themselves to their fate

[5]Ibid., p. 330.
[6]Ibid., p. 52.
[7]Ibid., p. 337.

and be tolerant; to have faith in God and leave themselves at his mercy; to make the poor and exploited masses believe that their present state of affairs is the upshot of deeds committed in a previous birth; and to sustain the existing social structure which serves their vested class interests. There are many for whom religious literature is a means to preserve their communal and caste interests. On the other hand, social reformers have drawn inspiration from religious texts to fight such social evils as untouchability, child marriage or *sati*, etc. Some political leaders have used religious texts to mobilize the people against imperialism by conceptualizing British rule as satanic or *Ravanraj* (rule of the demons) and *swaraj* as *Ramraj*—rule of God. Thus, it is of great importance to assess the use of religious literature by a peasant leader, Baba Ram Chandra, who used the *Ramcharitmanas* of Tulsidas, popularly known as the *Ramayan*[8] in the Oudh countryside, not only to expose and oppose the British, but also to highlight the inner contradictions of the Indian society. He used it to characterize the British, princes, landlords and the leaders of the national movement; to describe the condition of the peasants; to make the peasants aware of their exploitation and of the necessity to organize and assert their rights; to tell the peasants their duties during the national movement; and finally, what the achievement of independence meant to the peasants as against the upper strata of society.

Baba Ram Chandra had no formal schooling or education. He had, 'however, acquired previous experience of a working class movement as an indentured labourer in Fiji'.[9] After his flight from

[8] The title of Tulsidas's text is *Ramcharitmanas.* It has been mentioned as *Ramayan* by Baba Ram Chandra, the title by which it is popularly known in the Oudh countryside. Thus, we have also mentioned it as *Ramayan.* The English translation of the *Ramayan* verses is based on W. Douglas P. Hill, *The Holy Lake of the Acts of Rama,* Calcutta, 1971, and F.S. Growse, *The Ramayana of Tulsidas,* Delhi, 1978.

[9] Baba Ram Chandra Papers (hereafter BRP), Part I, Speeches and Writings (hereafter SW), F. No. 2, pp. 18–19, NMML. Ram Chandra has been described as a successful agitator in Fiji by the Deputy Commissioner of Partapgrah, V.N. Mehta Report, F. No. 753/1920, Revenue A, UP State Archives, Lucknow, p. 3.

Fiji to avoid arrest, during 1918–19 he moved about in the Jaunpur and Partapgarh countryside and gave religious discourses. The shift from *social* to religious work, on his own testimony, was due to some divine visions he had in his sleep.[10] In the course of this religious work he became familiar with the miserable condition of the peasants.[11] He was moved to see the tyranny of the landlords' managers and armed retainers, who forced the tenants to perform *begar* and cultivate indigo. His initial reaction was to work for harmony between the landlords and the tenants. Not sure whether he understood the situation well enough,[12] he was weighed down with a sense of his incapability to mediate effectively on the side of the tenants. He quoted Tulsidas to the following effect:[13] 'I have no education, no strength, nor money to spend. O God, only you can preserve the honour of a degraded person like me.'

He realized that the 'tradition of *Rambhakti* was extremely deep-rooted and popular' in the Oudh countryside, and decided to utilize it to do something for the upliftment of the peasants.[14] He started visiting various villages. He would carry on his back the religious literature related to *Ramayan* and *Gita* and would not part with it while he was moving, sleeping or eating.[15] As soon as he entered a village he would 'blow' the whistle of *Sita Ram*' to collect the peasants and recite passages from the *Ramayan*.[16]

The slogan of *Sita Ram* later on developed into a war cry during the peasant movement in 1920–1. Anybody in distress would raise the cry which would be repeated by whoever heard it. The cry would thus be relayed to the village and hundreds of peasants would soon converge at the point where the cry originated. The slogan not only created a bond of unity among different villages

[10] BRP-1, SW, F. No. 2.

[11] Ibid. For details of taluqdars' atrocities and peasants' exploitation, see Kapil Kumar, 'Peasants' Movement in Oudh, 1918–22', Meerut University thesis, 1980, pp. 30–91.

[12] BRP-2, RC, XI.

[13] BRP-1, SW, F. No. 2, p. 18.

[14] BRP-2, RC, XI.

[15] Ibid.

[16] BRP-1, SW, F. No. 2, p. 18.

but it also deterred the taluqdari agents from practising tyranny and forcing evictions. Jawaharlal Nehru has noted the significance of this slogan:[17] 'Sita Ram was an old common cry but he [Ram Chandra] gave it an almost war like significance and made it a signal for emergencies as well as a bond between different villages.'

Ram Chandra was successful in gaining the peasants' confidence by listening to their grievances. But the main task was to organize them for asserting their rights. The opportunity to do this came when Jhinguri Singh and Sahdev Singh, who had already formed a Kisan Sabha at the village of Rure in 1917, approached him to lead their organization.[18] After reaching Rure, Ram Chandra linked the name of the village with a verse from the *Ramayan*:[19] 'The two brothers reside in the assembly of kings as though beauty herself was dwelling in their persons' (*Balkand, chaupai* 240) and added on his own: 'Now Ram Chandra, Sahdev and Jhinguri are like them [Ram and Laxman] in Rure.'

Soon Rure became a centre of Kisan Sabha activity, and Ram Chandra, as the Deputy Commissioner of Partapgarh put it (not without some concern), became 'a magnet of attraction' who supplied 'som' mental *pabulum* to a people intellectually starved in these out of the way places.[20] Ram Chandra devised indigenous methods to propagate his programme[21] and to organize the peasants. He would suspend a cot horizontally with ropes tied to the trees and use it as a pulpit to address gatherings of thousands without

[17] J. Nehru, *Autobiography*, New Delhi, 1962, p. 52.

[18] This incident was described by Ram Chandra by citing Tulsidas: 'As destiny decrees, so help appears, either you go to meet it, or it comes to a man itself and leads him to safety'. (*Balkand, doha* 159b), BRP-2, RC, XI. For details of the formation of this Sabha at Rure, see M.H. Siddiqi, *Agrarian Unrest in North India*, Delhi, 1978, p. 104; D.N. Panigrahi, 'Peasant Leadership', in B.N. Pandey (ed.), *Leadership in South Asia*, New Delhi, 1977, p. 87; S.K. Mittal and Kapil Kumar, 'Baba Ram Chandra and Peasant Upsurge in Oudh, 1920-21', *Social Scientist*, Vol. 6, No. 11, June 1978, p. 38.

[19] Interview with Jung Bahadur Singh, village Rure, dist. Partapgarh.

[20] V.N. Mehta Report, p. 2.

[21] For details of his programme see Mittal and Kumar, op, cit., p. 39.

the help of loudspeakers.[22] He would, with his neat hand, write hundreds of pamphlets on various peasant problems. The words *Sita Ram* would be inscribed at the top of the pamphlet and appropriate verses from the *Ramayan* would be cited.[23]

Ram Chandra wanted to broaden the movement by drawing the attention of Gandhi towards it. With this aim he organized a march of about 500 peasants on foot from Patti to Allahabad, on the occasion of the *Saptami* bathing day. in early June 1920.[24] He started the march by quoting what Vibhishan had to say to Hanuman:[25] 'Hanuman, I feel more confidence, for without Hari's favour' there is no meeting with the good' (*Sundarkand*, ch. 7)

A fact worth mentioning here is that there were Muslim peasants also in this march.[26]

It is difficult to chronologically identify his writings. In this paper, I am not dealing with the ideological contradictions of Baba Ram Chandra but only taking up the thematic use of *Ramayan* by him which may be classified under the following headings:

CHARACTERIZATION OF THE BRITISH, OPPRESSIVE SOCIAL FORCES, LANDLORDS AND THE PEASANTS' CONDITION

In a piece written in the late thirties, Ram Chandra mentions that 'the highest *gaddi* (seat of power) of Indians is at Delhi or Pune, but today they are vacant and masterless. The foreigners have through treachery, made a *gaddi* at New Delhi. They are ruling according to their wish and forcing their laws and language on the Indians.'[27] Referring to the help rendered by certain sections of the Indian society to the British, he wrote:[28] 'They have bribed

[22] *Swatantrata Sangram Ke Sainik*, Vols. 13 and 26, Lucknow, 1972.

[23] There are several such pamphlets in BRP.

[24] *The Leader*, 23 September 1920; *Abhyudaya*, 12 June 1920; V.N. Mehta Report, p. 3.

[25] BRP-2, RC, XI.

[26] *Abhyudaya*, 12 June 1920.

[27] BRP-1, SW, F. No. 2, p. 113.

[28] Ibid.

the Indian rulers to their side and through them only are they avenging the *gadar* (revolt) of 1857 by torturing thirty-three crores of Indians'.

To expose the selfishness of the British and of their landlord allies and their callous exploitation of poor peasantry, he likened them to Indra, the king of gods, and quoted the following verse:[29]

> Though the king of gods, there is no limit to his guile and rascality; he loves another's loss and his own gain. The ways of Indra are like those of a crow—crafty, scoundrelly with no faith in anyone. Having in the first instance formed an evil plot and accumulating all the forces of deceit, he piled up trouble on the head of everybody. (*Ayodhyakand*, ch. 301)

It is striking that while citing this verse, Ram Chandra excluded the next verse, which is: 'Everyone was infatuated by the Gods' delusive power; their love for Ram was so violent that they would not be separated from him.'

To a certain extent he held the British responsible for diverting the taluqdars' attention from their subjects and differentiated them from their pre-colonial forebears.[30] Through *Ramayan* he described the peasants' condition and attributed it to the administration and policies of the British and the taluqdars. The verses cited by him relate to Ram's condition in the forest; Bharat's views about his mother, etc.[31]

> The people in their distress had the current of their ideas as disturbed as the water at the confluence of a river with the sea. Thus wavering in their mind they found no comfort anywhere; nor did any disclose to another the secrets of his heart. (*Ayodhyakand*, ch. 301)
>
> They wear deerskins, eat fruits, sleep on the ground strewn with grass and leaves, they live beneath the trees enduring cold and heat and rain and wind. (*Ayodhyakand*, *doha* 211)

By 'people' and 'they', Ram Chandra means the peasants and equates them with Ram, Sita and Lakshman. Further he quoted:

[29] Ibid., pp. 113–14.
[30] Ibid., pp. 114–15.
[31] Ibid., p. 115.

My mother's evil design, the source of all this mischief, was the carpenter who fashioned an evil adze out of our interests, and with the evil of wood jealously wrought an evil instrument and fixed it with the cruel, evil spell of the period of Ram's banishment. (*Ayodhyakand*, ch. 212)

'My mother's evil designs' are the intentions of the British who acted as a carpenter to create the 'evil instrument' of the taluqdari system; 'our interests' are the peasants' interests; and 'Ram's banishment' is the peasants' condition. Next: 'For my sake she fashioned this evil contrivance and ruined and confounded the whole world' (*Ayodhyakand*, ch. 212).

'My' here means the taluqdars and 'She' the British government; the message being that the British created the taluqdari system and ruined the peasants. Here he excluded the next line of the verse: 'These evil times will come to an end when Ram returns to Oudh. . . . There is no other way.'

This deletion suggests that he was not entertaining the idea of *Ramrajya*. No where did he mention or support this concept.

Ram Chandra was so much concerned about peasants' exploitation that he quoted the verses related to Bharat's worry about Ram:[32] 'It is this burning pain that ceaselessly consumes my chest so that I can neither eat by day nor sleep at night. There is no medicine for this fell sickness; I have searched the whole world in my thoughts' (*Ayodhyakand*, ch. 212).

After citing these verses Ram Chandra warned that 'only once will he ask the taluqdars . . . who are exploiting the peasants through illegal acts, to work for the benefit of the people . . . and if they fail we shall act on our Congress's advice.' The advice which he offered in the name of the Congress was: not to pay rent to taluqdari agents; not to obey any taluqdari dictates; not to pay a single pie as rent in the case of natural calamity and to pay only that much rent which has been advised by the Congress; and to have no relations with taluqdars, but only with the government, for only then peace shall prevail in the world.[33] This showed his hostility to the middlemen. Thus, without explicitly suggesting it, he asked

[32]Ibid., pp. 115–16.
[33]Ibid., p. 117.

for the abolition of taluqdari. He also warned the government officials, who looted the peasants and terrorized them with guns and rifles, to behave decently with the peasants. He suggested the formation of a committee to administer the country and to appoint everybody, from Viceroy to watchman. Indians should have the right to elect this committee and formulate laws which will solve all their problems.[34]

As part of his attack on the landlords and their connections with the British, Ram Chandra invoked a millenarian past that accorded beautifully with the popular remembrance of mythical antiquity. The ancient kings, he wrote, confronted many hurdles for the benefit of their subjects.[35] Moving on to more recent past, he found the existing landlords wanting woefully in comparison with their forefathers who had fought against alien rulers in 1857:[36]

> After foregoing their pride and with the help of the people of another country, these taluqdars, whose ancestors had fought the British in 1857, are now bent upon destroying their own subjects. . . . They should feel ashamed of their acts for there is no king of India . . . the king of another country is ruling here and everybody is a subject.

With the help of his favourite comparison with Indra, he described the unchecked oppression of the peasantry by quoting the following verses:[37]

> You are absolutely independent and there is no one to restrain you, so you do whatever you please. You make good evil and evil good, with a heart that feels neither grief nor joy. You have tested everyone by perpetually deceiving them; you fear nobody and you think it all good fun. You are not hindered by regard for good or evil deeds, and so far none has put you right. But now you have made fun of someone like me and you shall receive a due return for your act. (*Balkand*, chs. 136–7)

Imperialism was thus defined in the idiom of common folk. Like Indra, the British were the supreme sovereign who pursued their selfish interests without any restraint.

[34] Ibid., p. 118.
[35] Ibid., pp. 95–6.
[36] Ibid., p. 95.
[37] Ibid., p. 98.

While reposing faith in Gandhi and the Indian National Congress, Ram Chandra could see the duplicity of those who, although participating in the national movement, were motivated more by their narrow selfish interests. Such people had no qualms about exploiting the masses, including the peasantry, in the name of nationalism. He characterized these leaders thus:[38] 'At the moment the very persons whose shelter peasants had taken, are considering themselves the defenders of India, though in reality they are destroying the people with the help of *taluqdars, kings* and big *mahajans.*'

He quoted from the *Ramcharitmanas* to caution the peasants about the dual character of those who talked of serving the masses while remaining aloof from them. The verses he cited related to what Manthara had said to Kaikeyi about the prospective enthronement of Lord Ram:[39]

> Your rival queen desires to pluck you up by the root, so fence your garden round about with the stout hedge of a scheme. (*Ayodhyakand*, ch. 16)
>
> But now those days are past and gone, as soon as they get the opportunity, friends become enemies. (*Ayodhyakand*, ch. 17)

THE CONGRESS LEADERS BEFORE INDEPENDENCE

In this context Ram Chandra was alarmed by the relationship between the Congress and the landlords. The latter, he knew, joined the national body 'not to serve the people but in order to control the people through various legal provisions'.[40] In the pursuit of their narrow group interests, the landlords often got support from the Congress leaders. He compared such leaders to the gods who, for their selfish ends, had requested Saraswati to prepare the ground for Ram's banishment. Using Saraswati's reaction to their request, Ram Chandra described his feelings about these leaders.[41] 'High is their dwelling but low are their deeds; they cannot bear to look on another's prosperity' (*Ayodhyakand*, ch. 12).

[38] Ibid.

[39] Ibid., Printed Material (hereafter PM), A, F. No. 2.

[40] Ibid., Subject Files (hereafter SF), No. 3, p. 107.

[41] Ibid., p. 108.

Or they were like Lakshman as Parashuram had seen him: 'Though fair to see, his heart is evil, like a golden jar full of poison' (*Balkand*, ch. 278).

In these verses the urban Congress leaders are like Lakshman, and the taluqdars like villains and gods. Here, Ram Chandra clearly distinguishes between the landlords and the Congress leaders; but the latter's dual character is not hidden from him. The following verse, which is related to Ram's preaching to Sugriva, is cited to urge the peasants on to a total rejection of these persons:

> If a man hypocritically speaks fair words to one's face and slanders one behind one's back, a man whose soul is crooked and whose mind moves tortuously like a snake, then brother, it is better to have no dealings with such a disloyal friend.
>
> (*Kishkindhakand*, ch. 7)

Ram Chandra mounted a similar criticism against social workers who, without the slightest concern for the poor villager, used village upliftment programme as a cover for making money.[42]

The written programme of *gram sudhar* (village upliftment) is beautiful, but time servers have penetrated it. I have doubts how the government will be able to get the work accomplished through these people. . . . Unless all the petty and high officials related to *gram sudhar* are not kept in village huts, it all will be a big waste of money.

He further added:

> All those whom you see as reformers today are the ones who were idlers. They were worried about their stomachs (*unko apne pet ki hai hai pari thi*). By placing that *hai hai* (worry) on your head they have found a way out of their unemployment. They do not know your language, nor do they like your appearance, and they are not country dwellers.

These persons came to villages all dressed up and seated in cars, and, according to him, they were interested only in their own selves (*gram sudhar wale jivan sudhar kai pujari . . . ban baithai hain*).[43] Congressmen are 'flowing in the stream of office acceptance' and

[42] *Aba Bhi Ankhe Kholo Kisano*, 1938, ibid., P.M. (booklets) B.
[43] Ibid., SF, F. No. 3.

capitalists and police are bothered about their own interests. In spite of the fact that 'the theory or principle of the great Congress leaders is that there can be no great reform for *kisans* and *mazdurs* without achieving complete independence',[44] according to him some concessions could actually be implemented at the moment.

THE CONGRESS LEADERSHIP AFTER INDEPENDENCE

The realization that even Congress leaders could not be trusted to look after the interests of the poor assailed him with greater acuteness on the eve of Independence. The prospect of political power passing into the hands of these leaders inspired in him the kind of apprehension Lakshman had entertained about Bharat when the latter, accompanied by Shatrughan, was coming to see him in the forest.[45]

A worldly man, who has got power becomes infatuated and so foolishly betrays himself. (*Ayodhyakand*, ch. 228)

Gathering together an army with evil intent, he has come to make his sovereignty secure. Countless crooked schemes have the two brothers devised, and have assembled their army and come. If there was no treachery and wicked intent in his heart, why should he want to bring all these chariots and horses and elephants (*Ayodhyakand*, ch. 228).

The two brothers here appear to be capitalists and landlords. Ram Chandra admonished the Congress leaders turned rulers: 'Now that you have become king, you exceed in your actions all the bounds of duty' (*Ayodhyakand*, ch. 228).

He also gave expression to his sense of betrayal when he addressed the Congress leaders like the way Kaikeyi had rebuked Dasharatha.[46] 'If you were going to act like this in the end, on what strength had you pressed me to ask for the boon' (*Ayodhyakand*, ch. 35).

Ram Chandra hoped that the threat of being ruled by such

[44] Ibid.

[45] Ibid., PM, F. No. 1.

[46] Ibid.

people would oblige the peasants and workers to realizer:[47] 'For one bound by fate to live in the service of an enemy, death were far better than life' (*Ayodhyakand*, ch. 190).

He felt uncomfortable that in spite of seeing what was happening, he was being advised to do nothing to alter the course of events: 'How long must I endure and control myself, though my lord is with me and my bow in my hand' (*Ayodhyakand*, ch. 229).

He cited another verse to renew commitment to his 'lord' and 'master', the poor peasantry: I shall fight for my master on the battle field and illuminate the *fourteen worlds* with my glory' (*Ayodhyakand*, ch. 190).

Swaraj, to Ram Chandra, did not mean just the end of British *raj*. It also meant the end of people's miseries. Otherwise, if previously 'we were under the white government, now we shall be under the black government'.[48] He admitted that after acquiring power the Congress had brought some light to the dark life of peasants. But, on the whole, they remained 'entrapped by *thugs*'. The tragic situation, as he saw it, was that the Congress 'forgets its real self' and 'we have to face miseries'.[49] Believing the Congress promise to abolish capitalism and landlordism, he lamented that nothing had been done to set right the old character of capitalists and landlords. The two acted as follows:[50] 'Enemy, moreover of the warrior caste and a prince, he was bent upon furthering his own ends by force and fraud' (*Balkand*, ch. 160).

Still maintaining his faith in the Congress, Ram Chandra bemoaned the way capitalists and landlords 'are destroying our pious Congress'. He was not sure that the new constitution, towards which 'all eyes are centred . . . and which we are told will bring good days in future', would really benefit the 'uneducated society', because only '*brahmins*, *kshatrias*, *vaishyas*, the zamindar party, the taluqdar party, the ruling party, the *vakil* party or school masters will find a place in it'. These persons will 'get an opportunity to

[47] Ibid.

[48] Ibid., SW, F. No. 2.

[49] Ibid., SF, No. 3, p. 60.

[50] Ibid.

settle old scores'. They will 'raise their walls on *solah annah* (cent per cent) lies which they have been doing till now'. He cited the following verse: 'Even if by associating with good people they do some good, the wicked never wholly lose their innate wickedness' (*Balkand*, ch. 7).

And in utter despondency added: 'There is no medicine for this fell sickness.'[51]

He described the leaders of the day as 'hypocrites' who, being in league with the officials and the police, treated the tahsil as their property. In public they 'abuse officials and when they visit the latter they bribe them with sweets' (*janta mein afsar ko gali aur afsar ke yahan dali*). They 'want *laddus* (sweets) in both of their hands and mouth'.[52]

PEASANT MOBILIZATION

The *Ramayan* was utilized by Ram Chandra not only to expose and criticize the British, the internal oppressive social forces and the Congress leaders, but also to make use of it to mobilize peasants and acquaint them with the methods to be adopted for asserting their rights. The verses he cited related to the ocean's character as described by Ram:[53]

> To make petition to an adamant person, to treat a scoundrel with affection, to deal liberally with a born miser, to discourse of wisdom with a man absorbed in thought of self, to advise continence to a very avaricious man or to tell of Hari to a lecher, it is the same as to sow seed in a barren land. (*Sundarkand*, ch. 58)

He asked the peasants to remember: 'Only by pruning will a plantain bear fruit, though endless effort may be spent on watering; even so a mean man heeds not a prayer, only by threats will he learn humility' (*Sundarkand*, *doha* 58).

Obviously Ram Chandra had no faith in petitioning. He believed in direct action. This loss of faith in petitioning was an outcome of

[51] Ibid.
[52] Ibid.
[53] Ibid., SW, F. No. 2, p. 209.

his practical experience. Ram Chandra cited the words of Ravan, when the latter saw his warriors flee the battlefield:

> If I hear of anyone turning to flee from the battlefield, I will slay him with my dread sword. You have eaten of my bounty and feasted as you please, and now in the battle-field your lives have become dear to you. (*Lankakand*, ch. 42)

Here he himself is Ravan and the peasants are his warriors. The next verse cited relates to what Angad had to say to Ravan. Here Angad symbolizes Ram Chandra himself, Ravan the taluqdars, and monkeys and bears the peasants:

> Cut your throat and die you shameless destroyer of your race; are you not terrified at the sight of our power.
>
> You will reap your reward for this later on when the monkeys and bears cuff you. (*Lankakand*, ch. 33)

This citation was a direct challenge to landlords. Through the next verse he urged the peasants to rise in revolt against the taluqdars:

> The monkeys cuffed and kicked them and bit them with their teeth, and then belaboured them and threatened them with shouts of triumph: kill them, seize them, *seize and kill them*, smash their heads, clutch and tear out their arms. (*Lankakand*, ch. 33)

Suggesting an all out war against the taluqdars, he justified such means by citing Ram's advice to his teachers, Brahmins and to all citizens: 'Whoever crosses not the ocean of birth and death though he finds such means as these, is an ungrateful insensate and suicidal wretch' (*Uttarakand*, *doha* 44).

It is significant that Ram Chandra justifies his call to the peasants to rise against' the taluqdars in the name of Ram. For, the kind of struggle he justifies is in marked contrast with the means recommended by Ram; these means being 'ocean of morality, wind of God's grace and good teachers'.[54] Ram Chandra exhorted the peasants to stake everything they possessed or held dear:[55] 'Perish that wealth and home and pleasure and those friends and parents

[54] See Tulsidas, *Ramcharitmanas* (*Uttarkand*, ch. 44).

[55] BRP-1, SW, F. No. 2, p. 209.

and brothers that lend not cheerful aid to our quest for Ram's feet' (*Ayodhyakand, doha* 185).

Here 'Ram's feet' symbolized the cause of peasants. He wanted them to sacrifice everything in order to obtain their rights. The struggle against the landlords had to be part of the struggle for freedom. In a pamphlet written during the Congress ministry period, he stressed the need for a psychological liberation from the hold of the alien masters. He wrote:[56] 'It is only after destruction in every work that freedom comes. My guess is that the most important role in this is that of the ears.'

He quoted the following verse to strengthen his argument: 'Whoever hears and understands with joyful heart bathes with utmost devotion' (*Balkand, doha* 2).

This, according to him, proved that the 'ears are the root' of everything. But when 'everyone's ears are attentive to *videshi* (foreign) orders, how can they listen to the message of freedom?' Their 'feet are marching on *videshi* orders'. Not a single foot is marching 'towards independent India'. How is 'one going to realize the distance of the destination (*manzil*) of freedom?' Even 'hands are receiving food and clothing at the *videshi* orders' India, he felt, could not move towards freedom so long as the following message of the *Gita* was not propagated among the masses.[57] 'Killed you will obtain heaven; victorious, you will enjoy the earth' (ch. 2, *shloka*, 37).

CIVIL DISOBEDIENCE MOVEMENT AND GANDHI

Ram Chandra considered it imperative to remove fear from people's minds. Likening the freedom struggle, at the time of the Civil Disobedience movement, to a game of chess where the pawns had to make the first move, he wrote that of the 33 crore 'pawns of India, one weak pawn (Gandhi), without any army or crown, has moved forward'.[58] It was the duty of the peasants to march behind

[56] Ibid., SF, No. 1, p. 63.
[57] Ibid.
[58] Ibid., F. No. 2, p. 72.

Gandhi. As for the heavy odds against them in this apparently unequal struggle, Ram Chandra alluded to the fears expressed by Vibhishan as Ram confronted the mighty forces of Ravan in the field of battle. Seeing Ram on foot and Ravan mounting a chariot, Vibhishan asked Ram in apprehension.[59] 'Lord, you have no chariot, nor anything to protect your body nor shoes on your feet. How will you overcome this enemy?' (*Lankakand*, ch. 80).

He proceeded to cite Ram's reply:

> Heroism and courage are the wheels of my chariot, truth and virtuous conduct its firm set flags and pennants.
>
> The worship of God is its skilful charioteer, detachment his shield and contentment his scimitar.
>
> Alms giving is his axe and understanding his keen lance, and the highest wisdom his unyielding bow. His quiver is a soul stainless and unmoved, filled with the arrows of restraint, control and pious observance. Worship of *Brahmans* is his impenetrable buckler. There is no other way to win victory than this. My friend, one who rides upon this chariot of righteousness, for him there is no foe to conquer. (*Lankakand*, ch. 80)

When Gandhi went on fast against the Communal Award Ram Chandra wrote: 'If Mahatmaji dies there will be fire in the country . . . I will also commit suicide.'[60] Then he cited the following verses to warn against the result of not obeying Gandhi.[61] '(When Hanuman has burnt Lanka the citizens say) Such is the penalty for scorning the good; our city is burning as though it had no lord' (*Sundarkand*, ch. 26).

He was assured of Gandhi's eventual success because:

> Those, in whose hearts dwell desire for the good of others, find nothing in the world too hard to win. (*Aranyakand*, ch. 25)
>
> Gold is proved on the touchstone and a gem by the jeweller; so also are the men proved at the testing time by their character. (*Ayodhyakand*, ch. 283)

[59] Ibid., pp. 73–4. For peasants' attitude towards an understanding of Gandhi, see Kapil Kumar, 'Peasants' Perception of Gandhi and His Programme: Oudh 1920–2', *Social Scientist*, Vol. 11, No. 2, February 1983.

[60] BRP-1, SF, No. 2, p. 79.

[61] Ibid.

The British could not but come to grief in their confrontation with Gandhi for the simple reason that: 'For those monarchs, by whom hermits and ascetics are vexed, burn even though there is no fire' (*Ayodhyakand*, ch. 126).

Power of faith apart, even in more mundane and practical terms he argued that 'we had protected the British from the Germans, then how come we cannot take our kingdom back from these handful of white people?'[62]

As important as the fact of Ram Chandra's zealous support to Gandhi is his understanding of what Gandhi stood for. Imagining himself as the king in Gandhi's *raj,* Ram Chandra spelt out the following agenda:[63]

1. I would have given the land of my kingdom to the people.
2. Would not have kept my people under anybody's subjugation.
3. Would not have taken my people to courts on false charges.
4. Would not have maintained jails or courts in my kingdom.
5. Would have *offered the same food and the same clothes to everyone.*
6. The *banias* have looted our forefathers for ages through 'interest'. *I would have invested this looted money for opening industries in the countryside.*
7. Would have kept the people in good houses and myself stayed at the threshold, acting as their watchman.
8. I would not have imported anything and would have opened good industries in my kingdom.
9. Hindus and Muslims would have had equal place in my kingdom.
10. Would not have killed my people with bullets. Had they killed me I would have attained *baikunt* (heaven).

Ram Chandra requested Gandhi not to be annoyed with such a programme and cited a *drishtant* (illustration or a tale conveying a moral). A big frog used to trouble the smaller frogs in a pond. Some boys saw this and decided to liberate the smaller frogs from the tyranny of the big frog by either killing the latter or by throwing

[62] Ibid., p. 85.

[63] Ibid., pp. 87–8 (emphasis added).

him out of the pond. The youngest among the boys started pelting stones without bothering about the warning of the other boys that in this process some small frogs, too, might be killed. Seeing his determination, the others also joined in and killed the big frog. But some small frogs, too, were killed in the process. The young boy, Ram Chandra believed, did not incur the sin of killing some small frogs as he had acted in good faith for the welfare of others and had 'liberated the smaller frogs for ever'.[64]

CONCLUSION

The characters of *Ramayan* were living beings for Ram Chandra, very much alive in the present world. Ravan, Surpanakha, Manthara, Kaikeyi and Narad are regarded as evil characters by those who look upon *Ramayan* as a religious text. Ram Chandra did not hesitate to cite these characters approvingly if what they had to say was relevant to explain the present situation. In the same leaflet he would cite the verses 'which criticize Ravan and also the verses related to what Ravan has to say for mobilizing his army. Ram Chandra did not use *Ramayan* for the sake of devotion. Rather, he used it to expose the exploitative character of the given social organization and for its transformation.

Ram Chandra had the utmost regard for Gandhi. But he did not entertain the idea of *Ramraj*; nor did he make vague promises to the peasants in the name of *Ramraj*. For Gandhi *Ramayan* was the 'greatest book in all devotional literature', and *Ramraj* a rule of *dharma* or people's rule.[65] According to him:[66] 'All the sacred books, the *Gita*, *Ramayan* and the Bible, taught that there could be no cooperation between devils and good, no friendliness between saints and satans, no mutual help and cooperation.'

But the devil and satan for Gandhi were embodied by British rule which he so often described as *Ravanraj*. He did not look

[64] Ibid., p. 86.

[65] *The Collected Works of Mahatma Gandhi*, Vol. XIX, p. 77; Vol. XX, p.122; M.K. Gandhi, *My Experiments With Truth*, Ahmedabad, 1927, p. 83.

[66] *The Searchlight*, 10 December 1920.

upon the oppressive social forces within the Indian society as devils or satans.

For Ram Chandra the landlords, capitalists, moneylenders and all those forces that exploited the people were devils. He used *Ramayan* to mobilize the peasants for a struggle not only against the British but also against these internal oppressors. To Ram Chandra the British and their landlord allies were like Indra, the king of gods. He found in them all the wickedness, treachery and rascality of Indra, as depicted in Tulsi's *Ramayan.* According to Gandhi, 'the weapons that Rama used were purely spiritual'.[67] But Ram Chandra recommended the weapons used by monkeys and bears, the practical weapons of war, and justified their use by quoting Ram. Gandhi believed in trusteeship and change of heart whereas Ram Chandra cited Tulsidas to argue that the wicked may do some good by coming into association with good but their innate wickedness is never destroyed. He also used *Ramayan* to expose the double faced nationalist leaders.

A fact worth mentioning here is that though Ram Chandra often cited the example of Russia along with verses from the *Ramayan,* he never wrote a word about Marxism or Communism. He did refer to Lenin as 'the dear leader of the *kisans*', and wrote that the peasants 'are still slaves except in Russia.'[68] But there is no evidence to suggest any links that he might have had with the Communist Party of India, though he had contact with Manilal[69] while he was in Fiji and again during 1925–7 when he brought Manilal to Fyzabad to highlight peasant grievances.[70]

It is not only that Ram Chandra used religious literature to mobilize peasants, but also that he was aware of the progressive role of

[67] *Young India,* 1 December 1921.

[68] See Siddiqi, op. cit., p. 195.

[69] For Manilal's connections with communists see Sunit Chopra, 'Bourgeois Historiography and the Peasant Question', *Social Scientist,* Vol. 7, No. 11, June 1979, p. 78.

[70] BRP-1, SW, F. No. 2. During this period Manilal has been mentioned in the Intelligence Report as 'working for the Bolshevik Party in India of M.N. Roy along with Mahendra Pratap Singh'. Home Poll. F. No. 379-1, K.W/1924, National Archives of India.

literature and writers in building up a society. According to him, 'in all societies it becomes the duty of the leading persons to collect the literature of their society, resolve the deep meanings of every language and through their wisdom pick up the real text to use it for building up a *bara samaj* (big society) for the benefit of the world:' He added that 'through this only will they be able to generate the strength for removing vast contradictions' which 'will help in overcoming extremely difficult paths'.[71]

The Tulsi *Ramayan* is regarded as the peasants' text. But it has been and is still being used by the dominant social groups and castes to sustain their vested interests. For many it is just a sacred text of devotional literature, the reading and recitation of which leads one to heaven. It was Baba Ram Chandra who made a radical use of this devotional text, and used the peasants' tradition and culture to highlight the inner contradictions of the Indian society, and to fight oppressive social forces.

NOTE

The Kisan Sabha still existed in Rure and its membership was about 27,000 in 1977 when I toured these areas. Baba Ram Chandra is a legend for the peasants of Partapgarh and Rai Bareilly districts. In the course of interviews, the peasants would often recite a verse from the *Ramayan*, whenever I asked them the meaning, their reply was: *aap yeh nahin samjhenge* (you won't understand this). They were right. For, being a representative of the 'elite society', I did fail to understand their citations. It was only while writing this paper that I realized what the *Ramayan* is for the peasants of Oudh. Irrespective of their caste or religious identities, it has for generations provided the infrastructure, as it were, for their psycho-intellectual makeup.

[71] BRP-1, SW, F. No. 3.

CHAPTER 3

Ritualism to Radical Social Reality: Some Reflections on the Innovative Uses of Vedic Literature on the Eve of 1942, Baba Ram Chandra in Oudh*

The mightiest challenge to the British authority in India during the twentieth century came in the form of Quit India movement—a movement comparable only to that of the struggle of 1857. A number of studies have dealt with this massive upsurge of Indian people. Most of these researches highlight or hero worship the National level leadership—particularly Gandhi for giving the 'Do or Die' slogan and for launching the struggle. Similarly, a lot of debate has taken place as to the role of different political parties and individuals during the movement. Certain studies have highlighted the popular response to the movement and how parallel governments were established and administered during the movement. Yet, not much attention has been devoted to the attitudes, mental framework and mobilization efforts of the local leadership at a time when all eyes were centred towards the Congress Working Committee meeting at Bombay. The Congress ministries' resignation, the deliverance day celebrations by the Muslim League, the Pakistan resolution, Subhas Chandra Bose escape and the formation of INA along with the half-hearted individual satyagrah by Gandhi were the major events that preceded the Quit India movement. Though, the Congress had resigned from the government in the provinces, the very formation of these ministries had

*An earlier version of this paper was presented at a Seminar in March 1988 at Centre for Social Studies, Surat. I am extremely thankful to Late Prof. A.N. Pandeya and Prof. Ram Bapat (Pune University) for their valuable suggestions that helped me in improving this paper.

one positive impact on the people. It had become clear to the masses that freedom can be a reality and the British Raj was not going to survive for long. *And it was this psyche of the people that shaped the events of the Quit India movement.* With the leadership having been immediately arrested and the Congress having offered no definite programme of action, the people in different parts of the country initiated their own action programmes. The present paper investigates ideological inspiration and the methods of mobilization adopted by Baba Ram Chandra in the Oudh countryside on the eve of 1942.

Baba Ram Chandra had continuously utilized the *Ramcharitmanas* not only to expose and oppose the British, but also to highlight the inner contradictions of Indian society. I have elsewhere written on this aspect. The *Ramcharitmanas* was made political use of not only due to its popularity but for the kind of intellectual stimulation this text had provided the peasants for generations in relation to not only their psycho-intellectual make up but also in understanding the social realities.[1] While going through the Ram Chandra papers, I came across three of his writings which referred to certain Vedic *richas* (verses) and the dates were important, 30 June 1942; 4 and 9 August 1942.[2] A few days later he was arrested. It is worth noting here that Vedic literature was not at all popular in the Oudh countryside and was confined to religious ceremonies for ritualistic uses only. And here again one discovers that Baba Ram Chandra, as a real rural intellectual, liberates these *richas*, *mantras* and *sutras* from their ritualistic enclosures to explain the social reality and challenges the forces which hinder the development of a free man. In his translations the spirit remains the same as that in the text but his presentation is free from the ritualistic usage. It is applied to a domain that might have been the original intention of the creators of the text as such, i.e. providing a philosophical text to understand the worldly realities—social, political or cultural. But before I go to these aspects I would like to refer briefly

[1]See Kapil Kumar, 'The *Ramcharitmanas* as a Radical Text: Baba Ram Chandra in Oudh, 1920–1950', op. cit., pp. 311–33.

[2]Baba Ram Chandra's Papers (hereafter BRP): Speeches and Writings, NMML.

to his mental framework during this period in relation to the prevailing socio-political environment in the Oudh countryside.

The Congress ministry had failed to the expectations of the peasants. Their exploitation continued unabated and Ram Chandra was very critical of the linkages that had been established between the Congress, landlords and capitalists. Politics, he believed, was 'a dirty game':[3] 'Those who are masters in deceit, cleverness, jealousy, fraud, etc., are considered to be the participants in politics.'

And he added:[4]

> Many peasants have been to jail. What did they lose? They did lose their lands, orchards and wells. What the big people lost was restored to them but who will restore what the peasants lost? Peasants are more in numbers. But who will stand with these groups of crazy peasants.

He further stressed that:[5]

> Till the beginning of the movement the politicians run to their (peasant's) houses but once having got the leadership of the movement it becomes a big sin to look towards them. They even go to the extent of saying who should adopt their long line (of peasants). Shame on such leaders. The movement is lost among the educated people and the leaders become egoistic.

He was extremely critical of the double faced local Congress leaders. Yet he was prepared to go with Gandhi or Nehru for the freedom of the country.[6]

He considered the British as great exploiters and everything which they claimed to have done for the benefit of India was in fact meant to gain more profits for themselves only. He was warning England.[7]

> Oh Britain! You yourself have given space to a devilish Churchill in your parliament. And the other devil Amery was imposed on India. Oh Britain! Now also, get into senses. Bow before India, go to your own country and roam freely there.

[3]BRP: Writing and Speeches (1951).
[4]Ibid.
[5]Ibid.
[6]Ibid.
[7]Ibid., 29 May 1941.

During the period 1939–41, he organized a movement against the taking away of grazing lands by landlords under the UP Tenancy Act and as a protest had led a 10,000 strong procession of animals to the DC Partapgarh, with placards hung around their necks. This was a unique method of protest that surpassed many with comments like 'look the animals have also come to protest'.[8] He had participated in the Individual Satyagraha in 1940 and was arrested also.

By the beginning of 1942, he was touring all over the district and taking stock of conditions in villages—even conducting his own census. After analysing their problems as well as the national scene he came up with these writings.

The 30 June write-up starts with the *mantra.*

I don't wish for a kingdom, nor of a heaven
nor do rebirth
What I wish is that the suffering of the
aggrieved should end

Then he reminds the peasants:[9]

Whatever step you take, should be
a bold one
And the determination should be like a Kshatriya

As cited in *Ramayana*: 'The Raghukul tradition is that life may be lost but no going back on words.'

The write-up starts under the title 'Baba Ram Chandra–Jhinguri Singh dialogue on the ideas of Vedas' and the first *richa* quoted is from *Rigveda* 1 to 14 related to the worship of Indra, the king of Hindu gods:[10]

At they shout, wielder of the thunderbolt,
all things, movable or immovable, trembled;

[8]We find in his papers some of the names of the people and count of the animals like who sent how many oxen, cows, goats, etc., to join in the march.

[9]The translations of Vedic verses are from H.H. Wilson, *Ṛgveda-Sanhitā: A Collection of Ancient Hindu Hymns,* 6 vols. (London, 1850–88).

[10]BRP: Speeches and Writings, 30 June 1942.

Even Twastri shook with fear, Indra, at thy
wrath, manifesting their own sovereignty

Baba Ram Chandra gave the interpretation of this Indra worship as:

The whole world is afraid of a king who
is just, does not take sides, what to say
of others his own general—the leader of
the great force which defeated the enemy
is also afraid of such a king

He mentions that the most important word in this *mantra* is *manyu* which means 'anger'. But this is not ordinary anger. '*Manyu* is generated after much mature thinking. For example, when a crime is brought to notice it is only after going into all aspects of the crime that the anger falls on the accused. It is this anger which is termed as *manyu* and its natural to be afraid of it.' The message being carried is that if the truth incarnate gets angry (*krodh*), it can overwhelm everything. The literal meaning is that 'Manu performed a *yagya* to do away with misery'. But Ram Chandra in his message twists it to 'misery was done away with in the *yagya*', offering a more practical result oriented action.

After describing the anger of the 'just king', he mentioned of 'assurance' of people given to the king by citing:[11]

When thou (Indra), didst encounter with they bolt *vritra*, and the thunderbolt (which he hurled), then Indira, the strength of their determined to stay, *Ahi* was displayed in the heavens, manifesting thy own sovereignty. (*Rigveda* 1.80.13)

Ram Chandra's interpretation of this *richa* is:

As if the people are talking to the king

Oh King! If you will follow Swarajya according to a policy of dharma; will fully protect the wealth, honour and life of people; then the people will give you all help.

With this help from the people you will shine like a sun. In such a situation you need not be afraid of any enemy. You are capable of bringing destruction to

[11] Ibid.

the enemy. In the way the sun penetrates the clouds through its rays, scatters them and satisfies the earth.

You also meet the enemy with firearms and defeat him. And thus, add to the happiness of the people.

He states that such an assurance will always be there for a king who looks after his people. Implicit in this is the advice of launching the movement against the British without any hesitation. For he tells Jhinguri Singh that 'there is nothing surprising in such an assurance as the people stand by you due to their own interests, so use their strength. Or else if some other leader is there you follow him along with the people. Or any clever leader will utilize this (peasants') strength.'[12]

Thus, he explained the might of the people and how it was to be utilized. The message obviously is for the hesitant national leadership—particularly Gandhi—whom he refers to as a *Budha Tapasvi* during this period. But it could be for any leader to take the lead and not necessarily Gandhi alone.[13]

Systematically, he moved to the theme 'Rashtra Dharak Goon', i.e. 'merits for the preservation of the country'. Here he now quotes *Atharvaveda* hyms related to the worship of mother goddess Earth in the Prithivi Sutra:[14]

Truthfulness, simplicity, perfection, knowledge, spiritual reality, disciplined forms of life, capacity of affection and sacrifice, are the sources that sustain earth and are necessary values of survival. Earth is the protector of those born earlier and those to be born and grants us extensive space. [*AV*(*s*) 12.1]

From this purely ritualistic hymn Ram Chandra interpreted: 'whichever country has these virtues, its inhabitants never face problems either at home or abroad. *Subject people have no place even in their own country—what to say of in other countries.*'

Now he explains the features of equality by citing another verse:[15]

[12] Ibid.
[13] BRP, 29 May 1941, op. cit.
[14] BRP, 30 June 1942, op. cit.
[15] Ibid.

Earth, on which various human beings of a country learn to live without conflicts, confrontation and hurting each other, than alone they can utilize various plants and crops which the earth bears us. [*AV*(*s*) 12.2]

Ram Chandra, though maintaining the same spirit, makes a free translation of this:[16]

A country where there is no disharmony and contempt, no ill feeling for putting each other down; where all believe in the pious objective of equality, have good feelings for others; where the leaders are of the same opinion (*aikmut*); where there are all sources of production and the leaders look well of them, not only the freedom of that country is stable but its glory goes far. There no one is faced by shortage . . . all are content and flourishing.

This was not only a critique of the leadership in terms of differences of opinion during this crucial period with in the national movement but also suggestive of a code of behaviour for leaders.

Further, he cited another *richa* [*AV*(*s*) 12.3] the literal meaning of which is that in our country 'they are oceans, rivers, ponds, etc., various resources are there, where all sorts of crops are there, where all are happy, peasants and artisans are experts in their fields, that motherland should flourish'.[17]

Ram Chandra interpreted this as that 'this motherland should feed us with its juices instead of feeding others. *Purvapaiye* is the most important word in this *richa.* Whatever is produced in a country is first the right of its inhabitants. Only if there is surplus then it should be given to others. This is possible only when the country is free. A slave country has nothing of its own'. This was a direct attack on colonial system. He stressed that 'ours is a simple country. Such a nice country was handed over to strong people because of the lust for money and power.' He advocated that all have a right on the land. The *richa* he cites for justification is again from the *Matra Bhumika Sutra* of *Atharvaveda* (*S*) 12.15:[18]

All the human beings are born of you. They live and sustain through you—

[16] Ibid.
[17] Ibid.
[18] Ibid.

you sustain two legged ones—
you sustain four legged ones
The sun shines for us due to you
The five human communities wish to serve you

Here, Ram Chandra interprets *Pancha Manav* not into Brahmin, Kshatriya, Vaishya, Shudra and Nishad but as whites, reds, brown, yellow and black human races and asserts that all have an equal right on the resources provided by you (i.e. the earth). Thus, he converts the worship of mother earth into equality of all human races, equal sharing of resources and the concept of Vedic society is enlarged to absorb them and the *richa* is utilized for an anti-imperialist thrust. Ram Chandra in this section of the write up starts with *manyu* (anger) for peoples' support to a just king in the struggle against enemy to attain swarajya; lays stress on the importance of freedom, unanimity among the leaders, equality to enjoy earth's resources and ends with a concept of peaceful co-existence of all human races. All by quoting Vedas, he tells Jhinguri Singh that 'even if Swarajya is obtained it is difficult to preserve it and cites the *Rigveda* sutra Ahinaash Richa':[19]

Mighty wielder of the thunderbolt, when the priest had thus exalted thee (by praise), and the exhilarating Som juice (had been drunk), thou didst expel, by the vigour, *Ahi* from the earth manifesting thine own sovereignty. (*Rigveda* 1.801)

For this Ram Chandra's interpretation was that 'it is not so difficult to attain Swarajya as it is to preserve it due to (a) lack of awareness among the people as to what Swaraj is, (b) what is its relevance and importance?' Accordingly, 'firstly, people don't try to achieve it or if some how they attain it, they get exhausted in the process and thus become careless as to its perseverance.' And, at this stage the external foe or the hidden internal enemy strikes which again leads to (*Gadbad*) anarchy.' 'The Veda tells us that the invader has to be uprooted in full (Sarvath Nash)' only then the education, happiness and prosperity of the country will increase.' The quality of the Veda according to him is, that 'through

[19]Ibid.

the most simple words it communicates important teachings'.[20] For example: '*Ahi* is snake, snake is of wicked character, so the simple meaning of *Ahi* is wicked or wickedness.' It is not necessary to tell that how important it is to destroy the wicked in a country. *Ahi* and *Vritra* are synonymous in Vedic literature. *Vritra* means cover, or obstructer. Cloud is referred to as *Vritra* due to the same reason as it covers the sunlight. Thus, whoever obstructs or stops the happiness of people, of the development of knowledge is such as *Vritra.* Such a *Vritra* should be immediately turned out from the country. He quotes a fifteenth-century commentator Shri Sayanacharaya as to the treatment to be meted out to *Ahi* and that is its complete destruction.[21] 'It is only in a country where there are no internal or external enemies that the learned people through spread of education make people happy.'

After describing the practical polity through this *richa* he also looked at its philosophical aspect:[22]

> Human body is the kingdom of the soul but due to earlier or present misdeeds man loses his right or control over the body. The physical body prevails over him and though he is the king of his body he acts like its slave.

Accordingly the Veda says 'throw the *Ahi* out of your body'. But again, he comes back to practical polity. The *richa* he cites literally means 'That exceedingly exhilarating Soma juice, which was brought by the hawk from heaven, when poured forth has exhilarated thee, so that in thy vigour, thunderer, thou hast struck *Vritra* from the sky manifesting thy own sovereignty. . . . (*RV* 1.80.2)

Ram Chandra interprets this that the king takes taxes from the *praja* to defend *swaraj.* This is necessary as it is impossible to run the administration without it. But this ought to be just. Its realization or effects should not be based on suffering of the people. The people should feel that 'the tax collected from them will be spent for their defence and welfare. It won't be used to curb them.'[23] But how is this possible because 'Even if the crow is brought up

[20] Ibid.
[21] Ibid.
[22] Ibid.
[23] Ibid.

on feeding sweets with all love still he would not turn into a vegetarian.' Still 'Jhinguri Singh you make efforts for (the peasants) as with too much effort if someone crushes hard even a soft and cool wood like that of sandal catches fire'. 'You might be advised to give up the peasant movement or stop it. Don't agree to this.' Or 'penetrate in their society (*samaj*) and do some good for the peasants'.

He asserted that 'great men who have achieved swarajya do not want it for themselves only, but for all. To establish peace and equality in the world the countries that have attained swarajya should work for liberating slave nations. Else there will always be no peace in the world.' This it appears was an explanation he offered for the Second World War.

Again he tells Jhinguri Singh to listen to the concept of *Praja ranjan* (well wisher of the people) and cites:[24] 'Hasten, assail, subdue, thy thunderbolt cannot fail, thy vigour Indra, destroy men, slay *vritra*, win the waters manifesting thine own sovereignty' (*Rigveda* 1.80.3).

This *richa* he interprets as 'the king should have this knowledge that who is one's friend and who is the enemy. As soon as the enemy is identified then one should run it down. His attack should not be awaited. Those countries who sit and wait lose their freedom. Those who crush the enemy in its house are always victorious.' Again a call to the leadership to act timely for:

> When the people are all out to help the king his thunderbolt and arms cannot fail.
>
> The strength of a king who serves his people is his glory. The enemies also do not dare to face such a glorious king.
>
> Science, deed, worship and knowledge thy four means necessary for self sufficiency. To know the merits and features of all is science. On the strength of science only comes the knowledge of beneficial matters.

The word *prehi* is the *mantra* which refers to this.

> But only the attainment of knowledge is not at all beneficial unless scientific effort is not made. The success of scientific effort lies in *karma* (deed). That is why the Veda orders Abhihi Dhrishunhi.

[24] Ibid.

Meaning 'you' should win over friends and crush the enemy. He further breaks this *mantra* into:

O thou who lack courage,
the veda provides you that
mighty power
go attack. Your mighty effort to end evil will not fail.
For you are the mightiest.

He goes on to explain this *richa*:[25] 'How much sweet and beautiful are these words. How much encouraging are the preachings for life.'

To what extent or how is the swarajya beneficial? Ram Chandra tried to explain this by citing Vedic evidence. Though he admits that this *mantra* only gives a clue to that.

The literal meaning is: 'Indra has struck him (*Vritra*) on the temple with his hundred edged thunderbolt, and exulting, wishes to provide means of sustenance for his friends—manifesting his own sovereignty.'

On the basis of Indra as the king of Swarajya and *Vritra*, who has been stuck as enemy king Ram Chandra's explanation is:

> Enemy king (*Praja Raja*) only knows how to milch the people. He is not at all bothered about people dying of hunger or their being *Agyani*.
>
> But our own king takes proper care to feed the people physically as well as intellectually.
>
> The Enemy king will not let the people open their mouths (checks their speech). But our own king wishes to keep the speech open. He does not want to keep his people dumb.
>
> Difference—what a great difference.

Thus, we see that Baba Ram Chandra wished that the people should be able to clearly distinguish between self-rule (swarajya) and foreign rule; make an all out effort to end foreign rule and yet at the same time take all the precautions that they generate such virtues that would take care for the sustenance of the swarajya. Hence, the ideological thrust is to be taken from the Vedas for this practical activity minus religiosity and the ritual.

[25] Ibid.

The other writing dated 4 August 1942 is a document which speaks of the nature of the movement that was to come.[26] I am not discussing the details of the tense political atmosphere during this period. But obviously the document is an answer to the queries of the peasants regarding what shape the nationalist polity will take. He starts with a *mantra*: *Maunyam Sarva Sadhyet*, i.e. 'Silence can achieve everything.' This follows from the *updesh* of the Niti Shlokas; also represents the idea of *Arthashastra* and even *Smriti* texts. The policy is to be kept secret till fully achieved or implemented. There should be no premature leakage.

Ram Chandra asserted that our 40 crore people have not thought over this how and where this *mantra* has to be applied? And this is the reason for the miserable condition of the people of India.

The word *maunya* (silence) is (*gaunya*) meaningful, and so relevant that the entire country cannot pay for it. And now the writing deals with the existent situation, different trends and attitudes. Gandhi's position and what shape the movement will take. 'This is the last battle to depart from the world.' It is to be noted that he says this four days before the 'Do or Die' call on 8 August 1942. Further, he questions: 'It has to be seen that in this struggle which people will adopt which route and achieve freedom for India?' Implicit is who will participate and who will reap the benefits of the struggle. He adds 'which people will enjoy this freedom along with their friends? Today both the observers and those who guide (masses and leaders) are in a state of anxiety' and 'in which forest will the Yogi go to do his *tapasya* and *aradhna*? (Question on Gandhi).'

'*Maamlebazi*' (unnecessary discussions) in his words has 'not helped anyone nor will it help now'. And after making these statements Ram Chandra made a very pertinent prediction for he wrote 'now everyone has eyes and ears, they have their tongues, they have their hands and feet. Now no one will be able to control them. Everyone is going to act according to his own wishes.'[27] We know precisely what shape the movement took after the arrest of

[26] BRP: Speeches and Writings, 4 August 1942.
[27] Ibid.

national leadership and what Baba Ram Chandra had written and preached on 4 August 1942 became true all over the country—it were the people against the Raj and no leadership was there to direct them, nor were they in a mood to be directed and controlled.[28] The people acted on their own. It was a common man's war against imperialism.

The 9 August 1942 write-up[29] is incomplete and the one page that is available deals with the problems at a philosophical level in contrast to the earlier document. However, it encourages the people to be fearless.

Here is an example of ritualistic literature being used in different ways. Ram Chandra was not a prisoner of the text or merely a commentator of this cultural resource of the Indian society. He was not a divine worshipper in the sense that he related the text to practical utility in order to get rid of colonialism. For him Vedic literature was not divine but something very much of this world which provided clues and answers to everyday problems. He freely used it and at times twisted it according to his own vision to expose the existing social reality in terms of prevailing political and economic conditions. He was not reviving the past, nor going back to the past. He was explaining the present by using the cultural and religious idioms of the past to move ahead—to have a better future for the people. In fact even Swami Dayanand Saraswati in his commentaries on the Vedas did not link their relevance to explain imperialist exploitation in relation to contemporary polity, something which Baba Ram Chandra did to mobilize the peasants.

[28] Practically, all scholars who have researched on 1942 have demonstrated this aspect. For example, see Sumit Sarkar, *Modern India*, New Delhi, 1983, pp. 394–403.

[29] BRP, Speeches and Writings, 9 August 1942.

CHAPTER 4

Rural Women in Oudh 1917–1947: Baba Ram Chandra and the Women's Question*

Oudh (present-day central Uttar Pradesh) witnessed a massive peasant uprising during the early 1920s—an outcome of the oppression and exploitation faced by the peasants at the hands of the British Raj and its allies—the taluqdars (landlord of a taluqa, a group of villages).[1] Amongst the peasants was a doubly exploited section—women. On the one hand, women faced all the miseries of the tenants and agricultural labourers and, on the other hand, they also suffered as women due to the rigid traditional structure of rural society. The peasant movement, organized under the leadership of Baba Ram Chandra,[2] not only brought to the fore the oppressed condition of the peasantry as a whole but also, more specifically, the question of the position of women. Official documents and private papers provide some evidence of the various issues that formed part of the movement in rural Oudh.[3]

*The paper was first published in Kumkum Sangari and Sudesh Vaid (eds.), *Recasting Women: Essays in Indian Colonial History*, New Delhi, 1989 and New Jersey 1990. I want to thank Tanika Sarkar, Smita Tiwari Jassal, Gyanesh Kudasiya, Sudesh Vaid, Kumkum Sangari and Deepti Mehrotra. Discussions with them helped to give final shape to the paper. An earlier version of this paper was presented at the Women's Studies Conference, Chandigarh, October 1986 and History Department, University of Delhi, January 1987.

[1] For details of the movement see Kapil Kumar, *Peasants in Revolt: Tenants, Landlords, Congress and the Raj in Oudh, 1886–1922*, Delhi, 1984.

[2] Ibid. Also see S.K. Mittal and Kapil Kumar, 'Baba Ram Chandra and Peasant Upsurge in Oudh 1920–1921', *Social Scientist*, Vol. 6, No. 11, June 1978.

[3] The most valuable source of information in this regard is the Baba Ram Chandra Papers (BRP) collected by the author during his fieldwork. The papers are now preserved in the Nehru Memorial Museum & Library (NMML).

In spite of the advances made in the field of historical investigation, the role of women from the oppressed social strata—particularly peasant women—in transforming economic, social and political life in the countryside stands neglected in historical analyses. This study attempts to highlight some of these aspects. However, in approaching the subject, an exclusively gender-based approach cannot explain social reality because rural women were (and are) not a homogeneous social group. There were women taluqdars in the region who were as oppressive towards their tenants—male or female—as any other taluqdar.[4] Similarly, there were women moneylenders whose profession firmly puts them in the category of an oppressive group. The women of these categories, due to their control over the means of production, had a dominant position in society with greater privileges and social security. The problems of these women and those of women from landlord families who had no direct control over the means of production, were largely related to social customs and patriarchy while those faced by women cultivators and agricultural labourers were economic as well as patriarchal. That is why a gender-class approach to the 'history of feminism' is more useful than 'feminist history'.[5] This study is divided into sections dealing with the oppression of peasant women, Baba Ram Chandra's views on women and his personal experience, various issues related to women, political awakening amongst them and finally their participation in the freedom movement.

I

By the Taluqdari Settlement of 1858 the British government, in order to establish a social base in the Oudh countryside, recognized taluqdars as the 'natural leaders' of the masses with absolute ownership rights in the land. Thus, the peasantry was converted into tenantry and agricultural labourers. The peasantry had made common

[4] Various files of the Revenue Department and Settlement Reports give ample evidence in this regard.

[5] See Elizabeth Fox-Genovese, 'Culture and Consciousness in the Intellectual History of European Women', *Signs* 12, No. 3, Spring 1987, p. 530.

cause with the princes and taluqdars in opposing the British. But the ultimate result of this struggle was that the princes and taluqdars not only compromised with the British but threw in their lot with the colonial power. The peasantry then onwards faced double oppression both by feudal lords and by the imperial government.

I have elsewhere discussed in detail the various forms of oppression faced by the tenantry.[6] Here I shall confine myself to the issue of exploitation of women. The number of women in the rural areas of Oudh in 1921 was 5,497,147 and that of men 5,851,754. Amongst ordinary cultivators, there were 1,635,036 female and 2,895,552 male actual workers, with 3,711,437 dependents.[7] There were only 2.1 per cent secure tenants, while 97.9 per cent cultivators were tenants-at-will, mostly with a seven year lease. Amongst these, 85.8 per cent could be termed as poor peasants, 11.3 per cent as middle peasants and only 2.9 per cent as rich peasants.[8] Amongst agricultural labourers, 3,48,600 were women, 3,79,910 men along with 3,78,885 dependents. In the districts of Rai Bareilly, Fyzabad, Gonda, Baharaich, Unnao, Sultanpur and Partapgarh (i.e. in 7 of the 12 districts of Oudh), women outnumbered men as agricultural labourers. The agricultural labourers were a socially degraded class not only because of their occupation which kept them at the lowest economic stratum, but also because of the caste-structure. The bulk of the rural proletariat was drawn from 'low castes' who for generations had been prevented by the feudal aristocracy from owning land for cultivation in order to facilitate the supply of labour. They were not only paupers and serfs but 'untouchables' as well. The extreme economic and social pressure, to an extent, explains the large number of women amongst the labourers coming out to work. Moreover, the 'low castes' as compared to the 'high castes' were in greater number in these districts of Oudh. The number of actual workers whose income was from rent of agricultural land was 20,588 women and 57,279 men. There

[6] See Kapil Kumar, *Peasants in Revolt*, pp. 14–70.

[7] *Census of India*, 1921, United Provinces, Vol. 16, Part 2.

[8] Kapil Kumar, *Peasants in Revolt*, pp. 60–2, 218–20.

were 2,283 women moneylenders, as compared to 7,953 men in the trade.[9]

Foremost among the oppressive practices was the taking of *nazarana* (extra premium on rent) by landlords. This evil had penetrated to such an extent that some tenants were painfully forced to sell their daughters (*kanya vikray*) in order to raise *nazarana*:

> Bechai Misir sold his 12 year old daughter to a husband of 60 years for Rs. 300. Ishri Dubey sold one daughter five year old to a husband 40 years and another daughter, aged 12 years, to a husband 30 years for Rs. 300 each.
>
> The widow of Mahabadeo sold her daughter for Rs. 200. Mahabir Brahman married his 7 year old daughter to a husband aged 40 years and got Rs. 200. The minor son of Thakur Din (deceased) sold his 5 year old sister to a husband 40 years old for Rs.300. Gayadin Dubey, as a last resort to save his family from ruin, sold his 10 years old daughter to a husband about 40 years old for Rs. 400.[10]

We only have records of such cases reported from Partapgarh and that too only for the years 1919–20. They came to light during the enquiry conducted by the Deputy Commissioner (DC) to investigate the causes of agrarian disturbances in the district. No such efforts were made in other parts of Oudh, but it appears that the results would not have been different. The vicious practice of *kanya vikray* was intensified by the fact that 'there was enormous disparity in years between the ages of wife and husband' and the girl's marriage was often 'consecrated before the funeral pyre of her husband.' *Kanya vikray* 'is considered the most heinous sin amongst orthodox Hindus and punishment is eternal hell for the father'. The poor fathers were forced to take 'recourse to sale as a last resort to preserve the family holding from slipping away'.[11] Thus, in order to avoid a living hell in this world, they preferred incurring eternal damnation in the next world by selling their daughters. For the girls, it was a miserable existence. The parents who committed the sin, realized this, but felt helpless in the face of an oppressive

[9] All figures are from *Census of India*, 1921, Vol. 16, Part 2.

[10] V.N. Mehta Report (here after MR) on *Agrarian Disturbances in Pratapgarh*, F. No. 753/1920, Revenue, A, UP State Archives (UPSA), Lucknow.

[11] Ibid.

economic and social structure. Many broke down in tears in the presence of the DC while narrating their pathetic accounts of such transactions.[12]

Murdafaroshi (selling of holdings after the death of the lease-holder) was another weapon of the *taluqdari* (conferment of proprietary rights in land) system and the worst victims were again women. Legally, the heirs of a lease-holder could not be evicted till the end of the seven year lease, but in practice immediately after the death of the lease-holder, the holding was let out to the highest bidder at enhanced rates by the landlord. The heir could save the holding only by paying *nazarana.* But many a time even after payment the holding was not restored. It is worth mentioning some cases related to women heirs:

a. A widow was evicted after her son's death, since the holding was in his name. Another tenant gave Rs. 200 *nazarana* to get the holding, while she had to beg for her food.
b. A woman paid Rs. 21 as *nazarana* to the landlord, yet she was forcibly evicted and rendered destitute.
c. A holding of 4 *bighas* (a measure of land) was taken away from a woman and thus a family of eleven was left destitute.
d. A woman with 5 children paid Rs. 25 to the *zilledar* (landlord's manager) to get back her holding. Another Rs. 25 was demanded and, on this pretext, she was refused possession.
e. A Gadaria woman's husband and his brother died of influenza. Rs. 28 stood as arrears in their name. The widow was forced to pay Rs. 60 as *nazarana* but she could not get her 10 *biswas* (1/20th of a *bigha*) of land.
f. Rs. 600 were demanded as *nazarana* from a woman and since she could not pay the sum she was evicted.
g. A peasant paid Rs. 80 *nazarana* and obtained a holding in 1916. Next year, he died and his widow was evicted.
h. In 1915, a woman paid Rs. 7 per *bigha* as *nazarana* on the assurance that she would not be evicted. When her husband died she was asked to pay Rs. 50 and, on her failure to pay, she was evicted.

[12] Ibid.

i. Mussamat Sumera paid Rs. 100 as *nazarana.* The money was sent by her sons working in Calcutta. Her land was not restored to her.

j. Rs. 100 were demanded from a woman for retaining her holding. She was told that another tenant was willing to pay the amount to acquire her holding. As she could not pay and as the landlord was insistent, she committed suicide.

k. A landlord got some *maufi* (free grant) land assessed to rent. Mussamat Rahmani, a very poor *faqiran* (female religious mendicant; *maufi* land grants were sometimes given to religious mendicants) had to pay Rs. 30 as *nazarana* to save her ancestral holding of 3 *bighas.* This caused 'considerable resentment in the village', as it was considered a 'sacrilege to lay hands on a *faqiran's* property'.

l. A woman was evicted by the landlords's agent and left destitute. Her son had to migrate to Bombay to seek employment.[13]

During First World War, the taluqdars spared no effort to aid the British. In this process, they robbed their tenantry in the name of *larai chanda* (war donation) and *bharti chanda* (recruitment cess). False promises were made in order to lure peasants into recruitment. But the heirs of those who died at the front were evicted under the *murdafaroshi* proceedings. Numerous instances of such excesses can be cited.

a. Two members of a family died at the front. The widow of one of them was evicted under *murdafaroshi.* It was only at the intervention of the DC that the landlord returned 18 *bighas* to her. The DC commented: 'It would have been a very hard case had the landholder not agreed.'

b. A peasant died while his son was at the front. The landholder, a sub-inspector in the police, forcibly evicted the peasant's widow.

c. A soldier was killed at the front. His mother was evicted from their holding.

d. A pensioned soldier obtained a lease after paying *nazarana.* On

[13] All the cases cited are from MR.

> his death, the widow was evicted from her holding of 3 *bighas.* With her two children, she wept bitterly before the DC, as she had no means of livelihood whatsoever.[14]

Very often fights would break out among tenants due to the unscrupulous practices of landlords. A man died leaving behind his heir, a minor daughter, under the guardianship of her uncle. Without formally evicting her, the landlord gave the lease to another peasant after taking Rs. 250 *nazarana.* When the peasant went to take possession of the holding, the relatives of the minor girl opposed him and this resulted in a riot.[15] Here we find the relatives defending the rights of a minor girl because the encroacher was an outsider. However, in addition to harassment by the landlord, his zilledar and agents, women heirs—particularly widows—were very often harassed by male relatives who wanted to grab their holdings and property. Certain evidences show that women did hold leases in their own names but in most cases, they inherited them either as widows, mothers or daughters of the deceased male members of the family. This gave them a certain status as women controlling property land. But due to the lack of permanent occupancy rights both women and men tenants were equally insecure.

The taluqdars and their agents imposed fines on the tenantry, both women and men, according to their whims. *Kumarg* (moral delinquency) was one such extortion realized from tenants accused of having: 'illicit relations' with women from other families. These 'illicit' relations included not only cases of adultery but also of inter-caste sexual relations. Innocent peasants were often accused of having relations with this or that woman and, from fear of the landlords' power on the one hand and of social humiliation on the other, the peasants yielded to threats by landlords and paid fines as is borne out by the following instances:

a. Matabadal was fined Rs. 51 because his name was associated with a Kurmi woman.
b. In a joint tenancy, after the death of one partner, his widow was

[14] Ibid.
[15] Ibid.

made to complain, at the instance of the landlord, that her husband's partner was having relations with her. The partner was fined Rs. 51.

c. A charge was brought against the daughter of one tenant that she was on terms of familiarity with one Nidhan Singh. The father of the girl was fined Rs. 51 and one neem tree in addition.
d. In village Aspur Deosara, when an innocent tenant refused to pay *kumarg*, he was dragged and beaten up by the zilledar and his hut was burnt.[16]

At any given time we find a sizeable number of women taluqdars in the districts of Oudh.[17] In the estates managed by women taluqdars, as in those held by men, the peasants faced all kinds of hardships and exploitation. A *thakurain* taluqdar (Rajput woman landholder) in Partapgarh had a boil on her leg which turned septic. She distributed Rs.15,000 to *sants* (religious men) who prayed for her recovery. The entire sum was realized from the peasants in the form of *pakawan* (a septic cess).[18] Thakurain Ajit Koer of Patti Saifabad had raised rents illegally by 150 per cent in her estate.[19] The *thakurain* of Amargarh estate was a known offender of the Rent Act and practised all kinds of oppression on her tenants. In 1936, she even had the houses of her tenants looted.[20] We have the petition of Mussamat Wali, widow of Brahma, whose 5 *bighas* of land were forcibly taken in 1938 by the *thakurain* and given to the zilledar for planting an orchard.[21] These instances indicate the class character of the women taluqdars. The control over land was the ultimate factor in determining relations between landlords and tenants and, at times, between tenants and agricultural labourers. Thus, we find in the Baba Ram Chandra papers the case (July

[16] Ibid

[17] A study of the District Gazetteers of Oudh shows that at any given time each district had women taluqdars.

[18] F. Nos. 211–270/October 1886, Leg. Dept., National Archives of India (NAI), Delhi.

[19] *Oudh Revenue Administration Report, 1889-90*, p. 30.

[20] BRP, Subject Files (SF), No. 11.

[21] BRP, SF, No. 10.

1939) of a Brahmin peasant woman who would not pay wages to labourers. She was asked to appear before the Kisan Sabha (peasant organization). Her failure to do so was deemed an insult to the Sabha. The entire village socially boycotted her and this made her acknowledge the authority of the Sabha. She ultimately agreed to come under its protection.[22]

Another issue of concern, which indicates the status of women, was the marriage of infants and children, which was a common practice in the Oudh countryside. This is borne out from the following figures in Table 4.1:

TABLE 4.1: MARITAL STATUS IN OUDH (1921)

Age Group	Married Males	Married Females	Total
0–1	118	133	251
1–5	4,261	4,674	8,935
5–10	57,087	85,542	142,629
10–15	163,052	256,548	419,600
15–20	235,006	343,666	578,672

Source: *Census of India*, 1921, United Provinces, Part 2.

Closely linked with the practice of child marriage was the problem of the large number of child widows in Oudh. Table 4.2 gives the figures of widows and widowers in Oudh.

TABLE 4.2: MARITAL STATUS IN OUDH (1921)

Age Group	Widows	Widowers
0–1	23	2
1–5	271	174
5–10	3,611	2,562
10–15	8,736	7,261
15–20	14,052	13,047
Total	26,683	23,046

Source: *Census of India*, 1921, United Provinces, Part 2.

[22] BRP, SF, No. 10.

We shall discuss a little later how these inter-linked issues were taken up by the Kisan Sabha.

II

During 1917–18, Baba Ram Chandra came to the Oudh countryside and organized and led the most militant peasant movement of northern India in the course of the freedom struggle against the British. According to the DC of Partapgarh, Ram Chandra became 'a magnet of attraction' who supplied 'some mental pabulum to a people intellectually starved in these out-of-the-way places'.[23] His popularity knew no bounds. Not only men but women, with the permission of elders, would invite him inside the houses and discuss their problems.[24] This added to his knowledge on issues concerning women. It was a difficult task to raise issues related to women in a rigid, traditional feudal society like Oudh. Ram Chandra not only raised the issues but broke certain established norms in his personal life. His personal relations and experience with women shaped his attitude towards women in general and are worth recounting. Shridhar Balwant Jodhpurkar alias Baba Ram Chandra, a Maharashtrian Brahmin, left home at a young age. Though there was no *purdah* (seclusion of women) in his family, a lot of money had to be spent on a girl's marriage. He was critical of his father who brought in another wife: *Mere pita ne kalanka khada kiya* (my father brought dishonour and trouble to our family) but, as a child, could not protest in front of him. The relations between the two women were far from cordial and both Ram Chandra and his mother faced a great deal of hardship. Eventually, due to his stepmother's attitude, he left home. His mother gave him Rs. 25 as a parting gift and, of course, her blessings. Thereafter he met a *fakir* (religious mendicant) who was keen to take him on as his *chela* (disciple). Ram Chandra soon realized that the fakir was a fraud who 'pretended to cure Hindu women through divine powers, cheated them and lured their young daughters and daughters-in-law into prosti-

[23] MR.

[24] BRP: Speeches and Writings (SW), F. No. 2A.

tution' (*Hindu striyon ko jhadtā phunktā va unhe thug kar jawān bahu betiyon ko bhagāne vālon ke akhade me ja milātā thā*).[25] Soon he parted company with him. For some time, he stayed with Ganga, a Marathi girl, but their different lifestyles made them part company. Wandering through different parts of the Central Provinces and Maharashtra, he reached Bombay. During this period, he had the varied experience of working as a coolie, a vendor and a labourer at a coal depot. He must have earned some money, for now he visited the Bombay Race Course. In his autobiographical writings, he mentions that he put money on a horse in the name of his mother and, by a stroke of good luck, won Rs. 800. Out of this, he sent Rs. 700 to his mother by money order. He also worked on a coal ship and, out of his earnings, remitted another Rs. 400 to his mother.[26] We see here that Ram Chandra personally experienced the problems of polygamy in his parental house.

In 1905, Ram Chandra left for Fiji as an indentured labourer. The working conditions were extremely hard and punishments for workers were severe. His political activity began when the banana trees belonging to labourers were forcibly cut by an inspector. He had the trees loaded on carts and organized a procession to the Governor demanding redressal of the wrong committed. Under his leadership, the labourers were partially successful.[27] Ram Chandra was sentenced to three years imprisonment on charges of negligence of work. As a detenu, he was made to do domestic work at the Magistrate's house. As the memsahib was pleased with his work, his two-and-a half year term was pardoned on the condition that he would continue to work in the house.[28]

Ram Chandra has given an account of his stay in the house. The Magistrate (it is not known what nationality he was) had two daughters who tried various methods to attract him: *Ve apne kataksh chakshuon se apne vashibhoot karne ke liye kai prakar ke charitra kiya karti theen.*[29] (They used to look flirtatiously at me and try various means to seduce me.)

[25] Ibid.
[26] Ibid.
[27] Ibid.
[28] Ibid.
[29] Ibid.

Often he had to accompany them with soap, etc., to the pond for a bath. At times, he would join them and spend hours in the water. He complained that they ordered a tent and a phonogram machine from England without asking him and the cost was deducted from his salary. According to his own testimony, he accepted all this for two reasons. First, because if he refused he could be sent back to jail and, second, because he thought that since he had to stay in Fiji, he must get used to the lifestyle there. These two girls arranged his marriage to a 'beautiful Chamarin' through Fiji rites. On the pretext of meeting this Chamarin (women of the Chamar low caste), the girls would visit Ram Chandra for sexual pleasure: *Is stri ke bahane dono ladkiyan mere dhan, man haran ko mere paas aane lagin.*[30]

It was only when the two girls got married, that Ram Chandra shifted from their house along with his wife. Here two things need attention. First, that a marriage had taken place between a Maharashtrian Brahmin and a Chamarin; but Ram Chandra never reveals his wife's name, he only refers to her as a 'beautiful Chamarin'. Second, he blames the two girls for desiring sexual pleasure with him but is completely silent about his own feelings in the matter. Ram Chandra acted in close cooperation with Manilal, an advocate, for the cause of indentured labourers.[31] In spite of this political relationship Ram Chandra was sad to see that Manilal had a memsahib as his mistress and that his wife had to face problems which she did bravely: 'We and many Gujarati jewellers of Suva felt sorry for her and, at the same time, admired her courage and bravery.'[32] Due to his political activities, Ram Chandra had to flee from Fiji. But before he did so, he transferred his property (two houses and some lands) to his wife, 'the beautiful Chamarin'. This was followed by a mutual divorce. Commenting on the condition of indentured women labourers in Fiji, he wrote:

Regarding women it suffices to say that beautiful women are made to work at isolated places where both *gore* (white men) as well as *kale* (black men) seduce

[30] Ibid.

[31] For Manilal also see Suneet Chopra, 'Bourgeois Historiography and the Peasant Question', *Social Scientist*, No. 11 (June 1977).

[32] BRP, SW, F. No. 2A.

them. Pregnant women have to work right upto the time they deliver the child. Often this leads to miscarriage.[33]

During 1918–20, Ram Chandra was not only making efforts to mobilize the peasants against the British and the landlords but also attempting to articulate issues related to women. The very first programme he offered for the uplift of peasants in 1920 included the appointment of *updeshikas* (women teachers) to educate women in rural areas.[34] We shall discuss the role of women during the movement a little later.

Some time in the late 1920s Ram Chandra married Jaggi, a Kurmi by caste, and broke the caste norms once again. This marriage led to all kinds of vulgar propaganda against him by the landlords and by other opponents. Ram Chandra attributes this marriage to the advice of V.N. Mehta, a pro-peasant senior government official. A constant charge against Ram Chandra, levied by the landlords, was that he was an outsider, instigating peasants to 'rebellion' in Partapgarh. To counteract such attacks Mehta advised him to marry and settle down. Jaggi was the daughter of Kashi, his closest associate in the Kisan Sabha. He married her in the 'English style'. The marriage took place with Jaggi's consent.[35] But Ram Chandra's account makes it appear a political strategy. Jaggi accepts this and describes with pride the cordial relations between the two, and how under his influence she became an activist on the kisan front, on women's issues and in the freedom struggle.[36] It would be appropriate to mention here that though Ram Chandra died in 1950, Jaggi still continues to work as a Kisan Sabha activist in Partapgarh. She led a movement against levy collection on wheat in 1976—the emergency period—and went to jail. She also led a protest against a death in a family planning camp. As a consequence,

[33] Ibid.

[34] MR.

[35] BRP, SW, F. No. 2A. Personal interview with Jaggi, village Daudpur, tahsil Patti, Partapgarh district, 14 June 1987. For a different view on this marriage see Deepti Mehrotra, 'Women Participation in Peasant Movements in UP', M. Phil. thesis, Political Science Dept., University of Delhi, 1987.

[36] Personal interview with Jaggi in June 1987. She is no more now.

she lost her pension as a freedom fighter which was only restored in 1983.[37] Though well over 90, she walks 10 to 15 kilometres a day for Kisan Sabha work.

III

In a frontal attack on patriarchal domination in the Oudh countryside Baba Ram Chandra wrote:

> Howsoever meritorious the women may be, their partners are not up to the mark because after marriage they imprison their wives in house hold cages. They use them for sexual pleasure (*unka bhog karte hain*), make them cook food and trap them in many other social hypocrisies (*dhakosala*).[38]

He felt perturbed because: 'The women too regard their husbands as their *ishtdev* (gods) and dance to their tune.' On the other hand, he felt: 'Where the women get an upper hand, husbands become their slaves. They make all sorts of excuses in the name of their wives, when asked to participate in political activity or to fight for the redressal of their grievances.'[39] Ram Chandra was against domination of either sex by the other. In fact, what he had in mind was a monogamous, humane and moral form of family, based on greater rights for women. He preached: *Na joru se mard na mard se joru. Aisa koi ghar na rakha jaye ki joda na ho.* (No husband without wife, no wife without husband. There should be no home without a couple.)[40] He advocated that, 'if men and women are to be kept happy, then both should have equal freedom' (*nar nariyon ko sukhi rakhna hai to dono ki swatantrata ek saman ho*).[41]

Ram Chandra's concern for the problems faced by women is also reflected in the way he tried to make the peasants aware of the changes which had been made in the Indian Penal Code. In a pamphlet under the title *Tazerate Hind ki Dafain Badha di gain,* (Penalties in the Indian Penal Code have been Enhanced) he familiar-

[37] Ibid.
[38] BRP, SF, No. 3.
[39] Ibid.
[40] BRP, SW, F. No. 1A.
[41] BRP, SF, No. 11.

ized the peasants with the punishments for major offences—murder, dacoity, instigation to communal rioting as well as offences against women:

Attacking a woman with bad intentions—ten years jail
Abducting a *woman—kalapani* (penal transportation)
Abducting a woman for prostitution—kalapani
Raping a woman—kalapani[42]

To this, he added a footnote '*baint bhi lagenge*' (will be caned also). He cautioned that there will be a ten year jail term for those who kidnap a woman or use force to marry her and that such a forced marriage will have no legal status (*aisi zabardasti ki shadi ka koi kanuni asar na hoga*).[43] This establishes that Ram Chandra was opposed to the use of any form of violence or coercion on women. He regarded 'reforms a must for women' and this, according to him, 'would come when men reform themselves [in relation to women]'.[44] It must be noted that Ram Chandra managed to get such a resolution passed in a totally male attended conference of the Kurmi Sangh some time in the mid-1930s.[45]

Ram Chandra was very vocal against child marriage. In a leaflet titled *Ma Shatru Pita Bairi* (Mother Enemy, Father ill-wisher) he warned parents against the ill effects of child marriage.[46] It appears from this leaflet that many a time parents would sell their minor daughters in marriage to more than one person. The young girl then virtually led a prostitute's life. This practice also often led to disputes. Such marriages, it appears, took place due to extreme economic hardship as in the cases of *kanya vikray*. Another factor which contributed to the rise of such marriages was the absence of occupancy rights in this region. The peasants of the neighbouring regions of Oudh were reluctant to marry their daughters to peasant-tenants 'who may become beggars at the whim of their landlords'.[47]

[42] BRP, SW, F. No. 2A.
[43] Ibid.
[44] BRP, SW, F. No. 1A.
[45] Ibid.
[46] Ibid.
[47] Commissioner Fyzabad to Chief Sect. to Govt. of UP, 25 November 1920. F. No. 753/1920, Rev., UPSA.

Ram Chandra asked the peasants to show as much concern for their girls as they did for their animals.

> You make your animals mate only when they attain a particular age. You assert so much wisdom in the case of animals. If you do the same in relation to your child-daughters, the evil custom of child marriage will flee on its own from your houses.[48]

Ram Chandra accused old men and women (*budhe-budhiyan*) of committing the worst injustice against children by marrying young girls to aged men and young boys to aged women (*ye sabse bada anyaya hai*).[49] The sad part was that people were 'infected with the disease of pardon' and these old people 'were pardoned for their unjust acts only in consideration of their age'. He preached that, had he been the king[50] he would have made these old persons stay in separate houses where they would be looked after. But he also saw it as a welfare problem and demanded state pension for all men and women above the age of 55 as well as for all widows.[51]

Ram Chandra advocated that if adultery was to be checked, then boys and girls should be married by taking into account their respective merits—that is arranged marriages should be based on considerations of compatibility, such as Intelligence.[52] Here he was bringing in a new concept of conjugal relations based on the possibility of communication between partners.

Inter caste marriages were virtually absent due to rigid caste norms. The landlords upheld these norms and as part of their attempt to control social mobility, they would impose fines on

[48] BRP, SW, F. No. 2A.

[49] BRP, SW, F. No. 2B.

[50] BRP, SF, No. 16. According to Ram Chandra he used the word king because the people would understand *raja* (king) and *praja* (subjects) easily. BRP, SW, F. No. 2A.

[51] BRP, SF, No. 16. During the Congress ministry period Jaggi wrote to G.B. Pant, the Premier of UP, on 19 April 1938 demanding a pension for old men and women. She accused the government and the landlords of grabbing the lands of old men and women and this made them dependent on family members. The family members, she asserted, had a meagre income and were unable to look after the old people. BRP, SF, No. 15.

[52] BRP, SF, No. 16.

peasants for breaking caste customs. One Kallu had to pay Rs. 51 as fine to the landlord for bringing a wife from another sub-section of the Muslim community.[53] Thus, it was no surprise that Ram Chandra worked for reforms through caste *panchayats.*[54] Under his influence, the Kurmi Sangh resolved:

a. Marriage customs of the *biradari* (caste brotherhood) should be changed.
b. Marriage or *gauna* (post-puberty ceremonial bringing of girl bride to her husband's house) should take place with the signature/sanction of the head of the panchayat. If parents fail to do this, the marriage will have no legal sanction. It should be the duty of the *panch* (member of panchayat or village court) to ensure this practice or else he would be punished.
c. Reforms for women are necessary.
d. Women should not be sent to work in another person's house. Men should go upon payment of full wages only.
e. Reforms for women can be implemented only when men reform themselves in relation to women.
f. The fault of parents is that (i) on the failure to produce children, they make the women run after *fakirs, sadhus, ojhas, pirs* and *mazars* (holy men and religious places) (ii) if a child is born, they indulge in extravagance.[55]

This was an all male conference attended by 271 Kurmi representatives. Resolution (a) was to do away with the evils related to marriage, like child marriage and extravagant expenditure. Resolution (b) was for a kind of registration of marriage in village records. Here Resolution (d) should not be taken to mean a rejection of women's right to work but seen in the context of exploitative working conditions for women in the existing feudal structure. Women were the worst victims of *begar* (forced labour) as well as a target of

[53] MR.

[54] Among the various caste panchayats with which he was associated were the Kurmi Sangh, Harijan Sangh, Satnami Sabha and Tamoli Sabha, etc.

[55] BRP, SW, F. No. 2A.

sexual exploitation by the *karindas* (landlord's agents) and *sipahis* (soldiers) of landlords. At the same time the objective conditions were such that in order to be saved from sexual harassment women stood to lose their right to free movement and to certain forms of wage earning.

In another Kisan Council meeting at Rure—the headquarters of the Kisan Sabha—it was resolved that: (a) in household affairs all members of the family should have an equal say; (b) there should be separate means of livelihood such as shops, etc., for women, so that after the death of their husbands they and their children would not starve or stay unclothed; (c) old men and women should be looked after by everyone.[56]

But most important from the women's point of view were the resolutions brought forward by women themselves in this meeting. The initiative had been taken by Jaggi at the behest of Ram Chandra and Jhinguri Singh, another kisan activist.[57] These read:

a. Only men are free to marry two to three women, instead of one. This should be stopped with immediate effect. Whoever has done so should be punished. A woman should also not have a second *mard* (man). If so she should be punished.
b. One man and one woman can stay together. Their relations should not be treated as illegal. (Recognition to partners as a social institution?)
c. Such women (who stay with a man without formal marriage) should not be treated as belonging to any particular caste. They should not be dismissed as merely being there for producing children.
d. If a woman stays with a man and bears a child, she should be respected as a *devi* (goddess). Those who do not bear sons should be respected as *kanyas* (daughters).[58]

Radical in nature, these resolutions were accepted in the meeting.

[56] Ibid.

[57] Personal interview with Jaggi.

[58] BRP, SW, F. No. 2A.

They were aimed at obtaining social sanction for relationships otherwise regarded as *najayaz* (illegal). As women suffered in such relationships, these resolutions were also aimed at providing security for them. Here I would not treat Resolution (d) as merely an expression of patriarchal . . . values in relation to the birth of a son. I shall look at it from the point of view of the status of such women. They are generally regarded as *kulta*, *patita*, or *kalankini* (immoral, fallen or bad women) but now the status being demanded was that of a goddess and of a daughter. This indicated a radical break with existing social relations, but the irony of it is that they could achieve this radical break only by accepting a traditional value—that is, by producing sons.

Rural women in Oudh in the 1930s had not only made such radical demands, they had also got them accepted in the Kisan Sabha. This was a significant step forward towards a higher status for women. And they had been considerably influenced and inspired by Ram Chandra in this regard.[59]

It is significant that Ram Chandra would not spare his closest associates in the Kisan Sabha if they maltreated women. When Bhagwandin left his wife after a quarrel, Ram Chandra's comment was: *Aaj ghar mein kaliyuga ki paithaari ho gai* (today the age of corruption has begun for the family).[60] In his words, Bhagwandin was in the wrong as he wanted to stay with a rich woman and desert his poor wife: *Is bechari dhanheen ko adhar mein chhodna chahata hai* (he wants to abandon this poor helpless woman).[61] Ram Chandra was concerned about what would happen to Bhagwandin's wife if the latter did abandon her. Moreover this could also bring a bad name to the Kisan Sabha. Ultimately Bhagwandin was persuaded to return to his wife.[62]

I would also like to cite here some panchayat decisions found in Baba Ram Chandra's papers on petitions by women:

[59] Personal interview with Jaggi.

[60] BRP, SF, No. 6.

[61] Ibid.

[62] Personal interview with Jaggi.

a. *The case of Ramlal Satnami and Lilabai. Decision given by Devdas master and ten other members of the panchayat.*[63]

The panchayat admitted that a just arbitration in this complicated case was difficult. It appears that Ramlal and Lilabai were disciples of a Satnami *guru* (preacher) Baba Santdasji. Lilabai was a widow and had a son. A relationship developed between Ramlal and Lilabai. It is also possible that the son was an offspring from this relationship. The exact situation is not clear, but it appears that Ramlal disowned responsibility and Lilabai wanted compensation in the form of money. The panchayat judges made it clear that they would rule out giving money as compensation and would first enquire into the exact nature of their relationship from Santdasji. The final decision was:

> The panchayat has handed over Lilabai to Ramlal. From today, Lilabai is the wife of Ramlal. But at the same time, they both are declared guilty—*gurudrohi* and *santdrohi* (of violating precepts of preacher and holy man). They should be socially boycotted for life. Now Ramlal has a right over Lilabai and will look after her son. But a social boycott will continue and whoever breaks it will be subjected to punishment.

This judgement treated Lilabai both as property and as a deprived woman. As property where Ramlal is given a right over her and as a deprived woman when she gets her right as a wife. Moreover, she alone is not treated as a degraded person as both of them are to be socially boycotted; the latter punishment was inflicted perhaps to check or discourage such relationships in future.

b. *The case of Dhirajia Kurmin versus Sukhai Kurmi* (*April 1940*).[64]

Dhirajia petitioned that her husband Sukhai was not looking after her welfare (*hamara gujara nahin karta*) and asked that the

[63] BRP, SF, No. 20. Saurabh Dube pointed out to me that the strict moral code which Ram Chandra was advocating for the Satnamis in fact took away much of the freedom which the Satnami women had in terms of man–woman relationships.

[64] BRP, SF, No. 11.

panchayat should give her justice. The judges decreed that Sukhai should look after her, and if he failed to do so, a fine of Rs. 51 would be realized from him and his wife would then be free to leave him. At the same time, she was warned not to do anything violating customary norms (*bekaayda*) without his permission. If she did, she would not be given a hearing and any other man who took her with him would also be fined Rs. 51 and boycotted socially.

It appears from the judgement that the case was argued before the panchayat with both sides accusing the other of extra-marital relations. The judgement disproves the common belief that women could get no justice from the male-dominated panchayat. But at the same time the panchayat also tries to enforce a uniform but very strict code of sexual morality, perhaps as a means of gaining greater respectability for peasants.

c. *Petition of Lakhpati, village Maurahat* (*April 1947*).[65]

Lakhpati petitioned to get justice from the *biradari*, Jagan, her husband, had left her and for the last 18 years she had been looking after their daughter. She demanded: 'I should get the money I spent on her during the last 18 years. I should be told the fault of my daughter. My daughter's case should be settled.' Ram Chandra sent this petition to Guru Ramanugra of Kashi to explain. It appears that Jagan had become a *sadhu* (ascetic) and assumed the name Guru Ramanugra. His reply was that the girl should be sent to him: 'I love my daughter . . . . but you (Lakhpati) have no right to enjoy the happiness or sorrow of my house.' In fact, Lakhpati had never made a claim for herself but the demand made by her indicates a growing awareness among women of their right to seek maintenance. Even if Lakhpati was in the wrong, which apparently was the reason for their separation, why should she alone bear the expense of bringing up the daughter?

In addition to these cases, we find petitions addressed to Ram Chandra by a number of exploited women:

a. Sona Harijan's daughter, Koeli, complained on 12 September 1940 that Thakur Jagol Singh had forcibly sown her lands. She

[65] BRP, SF, No. 10.

had no faith in the *patwari* (village official), who was the zamindar's (*landlord's*) man. Her case, it was pleaded, should be taken up with the DC who must personally look into the matter.[66]

b. Kunau Kurmin, a widow residing in village Chandrahara, was forcibly evicted by the taluqdar of Ramganj. She sought Ram Chandra's advice. 'How should I live now?'[67]
c. Sumera Murain of village Fainha had 20 *biswas* land of a five rupee rental mortgaged to Jageshwar Pasi, a *mahajan* (moneylender). Jokhu Singh forcibly claimed the land. She had paid rent to the *mahajan* and now Jokhu also demanded it. On the other hand, the *mahajan* insisted that if she paid to Jokhu he would sue her. She asked Baba Ram Chandra, 'What should I do now?'[68]
d. On 25 April 1942, Mussamat Maharaji of village Gharoli complained to the Congress office that, after the death of her husband Khedu, the zamindar did not let her enter her holding. Whenever she tried, her bullocks and plough were thrown out. If the Congress 'does not take up her case she would starve, as she cannot resist the zamindar'. The president of the Partapgarh District Congress passed on the petition to Ram Chandra for action.[69]
e. Mussamat Hubrazi, a poor old Brahmin woman, complained that she had no one left in the house and, due to old age, she found it difficult to work. Two men—Devdutt and Suraj—would not let her enter her holding and beat her up whenever she tried to do so. She wanted the Congress to intervene and to make food and clothes available for her.[70]

All these problems were related not only to individual women but were a part of the wider problem—the exploitative character of the agrarian structure as a whole. They also indicated the faith reposed by women in Ram Chandra as the leader of the peasants.

[66] BRP, SF, No. 20.
[67] BRP, SF, No. 9.
[68] Ibid.
[69] Ibid.
[70] Ibid.

Ram Chandra argued for upward mobility for lower caste women. When the Sarda Committee was seeking evidence he advised the village panchayat heads to demand a similar status for the women of 'lower castes' as was enjoyed by 'high caste' women.[71] Peasant women, however, must earn their right to a higher status by changing themselves into highly austere, pious and moral persons. What he had in mind was the image of a new kind of woman who would also enjoy a greater measure of equality with her husband. It was this model of the new peasant woman that made him propose certain measures which in fact restricted the free movement of women. In a write up on '*Oudh ki Nariyon per Mere Vichar*' (My Views on the Women of Oudh), he started by quoting Maithili Saran Gupta:

> *Nari ninda na karo nari nar ki khan,*
> *Nari se nar hota hai Dhruv Prahalad saman.*
>
> (Do not talk ill of woman, she is the origin of man.
> From her are born men like Dhruv and Prahalad).[72]

But then he wrote: 'What should I do? I can't close my eyes to what's happening around.' He was highly critical of women's love for jewellery and regarded this as the prime cause for adultery. This weakness, he believed, exposed them to exploitation by men. Something concrete was needed to check this 'weakness'. One measure which he recommended was to discontinue the custom of inviting dancing girls on auspicious occasions, as women of the house and neighbourhood tried to imitate their dress and jewellery.[73] Another measure was to impose restrictions on women for going to fairs and markets as this would not only check their meetings with lovers but also prevent them from getting involved with bangle-sellers and other men.[74] But along with this strict moral code he worked for the uplift of women. Wherever he came across a woman who had the slightest education, he would inspire her to educate

[71] BRP, SW, F. No. 1A.
[72] Ibid.
[73] Ibid.
[74] Ibid.

other women in the village. Under his inspiration, Vidyavati wrote a booklet *Satnami Panch Kanya Daihati* and he published 2,000 copies of this.[75] The book dealt with various problems faced by women. When he was in jail (1942–5), he kept reminding his wife Jaggi to look after the education of their daughters.[76]

IV

We find the first instance of active political participation by women in the peasant struggles of August–September 1920. When Ram Chandra was arrested for the first time, about 40,000 peasants surrounded Partapgarh jail and the government was forced to release him.[77] Women had taken an active part in this agitation and after this there was no going back. Incidentally, Ram Chandra and 32 other peasants had been arrested by the police on the complaint of a woman taluqdar—Chabiraj Kunwar—who was notorious for being very oppressive.[78]

Thakur Din Singh rose in revolt against the Raja of Parhat in October 1920. He directed the movement against landlords, money-lenders and traders. The police and taluqdari agents crushed the uprising with great difficulty and women were the worst sufferers. Villages were plundered and women molested in eight villages during the hunt for Thakur Din.[79]

The Ayodhya Kisan Conference of December 1920 was a unique spectacle in the history of peasant struggles in India. About 50,000 to one lakh peasant men and women reached the town in spite of the cold weather. On his way to the meeting ground, Ram Chandra saw some very old women sitting exhausted by the long journey they had undertaken in order to attend the conference. He arranged an *ekka* (horse cart) to take them to the venue.[80] For the first time, women's presence was asserted separately from men in this historic

[75] BRP, SF, No. 4.

[76] Ram Chandra to Jaggi, 14 April 1944, BRP, SF, No. 26.

[77] Kapil Kumar, *Peasants in Revolt*, pp. 96-102.

[78] BRP, SW, F. No. 2C.

[79] *Abhyudaya*, 11 December 1920.

[80] BRP, SW, F. No. 2A.

meeting. Satya Devi spoke from the stage on behalf of women and assured their participation in the movement. This was greatly applauded from all sides.[81]

As if to test this assurance, the opportunity came that very day on the 20th of December. On the return journey there was trouble at the railway station. A clash took place over tickets and peasants offered *satyagraha* (passive resistance) by prostrating themselves on the railway tracks. Ram Chandra mentions that 'women feeding their infants lay flat on the rail lines and would not budge. Hot water showers from rail engines and police lathi charge could not deter them.' Ultimately they were allowed to board the trains.[82]

The peasant movement in Oudh assumed the dimensions of a class war as the desperate peasantry resorted to militant action on a large scale in Rai Bareilly district. The year 1921 began with the *jacqueries* of Oudh peasants. The peasants, in their thousands, moved from one estate to another destroying the crops of the taluqdars.[83] Here, I shall confine myself to the role of women during the uprising.

On 5 January the peasants surrounded the *kothi* (palatial house) of taluqdar Tribhuwan Bahadur Singh at Chandania. The taluqdar was hated by his tenants because of his immoral and oppressive practices. The estate was virtually ruled by a prostitute, Achhijan, who was the taluqdar's mistress or 'keep'.[84] The peasants demanded the expulsion of Achhijan and the restoration of the real Rani (taluqdar's wife), exemption from *nazarana* and no more evictions.[85] The first demand indicates that the opposition to Achhijan was not only on account of her oppressive practices but also on grounds of morality as she had infringed on the rights of another woman—the wife. Of course, the person responsible for this infringement was the taluqdar himself. He refused to meet—the demands of the peasants and many were arrested by the police.[86]

[81] C.I.D. Report on Ayodhya meeting, F. No. 358/1920, Police, UPSA.

[82] BRP, SW, F. No. 2A.

[83] F. Nos. 195-216A/February 1921-B, Home Pol., NAI.

[84] Personal interviews with Kanhai Singh and Parag Singh, village Harnirmau, Rai Bareilly district, 12 June 1977.

[85] *Pratap*, 16 January 1921.

[86] *Independent*, 11 January 1921.

On 24 January there was a pitched battle between the police and taluqdar's men on the one side and peasants on the other in village Sehagaon Panchimgaon. One constable was killed with *lathi* (thick wooden staff) blows and two others were injured. In spite of firing by policemen, the women of the village did not remain passive in the struggle. They pelted brickbats from their housetops on the policemen.[87] The DC of Rai Bareily was perturbed by this development in the peasant movement.[88]

In Fyzabad district, on the 13 and 14 January, large crowds consisting mainly of landless labourers moved about the Baskhari and Jehangirganj police circles, 'looting' the zamindars, moneylenders, merchants and goldsmiths. The main targets of attack were the grain stores of the zamindars and *mahajans.* These crowds, numbering between 1,000 to 5,000 men, were followed by crowds of women who carried off the 'booty' of their 'pillage'.[89] In many instances, women belonging to upper classes were subjected to humiliation, maltreated and abused by groups of oppressed women.[90] This demonstrates the awareness on the part of women of the class-contradictions of rural society. It would be interesting to mention here that two peasant leaders, Deo Narain and Kedarnath, were assaulted by Alopi, a Brahmin zamindar, on 19 January. Alopi regarded them as instigators and as such responsible for the 'insult of his womenfolk during the riots'.[91]

There was considerable interaction between the peasant movement in Oudh and the Non-Cooperation movement. Gandhi's name surfaced in different contexts during the peasant movement. Faruq Ahmed, a *fakir,* proclaimed that 'Gandhi would ascend the throne of Delhi on 15 February' and 'three lakhs of English ladies' would be 'distributed at the Guhuana Sabha'.[92] The talk of Gandhi ascending the throne is understandable but why English ladies are to be 'distributed' is not at all clear. Is it to be seen as a sexually moti-

[87] Shereff to Kaye, 24 January 1921, F. No. 50/1921, Gen., UPSA.

[88] DC, Rai Bareily to Commissioner, 24 January 1921, ibid.

[89] Nos. 195-216A 1921, Home Pol., NAI.

[90] Porter to Hailey, 19 January 1921, F. No. 50-3/1921, Gen., UPSA.

[91] Nos. 195-216A 1921, Home Pol., NAI.

[92] *Leader,* 24 June 1921.

vated statement to attract the men or was it a revengeful statement against the treatment meted out to peasant women by landlords? (There were a few British landlords in Oudh.) Or was there any case involving the honour of any local woman at the hands of an Englishman? There is no evidence to support any of these conjectures. However, Gandhi was projected in a totally different manner at the Guhuana Sabha on 27 January. Ram Devi compared Gandhi's agitation with the *Mahabharata* (Hindu epic) war: just as in the *Mahabharata* Draupadi's honour was at stake, Gandhi's agitation was seen to maintain the honour of Bharatmata (Mother India).[93] In fact, the peasants had their own perception of Gandhi and of his programme and were anxious about their economic emancipation.[94]

Active participation by women was a significant feature of the peasant movement in Oudh. The pelting of stones by women on the police party, their presence in hundreds during the Fyzabad uprising and the humiliation of upper class women at the hands of oppressed women, exhibited the revolutionary potential of the peasant women in the countryside.

On 19 February 1925, in Partapgarh, an all women conference was held under the Presidentship of Jai Kumari. It was described as a 'Kisan devi ki sabha' and the following resolutions were passed:

a. A cow should be maintained by the panchayat in every village so that milk is available for small children.
b. After the death of the husband, and on confirmation of the proof of marriage, the wife should get her right. If the wife is not there then the son or daughter should have it.
c. For achieving these demands of kisanin (peasant women) we shall organize meetings in every village.
d. We will contribute one anna per woman and form women panchayats in every village.
e. We shall hold meetings in our own villages and for the redressal

[93] CID Report on Guhuana Sabha, F. No. 50/1921, Gen. UPSA.

[94] See Kapil Kumar, 'Peasants' Perception of Gandhi and his Programme, Oudh 1920–1922', *Social Scientist* 11, No. 2, February 1983.

> of our grievances we shall get our own laws constituted from the government.[95]

Whether future meetings were held or not we do not know, but this meeting itself was a turning point for women as it is, till today, the first known recorded charter of peasant women's demands.

Concrete efforts were made in the 1930s to form peasant women's organizations. Among the activists who took the initiative were the wives of the Kisan Sabha leaders. A Kisanin Panchayat was formed with Jaggi as its leader. This organization functioned as a branch of the Praja Sangh organized by Ram Chandra.[96] The aims of the Kisanin Panchayat were:

a. To fight the grievances faced by them as women.
b. To fight the grievances faced as peasants and agricultural labourers.
c. Political mobilization for the national movement.[97]

Quite important was the pledge—almost a kind of demand charter—which a kisanin had to sign and to promise to work for its attainment:

a. After the death of the husband, without paying anything [this seems an indirect reference to *nazarana*], we should have full right over the holding. And, there should be no eviction for five years.
b. The women from kisan families should not be forced to work under the threats of lathis, *dandas* (sticks), chains, etc.
c. Those who work as labourers should get full wages.[98]

Both the aims and the pledge of the Kisanin Panchayat were an overt expression of the oppression faced by women in the countryside. They demonstrate an awareness and a determination on the part of women to fight against such oppression.

[95] BRP, SF, No. 4.

[96] In an attempt to forge unity amongst various strata of peasants and small zamindars Ram Chandra had organized the Praja Sangh in the early 1930s.

[97] BRP, SF, No. 12.

[98] BRP, SW, F. No. 2B.

Baba Ram Chandra used traditional customs and ceremonies to mobilize peasants against taluqdars and the British.[99] The Kisanin Panchayat also adopted such methods to create awareness amongst women. On 14 July 1933, a circular in Ram Chandra' handwriting read:

Due to Jaggi's efforts, the benefits which kisanin have got will be celebrated by a *yagya* (religious rite) of Bala Devi (local goddess) *pujan* (worship). Jaggi will go with prominent members of her panchayat.[100]

What exactly the benefits were is not clear from this circular but in all probability the celebration was in connection with the acceptance of women's demands by the Kisan Council and Kurmi Sabha as mentioned earlier. The celebration of success through a *yagya* indicates that those very women who demanded a radical change in their economic and social status were not prepared to break away from rituals.

The Kisanin Panchayat organized exhibitions to educate the kisanin and these were financed by the Praja Sangh. In the account papers of the Sangh we find reference to one such exhibition held on 7 February 1934: 'Bhagwandin and Jaggi's exhibition for kisanin was attended by kisanin from distant places. They stayed overnight. The expenditure was Re. 1 for inkpot, 8 annas wood, 8 annas food (*chabena*) Rs. 3'. . . . [101] This indicates that women were undertaking journeys on their own to make themselves aware of various issues related to them and to strengthen their organization. We have on record two meetings (3 September 1933 and 25 April 1934) of the Praja Sangh which were largely attended by women from the three tahsils (district subdivisions) of Partapgarh.[102] The Kisanin Panchayat would send separate invitation slips to women

[99] Kapil Kumar, 'Using the *Ramcharitmanas* as a Radical Text: Baba Ram Chandra in Oudh, 1920–50', in *Social Transformation and Creative Imagination*, (ed.) Sudhir Chandra (Delhi, 1984), pp. 311–34.

[100] BRP, SF, No. 11.

[101] BRP, SF, No. 12.

[102] BRP, SF, Nos. 6 and 25. In these meetings drug addition and prostitution were denounced.

for such meetings: *Kisanino ki panchayat mein kisano ki mang ke sath milne ka utsav kiya jayega* (In their meeting the women will celebrate their joining the peasants in their demands).[103] These invitations, though signed by Jaggi, are in Ram Chandra's hand-writing.

Some time in the mid or late 1930s a petition titled *Anath Ablaon ki Pukar* (The Helpless Women's Appeal) was sent to Prof. Braj Gopal Bhatnagar.[104] The petitioner signed herself as a *dukhit praja ki abla* (A helpless woman of the oppressed masses). The petition listed five grievances:

a. We are beaten with lathis.
b. Being forced to stand on a mudpot in the glaring sun we are watched with lustful eyes (obviously by landlords or their agents).
c. During *begar* they make us grind. If we refuse, we are beaten with lathis. They break our heads.
d. After the death of our husbands we are evicted from our holdings, houses, orchards, etc.
e. Thus, we cannot repay loans nor manage our family.

The petitioner further questioned *Kya ham kisi ki byahata nahin hain* (Are we not wives too), *Is apman ka dava kahan karen?* (Where should we appeal against such humiliation?); *Ham dukhi abla kya karen?* (What should we, the aggrieved and oppressed women do?). A significant move to attract the attention of intellectuals towards the plight of oppressed rural women, this document too, like many others, was penned by Ram Chandra.

The late 1930s witnessed a sharp ideological struggle within the Indian National Congress.[105] The right wing leadership was particularly hostile towards the Kisan Sabha and at many places, peasant members of the Congress were not allowed to vote in the organizational elections. In the Partapgarh countryside women had

[103] BRP, SF, No. 10.

[104] BRP, SF, No. 4.

[105] See Kapil Kumar, 'Ideology, Congress and Peasants in 1930s: Class Adjustment or Submission?', *Social Scientist* 14, Nos. 2–3, August–September 1986.

enrolled themselves in large numbers as 4 anna members of the Congress. These women were not just passive members. They played an important role not only during the direct action struggles but also in organizational matters. When a large number of women found their names missing in the voters list for organizational elections they flooded the DCC (District Congress Committee) office with representations during 1938-39.[106]

Certain changes had been made in the tenancy laws during the Congress ministry in UP, but they failed to meet peasant expectations. On the contrary it was the landlords who were able to extract some concessions from them. One among these was the enhanced power of the landlord to take over the lands which had been used for generations by the peasants for grazing their animals. In October 1940 Baba Ram Chandra organized a movement against this and more than 10,000 animals were taken in a procession to the DC's office in Partapgarh. It was a unique spectacle and in the words of Ram Chandra, 'people were surprised to see that even animals had come to petition'.[107] Women played a vital role in organizing this march. Maharani Devi, Gainda Devi and Paiga Devi had sent one ox each and many other women sent their animals which included cows, asses, goats, horses and even camels.[108] Laxími Kurmi has been mentioned as the most active participant in the movement.[109]

On 4 December 1940 during the individual satyagraha Jaggi made a request to the president of the Partapgarh DCC saying that since she was a Congress member from mandal 7, she should be issued a satyagrahi pass. She wanted to issue a statement before the DC and it was the responsibility of the DCC to take her to his office. She asserted that her statement should be printed and distributed by the DCC to all kisans and *mazdurs* (labourers). She wanted to offer satyagraha because: (a) peasants were oppressed; (b) the government had insulted Mahatma Gandhi and all this

[106] BRP, SF, No. 20.
[107] BRP, SF, No. 18.
[108] Ibid.
[109] BRP, SF, No. 9.

had become unbearable.[110] It is important here to note that while offering satyagraha for the nationalist cause she stressed peasant oppression and this signifies the peasants' own perception of nationalism. A handwritten leaflet was issued under her signature appealing to the peasants to:

a. Never believe the alien government or its servants and allies, nor help them in any way.
b. Not help or be with rajas and maharajas as they are the friends of the alien government.
c. Look after your homes, family, lands and animals yourself.
d. Break all caste norms in crisis.
e. Not side with those who indulge in violence and looting.
f. Be with the poor and not with the rich as they are all one and at many places the taluqdars, small zamindars and capitalists, with the help of high classes and arms want to create disturbances.

She declared that she was marching fearlessly and that they should all do the same. 'Don't get stuck at home' (*ghar na reha jana*).[111]

The Partapgarh DCC had made no call to women to participate but Jaggi insisted: 'We women have come to offer satyagraha at Gandhiji's order.[112] Under her leadership ten other women offered satyagraha. Out of these eleven, nine went to jail but Jaggi and Sundra Devi were not allowed to do so by the DCC. The explanation given to them was that Mahatmaji had ordered that no women with small children could go to jail. Both of them had children in their laps and when I interviewed them, with great anguish they told me how they were deprived from going to jail and separated from their sisters due to Gandhiji's orders.[113]

All these women were from poor peasant families and belonged to different castes:

[110] Ibid.

[111] Ibid.

[112] Personal interview with Jaggi: also with Sundra Devi, village Deosara, tahsil Patti, Partapgarh district, 16 June 1987.

[113] BRP, SF, No. 9.

Mussamat Putta	–	Harijan (Chamar)
Sampati	–	Kurmi
Razi	–	Kurmi
Sukhi	–	Teli
Sukhmani	–	Pasi
Bubai	–	Kurmi
Putra	–	Kurmi
Abhilakhi	–	Kurmi
Basanti	–	Brahmin
Sundra Devi	–	Ravidas[114]

This caste composition was an important development as these women had joined hands cutting across rigid caste norms and demonstrated through this that satyagraha could be a combined effort of the oppressed.[115] But the high caste *vakil* (lawyer) leaders in the DCC did not appreciate this as they were opposed to the peasants organizing as a class. Munishwar Dutt Upadhyaya, an important Congress leader, commented: 'Had the women from high families offered satyagraha it would have brought fame to the Congress. What could the women from Shudra (low caste) families bring?' This was strongly resented by Sita Ram, Sundra Devi's husband. On 27 December he wrote to Baba Ram Chandra that Munishwar Dutt had insulted the Devis and as such he and many other men might not offer satyagraha.[116] But on Ram Chandra's advice they continued with the satyagraha.

I did get certain information in relation to the life and activities of the prominent women activists in the Kisan Sabha through interviews conducted during my fieldwork. Mussamat Putta's husband was an agricultural labourer who never participated in the Kisan Sabha. He earned his wages and looked after the house whereas Putta was a Kisan Sahba wholetimer, very vocal and very active. She was given the name Laali (red) by the peasants due to her militant and aggressive participation. Her husband did not oppose her

[114] The first four among these were widows. For caste–class relationship in Oudh countryside see Kapil Kumar, *Peasants in Revolt*, pp. 223–4.

[115] Sita Ram to Ram Chandra, 27 December 1940, BRP, Correspondence.

[116] Ibid.

participation.[117] Sampati was herself a peasant-tenant and was in the forefront of the kisan movement. The husbands of Abhilakhi and Putta were not active in the Kisan Sabha—the former's because of his occupation in agriculture and the latter's because of fear.[118] According to Jaggi, men never opposed the participation of their wives in political actions, rather they encouraged it and the wives of all Kisan Sabha leaders were active at the same level as the men. Even if they had objected the women would have defied them for 'did not Ram tell Sita not to accompany him to the forest but Sita on her own decided to go.'[119] Sita to Jaggi is a symbol not of a woman who followed her *pati Parmeshwar* (husband-god) but of a woman who took her own decisions.

Sundra Devi had no political education in her parent's house. Hers was an arranged marriage with Sita Ram whose first wife had died after giving birth to a son. This was a political family. Sita Ram's father was a contractor and later on he bought a small zamindari in his wife's name. After his death his wife became a Kisan Sabha activist and in 1938 transferred her zamindari lands to the Congress.[120] Sundra Devi was encouraged by her mother-in-law and her husband to become active in the Kisan Sabha. During the 1942 movement Sita Ram was arrested and Sundra Devi went underground with her children. Soon Jaggi joined her and they faced tremendous hardships.[121]

It is important here to mention the kind of symbols Ram Chandra

[117] Personal interview with Mathura s/o Putta Lali, village Atraura, tahsil Patti, Partapgarh district, 14 June 1987.

[118] Personal interview with Mathura and Jaggi; also with Ram Bahadur Singh, village Rure, tahsil Patti, Partapgarh district, 14 June 1987.

[119] Personal interview with Jaggi. Personal interview with Sundra Devi. During my visit to Deosara I collected the papers of Sita Ram from Smt. Sundra Devi. The papers contain references to her mother-in-law and her small zamindari. The papers have been deposited in the NMML.

[120] Personal interview with Sundra Devi.

[121] BRP, SW, F. No. 2B. Within Hindu religious thought cosmic time is divided into four recurring *yugas* (periods)—*sat-yuga* is the golden period of virtue, *treta* wherein virtue and vice are in a proportion of three to one, *dvapara* where they are in equal proportion, and *kali-yuga*, the age of corruption.

was using to mobilize peasants. Kaikeyi in the popular imagination, is regarded as an evil character who sent Rama to the forest. But Ram Chandra was all praise for her:[122]

> In the *treta yuga,* when the freedom of India was abducted by Ravana of Lanka; there was a mother like Kaikeyi who created a way out to achieve independence. Had she not sent Rama to the forest who would have killed Ravana? Today in this *kaliyuga* if mothers act like Kaikeyi and offer their sons in the service of the country the *kalank* (shame) of mother India will go. But alas these days there are as many different feelings and opinions as there are mothers.

Jaggi very proudly narrates how Ram Chandra used to advise her and other women to work for the upliftment, of women of peasants and for the freedom struggle.[123]

V

This study is largely based on Ram Chandra's papers and there is ample scope for further investigation in the field. Yet, I have attempted to reconstruct the history of the rural women in Oudh. Three distinct voices are discernible in the study; (1) statements of women themselves cited in the Mehta Report and also found in the Ram Chandra papers; (2) issues raised by women under the tutelage of Ram Chandra; and (3) the concern shown by Ram Chandra and other kisan leaders for the plight of women in the countryside. These indicate that not only was there awareness of women's issues amongst both men and women but that both made a conscious effort to remedy specific grievances. This was not a one way process.

Ram Chandra's personal experience in relation to women did affect his views considerably—the stress on monogamy and sexual morality particularly was the direct result of what he had seen and experienced. Polygamy was described as a game of the rich (*bade logon ka khel hai*),[124] something which the poor peasant could not afford and should not think of. Moreover the justification for mono-

[122] Personal interview with Jaggi.

[123] Ibid.

[124] Ibid.

gamy was sought by citing Rama who had only one wife—Sita.[125] He learnt a great deal from women about their problems either through direct dialogue or through intermediaries. He would urge the women to stand on their own feet, but being aware of the existing social reality he knew well that their amelioration would not come through their own efforts alone. The attitude of the men towards women had to be changed. Like all political and social reformers he was patronizing towards women but did not want them to be submissive. He struggled for transformation in the condition and status of women which he sought by using traditional and cultural idioms to mobilize them not only as peasants but also as a separate group—women. The organization of the Kisanin Sabha was an effort of this kind.

Once the women were organized and out in the movement did any tension emerge between them and Ram Chandra? There is no evidence yet to indicate this. Rather the evidence speaks otherwise. The entire women's movement collapsed after his death in 1950. What the situation is today is subject for another study.

[125] Ibid.

PART 2

THE PEASANTS OF CONGRESS

CHAPTER 5

Peasants' Perception of Gandhi and his Programme: Oudh, 1920-1922*

The role of Gandhi in the Indian national struggle has been constantly analysed by the historiographers of modern India. We have a heap of literature[1] on Gandhian studies which emphasize on Gandhi's initiatives in resisting the colonial dominance. This emphasis partly reflects the hold of the dominant social groups and their intelligentsia on the national struggle. The initiatives on the part of the peasantry in responding to the Gandhian call are a subject to which few historiographers have paid attention and this needs further investigation. It is necessary to note that in the field of Gandhian studies a vacuum will persist so long as we do not analyse the peasants' response to Gandhi and the attitude of Gandhi towards this response. How did the peasants look upon Gandhi? Why and how did they follow him? We have discussed the attitude of national leaders towards the Oudh peasants elsewhere.[2] This study is an attempt to analyse, at a regional level, the peasants' attitude and response to Gandhi and his programme of non-cooperation—an attempt to look at Gandhi from below—and Gandhi's attitude towards this response in the light of contradictions within the anti-

* This paper was earlier published in *Social Scientist*, Vol. 11, No. 2, February 1983.

[1] Also see, Shahid Amin, 'Gandhi as Mahatma: Gorakhpur District, Eastern UP, 1921', in Ranajit Guha (ed.), *Subaltern Studies-3: Writings on South Asian History and Society*, New Delhi, 1984. Amin's concern has been on the making of Gandhi's image in the countryside whereas my concern is on not only the image building but also on how that was translated into political action. See my review of Amin's article in *Social Scientist*, Vol. 16, No. 3, March 1988, pp. 3–5 (produced as Annexure I in this article).

[2] S.K. Mittal and Kapil Kumar, 'Anti-Feudal and Anti-Colonial Struggles of the Oudh Peasantry in Early 1920s', *Social Scientist*, Vol. 8, No. 12, July 1980.

imperialist struggle during 1920–2 in Oudh, a taluqdari region of the United Provinces in British India.

The Non-Cooperation movement was the first major attempt on the part of the Indian National Congress leadership to broaden its mass base against imperialism. The credit for this breakthrough goes to Gandhi, the originator of the movement, who was fully aware of the necessity to enlist the peasants' support for the programmes of the national movement as visualized by the Congress leaders. This is apparent from his observation in 1916: 'Our salvation can alone come through the farmers. Neither the lawyers, nor the doctors, nor the rich landlords are going to achieve it.'[3] Again, in January 1921, Gandhi told the merchants of Calcutta: 'Swaraj depends on the agriculturists. If they do not help then Swaraj cannot be attained. If they cooperate with the Government, then all your virtues will not help in winning Swaraj.'[4]

Gandhi was fully aware that the 'zamindars would prove the chief stumbling block to . . . the Non-Cooperation programme' and they 'could be brought to senses if the tenants could be induced not to pay rent'.[5] But the crucial issues of concern to the peasantry such as high rents, evictions, cesses, high prices, social humiliation and exploitation at the hands of the *Raj* and the *zamindars*, etc., were not taken account of in the Non-Cooperation programme. Not only were the peasant issues sidetracked, but Gandhi wrote in *Young India* that it was 'dangerous to make political use of peasants and workers';[6] and a year later, after the Chauri Chaura incident, he suspended the entire movement. This was a time when there was widespread awakening among the peasants and an immense pressure from below to include the 'no-rent' demand in the programme of the movement.[7]

[3] Gandhi's address to Banaras Hindu University students on 6 February 1916, *Collected Works of Mahatma Gandhi*, Vol. XIII, p. 213.

[4] Speech at merchants' meeting in Calcutta, ibid., Vol. XIX, p. 281.

[5] F. No. 75/January 1921, Home-Political, Deposit, National Archives of India, New Delhi, p. 8.

[6] *Young India*, 9 February 1921.

[7] In UP, Bihar, Orissa, Andhra and in many princely states of Rajasthan the peasants had spoken of and even practised no-rent campaigns. Gandhi also

This abrupt withdrawal of the movement is understandable from the very fact that despite his acknowledgement of the peasants' role in winning *swaraj*, Gandhi had offered nothing for the peasantry in his programme of political action. While launching the movement he had clearly stated that he wished to 'begin with the educated classes'.[8] Thus, the Congress resolution on Non-Cooperation read:

And in as much as *a beginning should be made by the classes who have hitherto moulded and represented opinion* and in as much as Government consolidates its power through titles and honours bestowed on the people, through schools, controlled by it, its law courts and its legislative councils, and inasmuch as it is desirable in the prosecution of the movement to take the minimum risk and to *call for the least sacrifice* compatible with the attainment of the desired object. . . .[9]

Who were these classes which 'moulded and represented opinion'? Precisely the dominant sections and the oppressive social forces which did not mould opinion but forced their opinion through coercive acts under imperial instigation and support and then claimed to represent public opinion. The British depended on these forces to strengthen and consolidate the hold of imperialism and now the Congress leadership was looking to them to challenge the British. Obviously in both situations the dominant groups were the gainers and Bipan Chandra, in his earlier writings rightly mentioned that the national integration was promoted at the 'unilateral cost' of the peasantry.[10] It is precisely from this juncture onwards that the Congress leadership attempted to establish its dominance over the peasants' initiative in the national struggle.

The 'constructive programme' was 'a success politically and a

---

wrote, 'The idea of non-payment of taxes is in the air', *Young India*, 26 January 1922.

[8] Speech at a Gujarat political conference, 28 August 1920, *Collected Works*, Vol. XVIII, p. 202.

[9] Ibid., p. 230, emphasis added.

[10] Bipan Chandra, 'Indian Peasantry and National Integration', *Social Scientist*, Vol. 5, No. 2, September 1976, pp. 19, 27.

failure on social and economic fronts'[11]; it was successfully used by the Congress leadership for 'tension management'.[12] The Non-Cooperation programme offered nothing concrete to achieve or struggle for, except mentioning the attainment of *swaraj*, and the Congress leadership itself was not clear about the meaning of *swaraj*. Gandhi, who gave the catchy slogan of '*swaraj* in a year', on his own failed to spell out his exact understanding and meaning of the concept of *swaraj*. On different occasions *swaraj* was defined differently by him: '*Swaraj* means a state such that we can maintain our separate existence without the presence of Englishmen. If it is to be partnership, it must be a partnership at will';[13] '*Swaraj* is *Ramrajya*'[14]; 'My *swaraj* is the parliamentary Government of India in the modern sense of the term for the time being';[15] at times *swaraj* meant redressal of Punjab and Khilafat wrongs[16] and by 1922 it meant the practice of national virtues of *charkha* (spinning wheel), *khaddar* (hand spun and hand woven cloth), non-violence and equal treatment of untouchables.[17] Yet, there was a promise for the masses—the promise of 'swaraj in a year'—a *swaraj* which would end their grievances. In fact, *swaraj* 'was very much in the air and in people's thoughts, and frequent reference was made to it in innumerable gatherings and conferences'.[18] On a number of occasions nationalist leaders like Motilal Nehru, Jawaharlal Nehru, Abul Kalam Azad, Gauri Shankar Misra and ultimately Gandhi himself had impressed upon the peasants of Oudh that they should work

[11] David Hardiman, 'Peasant Agitations in Kheda District, Gujarat, 1917–34', Ph.D. thesis, Sussex, 1975, p. 219.

[12] D.N. Dhanagre, *Agrarian Movements and Gandhian Politics*, Agra, 1975, pp. 94–5.

[13] *Young India*, 29 September 1920.

[14] *Aaj*, 27 November 1920.

[15] *Young India*, 20 December 1920.

[16] Ibid.

[17] Ibid., 16 January 1922. Jawaharlal Nehru, commenting on the principles and objectives of the Congressmen in 1921–2, wrote that it was a 'vague *swaraj* with no clear ideology behind it'. Jawaharlal Nehru, *An Autobiography*, New Delhi, 1962, p. 86.

[18] Nehru, ibid., p. 63.

for the attainment of *swaraj* through which they could gain deliverance or that *swaraj* was the only remedy for the redressal of their grievances.[19] The peasants' interest in *swaraj* was imparting a nationalist dimension to their own programme for redressal of grievances. Their understanding of *swaraj* made it synonymous with self-rule and they believed in the Congress leaders' assertion that *swaraj*, and a fast approaching *swaraj* at that, would ameliorate their pathetic condition and that they would enter the 'golden age of *Ramrajya*'. To them *swaraj* meant their own rule, the end of the British raj and with it of all the oppressive social forces.

The Congress was yet to find a base in the Oudh countryside but the response it had from the rural areas was more encouraging and radical than the response from urban centres during the 'non-cooperation' phase of the national movement. The credibility of the British and *taluqdari* regime was seriously challenged in the Oudh villages.[20] Unlike in the case of the urban leaders, the attacks of the peasantry were not confined to the fringes and outer manifestations of Imperialism; besides the colonial administration, the targets of such attacks included the pillars of the *raj*—the *taluqdars*. Quite distinct from the Non-Cooperation movement, a strong peasant movement had emerged in Oudh under the Kisan Sabha banner. Although 'anterior to and independent' of non-cooperation, the Kisan Sabha movement soon adopted the non-cooperation programme along with its economic struggle. In due course it became difficult to distinguish between Non-Cooperation, Kisan Sabha or a Khilafat meeting[21] as the triple programme was discussed and propagated from the same platform. The boycott of law courts and the promotion of *swadeshi* (indigenous products) was 'greatly helped by the activities' of the Kisan Sabha.[22]

[19] *Leader*, 6 December 1920; *Independent*, 2 July 1920 and 11 January 1921.

[20] For details see Kapil Kumar, 'Peasants Movement in Oudh 1918–22', unpublished Meerut University thesis, 1980. This has subsequently been published. Kapil Kumar, *Peasants in Revolt: Tenants, Landlords, Congress and the Raj in Oudh 1886–1922*, Delhi, 1984.

[21] Superintendent of Police to Deputy Commissioner, Rai Bareilly, 25 February 1921, F. No. 50/1921, General UPSA.

[22] F.No. 21, Bulletins of Congress, All India Congress Committee (supplementary) Papers, 1921, Nehru Memorial Museum & Library.

CLASS BASIS OF THE PEASANT AWAKENING

Before we go further, it is necessary to identify the sections of the peasantry that participated in or directed the Kisan Sabha and Aika movements, for it was they alone who responded to the Gandhian call in the countryside.[23] Eric Stokes applies to these movements the conclusions drawn by Jacques Pouchepadas and Judith Brown in the case studies of Champaran and Kaira that political mobilization was based on the rich peasants.[24] We, however, have evidence to suggest that the rich peasantry was conspicuous by its absence and that it was the poor peasantry, who, along with the agricultural labourers, challenged their oppressors in Oudh.[25] In Sultanpur, the movement was initially of landless agricultural labourers.[26] In Fyzabad, the movement was given a radical turn by the ploughmen, landless agricultural labourers and tenants-at-will and the targets were *zamindars, banias* (traders), *mahajans* (money-lenders) and well-to-do cultivators.[27] In Rai Bareilly, Mata Badal, the tenant who was instrumental in launching the first Kisan Sabha at Rasulpur, was an evicted tenant who paid Rs. 30 per year as rent (his holding would have in no case been more than 2.5 acres for, belonging as he did to the Koyari caste, his rent would not have been less than Rs. 12 per acre[28]) per year. In Partapgarh, the members of the Kisan Sabha were poor and evicted tenants. Amol Sharma resorted to direct action at Chandania only after he had been evicted by the landlord.[29] The peasants that moved about in

[23] For details against the rich/middle peasant thesis see Kumar, *Peasants in Revolt*, op. cit., pp. 218–22.

[24] Eric Stokes, *Peasant and the Raj*, New Delhi, 1978, p. 277.

[25] See also D.N. Dhanagre, 'Congress and Agrarian Agitation in Oudh, 1920–2 and 1930–2', *South Asia*, No. 5, December 1975, p. 71.

[26] Hailey to Keane, 6 October 1920, F. No. 358/1921, Police, UP State Archives, Lucknow.

[27] Hailey to Butler 24 January 1921, F. No. 50-3/1921, General UPSA; F. Nos. 195-216A/February 1921-B, Home Political, National Archives of India, New Delhi.

[28] Farnon Report, F. No. 50/1921 General, UPSA.

[29] See Kumar, thesis, op. cit., p. 155.

Partapgarh, Rai Bareilly, Fyzabad and Hardoi districts and the peasant gatherings at various Kisan Sabha and *aika* meetings numbered between 300 and 5,000 including women. These could hardly be described as rich peasant gatherings. The percentage of rich tenants who paid Rs. 100 or more as rent was only 2.9 of the total tenantry in Oudh. The percentage of those tenants who paid rent between Rs. 50 and 99, who may be placed in the category of middle tenants, was 11.3. The percentage of those tenants who paid rent between Rs. 1 and 50 was 85.8[30] and I place them in the category of poor tenants. The demarcation line between the poor tenants and the agricultural labourers was a thin one as 97.9 per cent[31] of the total tenants had no rights of occupancy and, once evicted by the landlords, they had no source of livelihood other than becoming agricultural labourers or migrating to cities in search of petty jobs.

GANDHI IMAGE

Gandhi had in reality exercised a restraining influence on the revolutionary potentiality of the peasants at Champaran which might have erupted into militant struggles but for his intervention.[32] Yet, it can hardly be disputed that the image he got after Champaran was of a 'liberator of the peasants' or a 'messiah who could ameliorate the peasants' lot'. And it was this image that made Baba Ram Chandra appeal to him to come and lead the Oudh peasants.[33] What made Gandhi popular in the countryside was not his *satyagraha* in South Africa or his undisputed leadership of the Congress but the association of Champaran with his name—his work amongst the peasants.[34] It was against the logic of Gandhian

[30] Figures extracted from the Report of an Informal Committee Appointed to Examine and Advise Regarding Paragraphs 212 to 259 of the *Report on Indian Constitutional Reforms*, Allahabad, 1918.

[31] Ibid.

[32] See S.K. Mittal and Krishan Dutt, 'Raj Kumar Sukul and Peasant Upsurge in Champaran', *Social Scientist*, Vol. 4, No. 9, April 1976.

[33] Ram Chandra Papers, NMML; *Leader*, 9 September 1920.

[34] Ibid.

politics[35] to fight the Indian landlords[36] and to expect help from Gandhi in a struggle against the landlords and other oppressive social forces was an illusion on the part of the peasantry and the indigenous peasant leadership. Yet it is worth investigating how Gandhi's name figured in the peasant movement.

A CID officer, while reporting on the activities of the Kisan Sabha around Allahabad and Partapgarh, observed: 'The fact must be faced that Gandhi's word is supreme.'[37] How did this happen? The answer is that the local newspapers played a vital role in building up the image of the Mahatma and in the countryside rumour added much to his popularity. Both attributed to him unknown powers and quoted statements which he had never made. The *Awadh Bhashi* published four miracles of Mahatma Gandhi:[38] (1) An old man in Lucknow got back his lost eyesight in a night by believing in Gandhi. (2) A police inspector arrested a non-cooperator and so a brick from the sky fell on his head and wounded him severely. (3) An *Arya Samajist* lady became a non-cooperator and when, against her will, her husband bought foreign cloth, she cursed him and so whatever he wanted to eat became filth. (4) A Muhammadan *rais* (rich man) of Lucknow wanted to have a dancing party against Gandhi's instructions and so a fire broke out in his palace.

The *Bhavishya* reported a speech of Gandhi in which he was said to have remarked: 'One hundred thousand of whitemen would be blown away by the very breath of thirty crores of Indians.'[39] The editor of *Vartaman* had several 'Gandhi notes' printed and the income from these was to be utilized in the non-cooperation movement.[40] At Ajodhya a rumour went around that 'Gandhi was to rise from the river'. Hundreds of peasants rushed to witness the

[35] See also Sumit Sarkar, 'The Logic of Gandhian Nationalism: Civil Disobedience and the Gandhi–Irwin Pact 1930-31', *Indian Historical Review*, Vol. III, No. 1, July 1976.

[36] See Mittal and Kumar, 'Anti-Feudal and Anti-Colonial Struggle of the Oudh Peasantry', op. cit., p. 39.

[37] F. No. 13, February 1921, Home Political, Deposit, NAI.

[38] *Awadh Bhashi*, 19 April 1921. Also see Amin, op. cit.

[39] *Bhavishya*, 1 November 1920.

[40] *Vartaman*, 25 November 1920.

scene and this resulted in a stampede.[41] Similarly, a 21-foot tall figure dressed in white was said to have appeared in a temple and vanished in the garb of a little boy after disclosing that his name was on everybody's lips in India. It was assumed that Gandhi had come.[42] The CID report read:

The currency which Mr. Gandhi's name has acquired in the remotest villages is astonishing. No one *seems to know quite who or what he is*, but it is an accepted fact that what he says is so, and what he orders must be done. He is a *Mahatma* (sacred soul) or *Sadhu* (Saint), a *Pandit* (priest), a *Brahman* (learned one) who lives at Allahabad, even a *Deota* (angel). One man said *he was a merchant who sells cloth at three annas a yard.* . . . The most intelligent say he is a man who is working for the good of the country, but the *real power of his name is perhaps to be traced back to the idea that it was he who got bedakhli* (ejectment) *stopped* at Partapgarh. It is the curious instance of the power of a name.[43]

In fact, it was Baba Ram Chandra who had organized the peasantry to offer resistance to *bedakhli* in Partapgarh,[44] but as he had marched with some 500 peasants to Allahabad to persuade Gandhi to come to Partapgarh,[45] the credit for organizing the peasants had been attributed to Gandhi through rumour in the countryside. There are other interesting observations too. At places, Gandhi was not thought of being 'antagonistic to government, but only to zamindars'. The reverence for Gandhi was 'undoubtedly partly due to the belief that he has great influence with the government' which led some peasants to say 'we are for Gandhi and the *sarkar* (government)'.[46] Thus, Gandhi was looked upon as an emancipator of the peasants with the help of *sarkar*. This was perhaps a refracted understanding of the Champaran compromise.

The *Independent* was constrained to make the following observation:

[41] See D.N. Panigrahi, 'Peasant Leadership', in B.N. Pandey (ed.), *Leadership in South Asia*, New Delhi, 1977, p. 84.

[42] Ibid.

[43] F. No. 13, February 1921, op. cit., emphasis added.

[44] See S.K. Mittal and Kapil Kumar, 'Baba Ram Chandra and Peasant Upsurge in Oudh 1920–1921', *Social Scientist*, Vol. 6, No. 11, June 1978.

[45] Ibid., p. 40.

[46] F. No. 13, February 1921, op. cit.

It has almost become a trite saying that political leadership has passed from the educated class to vast rural democracy. The saying is strictly true. Now we have a famous *Kisan* leader (Baba Ram Chandra) making a profession of faith before an urban audience and challenging the emasculated children of Western culture to the high task of national participation and regeneration.[47]

Baba Ram Chandra made strenuous efforts to propagate the non-cooperation programme. He would tell his audience not to tolerate the *zulum* (tyranny) of district and police officials and to take to *swadeshi* and handspun cloth.[48] He described the government as 'treacherous, tyrannical and dishonest' and would not rest 'until he had driven the British government out'.[49] He often referred to the government as *phupha* (uncle) and referring to the King he would say, '*Bad-zat kafir ko badshah na manna chahiye*[50] (we should not recognize the outcast as our king).' His dramatic methods included the auction of his *lungi* (lower dress) proclaiming that the amount thus collected would go towards the construction cost of a national school.[51] The Ajodhya conference, which was attended by nearly one lakh peasants,[52] 'had assured the Congress leaders of the peasants' support for the cause of non-cooperation'.[53] The apostles of the non-cooperation movement had succeeded in injecting a considerable dose of nationalist ideology in the villages. The political programme of the Aika Movement included the formation of *aika* (unity) to win *swaraj*; use of swadeshi and *charkha* (spinning wheel) as Mahatma Gandhi's raj was soon to appear; boycott of courts and establishment of village panchayats (village courts).[54] This programme reflected how deep the philosophy of non-

[47] *Independent*, 28 January 1921.

[48] Ibid., 1 January 1921.

[49] Ibid., 10 and 25 March 1921.

[50] Superintendent of Police to CID, 15 January 1921, F. No. 50/1921, General, UPSA.

[51] *Independent*, 10 March 1921.

[52] This is based on contemporary newspapers and Baba Ram Chandra Papers.

[53] *Leader*, 23 December 1920.

[54] Faunthorpe Report on Eka Movement, *United Provinces Gazette*, 13 May 1922, part VIII, p. 275.

cooperation had gone into villages. The more conservative village folk who refused to join *aika* were told, or came to believe, that by not joining they would not get the benefits which were to come when Gandhi's *swaraj* materialized.[55] Social boycott was carried against the *zamindars* and the bureaucracy in the form of *nai-dhobi band* (refusal of services by barber and washerman). At Sandila, the Sub-Divisional Magistrate could not find a barber to shave him.[56] But the peasants opposed the move of the Congress leaders to form *aika* with zamindars in opposing the government. The former wanted to have *aika* among themselves against both the *zamindars* and the government.[57]

Gandhi's name was associated with the 'looting' of markets and *taluqdari* property, travelling without tickets and mobilization. At Fursatganj *bazar* (market) in Rai Bareilly district, under the cries of *jai* (hail) Ram Chandra, Mahatma Gandhi, Shaukat Ali and Mohammad Ali, the peasants accused the *banias* (traders) of making heavy profits at the cost of the peasantry. The *banias* were urged to sell cloth at four annas a yard and flour at eight seers a rupee or else face plunder. The peasants were dispersed after the use of firearms, leaving six dead and 24 injured.[58] Before the Munshiganj firing, many peasants believed that Gandhi had been arrested and that he was in Rai Bareilly jail.[59] Oaths had been administered to the peasants to reach Rai Bareilly and the failure to reach was supposed to be tantamount to eating nine pigs if they were Muslims and of killing nine cows if they were Hindus.[60] The peasants boarded the trains at Fyzabad and Sultanpur railway stations without tickets on their way to the Unchahar meeting.[61] It was reported that the peasants had been informed by the Kisan Sabhas 'that it was Gandhi's

[55] Ibid., p. 273.

[56] *Pioneer*, 10 March 1922.

[57] Police Abstract of Intelligence, 3 March 1922.

[58] SDM's Report, F. No. 195-216A/ February 1921, op. cit.

[59] Farnon to Deputy Commissioner, Rai Bareilly, F. No. 50/1921, General UPSA.

[60] *Leader*, 23 July 1921.

[61] For details see Mittal and Kumar, 'Baba Ram Chandra and Peasant Upsurge in Oudh, 1920–1921', op. cit., p. 47.

order that they are to go' and that 'they will be provided (food) in the name of Gandhi'.[62] There was no need to purchase tickets in Gandhi *raj*.[63] Shah Mohammed Naim Ata, the *sajjadnasin* (head) of a dargah (Muslim shrine), declared himself the 'king of Salon on the advent of Gandhi *raj*'[64] during the peasant movement.

In Fyzabad it was 'Gandhi's order to loot' *taluqdari* godowns, *mahajan* (moneylender) houses and those of well-to-do cultivators.[65] Many peasants publicly confessed to Jawaharlal Nehru of having taken part in the 'loot of Gandhi *baba*'.[66] Kedar Nath, a local peasant leader and a non-cooperator, sat in *dharna* (strike) outside the Baskhari *thana* (police station) after he was assaulted by a *zamindar*. He lectured to the peasants:

> . . . Either we shall die or the police will die. Make room and arrangements for food for those who will gather. Mahatma Gandhi will not come but they will show their strength. I do not think it proper to call Mahatmaji; either *he will die or overthrow the police*. These *londaharu* (policemen) will see how they will be treated, and you will see the dropping of bomb in Baskhari.[67]

On the other hand, his colleague, Deo Narain, after hearing the complaint of district authorities that the crowd was armed, removed the peasants from the front of thana and made them surrender some 300 *lathies* (sticks).[68] Faruq Ahmed, a village *faqir* (saint), proclaimed: 'Gandhi would ascend the throne of Delhi on 15 February and three lakh English ladies would be distributed at the Guhana *sabha* (meeting).'[69] The talk of ascending of the throne by Gandhi is understandable but why the question of English ladies appeared

[62] Hailey to Lambert, 13 Janunary 1921, F. No. 50-3/1921, General, UPSA.
[63] Ibid., 14 January 1921.
[64] F. Nos. 195-216A, op. cit. For details see M.H. Siddiqi, *Agrarian Unrest in North India*, New Delhi, 1978, p. 155.
[65] *Independent*, 26 January 1921.
[66] CID Report on Guhuana Sabha, 28 January 1921, F. No. 50/1921, op. cit.
[67] Hailey to Lambert, 31 January 1921, F. No. 50-3/1921, op. cit., emphasis added.
[68] Ibid.
[69] *Leader*, 24 June 1921.

is not at all clear. Is it to be discarded as a sexually motivated statement or was it a revengeful statement in retaliation against the treatment meted out to the peasant womenfolk by the landlords? Or was there any case involving the honour of any local woman at the hands of an Englishman? There is no evidence to know the truth.

On 27 January 1921, 30,000 to 40,000 peasants gathered at Guhana, a village in Fyzabad district. The meeting, which was supposed to give the results of Baskhari affair, was now dominated by the Congressmen and Jawaharlal Nehru presided. The Congress leaders called upon the peasants to work for the attainment of *swaraj* and carry on non-cooperation. Speeches were directed mainly against the government and there was no mention of *taluqdari* oppression. Jawaharlal told the peasants that 'only by coloured clothes they should not believe that every person was a real sadhu and a messenger of Mahatma Gandhi' as the latter 'never advises irreligious or unlawful acts'.[70] Sarju Pande lectured that if 'the *khufia* (secret) police come and say they are Gandhi's messengers they are not to be believed'. Ram Devi compared Gandhi's agitation with the *Mahabharata.* (Hindu epic war). In the *Mahabharata* Draupadi's respect was at stake and 'Gandhi's agitation was to maintain respect of *Bharatmata*' (mother India). Phool Chand described Mahatma Gandhi as a doctor who was suggesting medicine to cure the condition of India. In the course of the speeches it was suggested that the peasants should consider Mahatma Gandhi as their *raja* (king) and act on his advice. They were told that so great was Gandhi's influence that a *daroga* (police inspector) returned bribes when he came to know that 'Gandhiji's disciples had also reached the spot'.[71] To all this the peasants listened peacefully but when they were asked to vote a resolution which condemned the 'plunderers' during the agrarian upsurge, they became unruly and Jawaharlal, after postponing the speeches, made use of music played on the harmonium to quieten the peasants.[72] Nehru, it appears, was following Gandhi's instructions as the latter had suggested the use of music to control

[70] CID Report on Guhana Sabha, op. cit.

[71] Ibid.

[72] Ibid.

'mobocracy'.[73] It appears that the enthusiasm of the peasants was somewhat dampened by the sermons of the Congress leaders; the exuberant shouts of *jai*, which were raised on the way to the meeting, were absent on the return.[74]

But the preaching of direct action was readily followed. One Nageshwarlal had lectured: 'The audience should be careful of the CID. . . . If they catch a *khufia* policeman they should keep him in their custody for 7 days and should never let him go as they blame the name of their Mahatma (Gandhi). Such *khufia* police should be shown to his uncle (British officer) to look into the acts of his nephew (*khufia* policeman).'[75] The preaching soon had effects. Two policemen who had gone to report on a Kisan Sabha meeting were assaulted on 29 January at Baskhari.[76]

To the peasantry, Gandhi was a symbol of opposition to the oppressor, whosoever he may be. During the popular protest at Karahia, Brijpal Singh told the peasants: 'Mahatma Gandhi would arrive at 11 o'clock and he would regulate the Deputy Commissioner's action.'[77] This was welcomed by the peasants with great shouts of 'Mahatma Gandhi ki jai'.[78] When 660 peasants were released from the Rai Bareilly jail on the ground that the jail was not a 'lunatic asylum' it was rumoured in the countryside that '. . . the recent wholesale releases from jail were carried out on receipt of orders from Mr. Gandhi and that further releases would be similarly arranged for'.[79]

During the Aika movement a widespread rumour in Baharaich was that 'Gandhi will lower the cash rents'.[80] Gandhi's image as a helper of the oppressed was so deep-rooted in the countryside that Farnon observed:

[73] *Young India*, 8 September 1920.

[74] Hailey to Lambert, 31 January 1921, op. cit.

[75] CID Report on Guhana Sabha.

[76] F. No. 195-216A/February 1921, op. cit.

[77] Statement of Bryan, Assistant Opium Agent, F. No. 50/1921, General, UPSA.

[78] Ibid.

[79] S.R. Mayer to A.G. Sherreff, 25 January 1921, ibid.

[80] *Leader*, 14 January 1922.

'. . . Any person whether actually a disciple of Mr. Gandhi or not, who set up the cry of 'Gandhiji *ki jai*' was assured of a following of hundreds for the sake of excitement and thousands out of mere curiosity—where excesses would be committed by the few, and provided that the taluqdars were the only sufferers, condoned by many.[81]

The peasantry of Oudh attempted in reality to practise the theoretical *swaraj* of Congressmen by raising parallel administration in the countryside. In Fyzabad, Sultanpur and Sitapur districts, peasants established their own *swaraj* by taking over the village administration in some villages.[82] They appointed officials, such as deputy commissioner, *daroga sahib* (police inspector) and captain *sahib* (superintendent of police), from among themselves. Along with one such document which described these appointments the police seized a number of petitions to Gandhi regarding peasant grievances.[83] The establishment of *swaraj* in Tazuddinpur, a village in Sultanpur district which was administered by the Court of Wards, was a direct challenge to the imperial authority and the latter could be re-established only with the help of the military.[84] Suraj Prasad alias *Chhota* (younger) Ram Chandra started by preaching *swadeshi* and ultimately uprooted the *taluqdari* authority in his area of influence in the Fyzabad district, distributed land to the evicted and landless peasants, fined government pensioners and arrested policemen on patrol duty.[85] All this he did under the name of Gandhi and this signifies what he and the oppressed peasants hoped to gain from Gandhi and his programme. As expected, the administration described his radical acts as 'loot pure and simple' and 'blackmail in the name of Gandhi'.[86] It was a common practice on the part of officials and landlords to label as 'bad characters, bandits, ex-convicts, absconding offenders, criminals' all those peasants and

[81] Farnon to Deputy Commissioner, Rai Bareilly, F. No. 50/1921, op. cit.

[82] For details see Kumar, thesis, op. cit., pp. 188, 189, 263.

[83] F. No. 195-216A/February 1921, op. cit.; *Pioneer*, 4 February 1921.

[84] Deputy Commissioner's Report on the passage of Column of Troops through Sultanpur, 4 March 1921, F. No. 50-3/1921, General, UPSA.

[85] Note on Spurious Ram Chandra, F. No. 50/1921, General, op. cit.

[86] Hailey to Lambert, 29 January 1921, ibid.

their leaders who offered resistance to the oppression practised by the officials and the landlords.[87]

GANDHI REACTION

Gandhi's reaction to the peasants' initiative has been dealt with by scholars[88] and here I will briefly discuss some aspects which further need to be mentioned. The more direct forms of action adopted by the peasants against the landlords and the *raj* were matters of great concern for Gandhi as they surpassed the limits of his programme of political action. He described these actions as 'madness' and 'mobocracy' and did not want anybody to 'commit mischief' in his name.[89] At no stage of non-cooperation did he want to deprive the *zamindars* of their rent.[90] He condemned the peasants for '*not making wise use* of their newly found power'.[91] He warned the peasants that in case they did not conduct themselves on his methods and follow the Congress and Khilafat decrees, he would 'not tolerate them'. He even went to the extent of declaring that the 'tenants went mad at Fyzabad'.[92] The Gandhian methods through which the peasants could make 'wise use' of their power were: complete adherence to non-violence; not to stop services to the landlords; to follow the advice of the Nehrus; to carry out all government orders;

[87] For a detailed discussion, see Kapil Kumar, *Peasants in Revalt*, New Delhi, 1984.

[88] See Walter Hauser, 'The Indian National Congress and Land Policy in the Twentieth Century', *The Indian Economic and Social History Review*, Vol. 1, No. 1, July-September 1963; W.F. Grawley, 'Kisan Sabhas and Agrarian Revolt in UP', *Modern Asian Studies*, Vol. 5, 1971; Judith Brown, 'Gandhi and Indian Peasants', *The Journal of Peasant Studies*, Vol. 1, No. 4, 1974. Mittal and Kumar, 'Anti-Feudal and Anti-Colonial Struggles of the Oudh Peasantry', op. cit.; Gyan Pandey, 'Peasant Revolt and Indian Nationalism: The Peasant Movement in Awadh, 1919–22', in Ranajit Guha (ed.), *Subaltern Studies I*, Delhi, 1982.

[89] Gandhi's speech at Banaras, 9 February 1921, F. No. 87/1921, Home Political Department, NAI.

[90] *Collected Works*, Vol. XX, pp. 105–6.

[91] *Young India*, 18 May 1922, emphasis added.

[92] Gandhi's speech at Fyzabad, 10 February 1921, F. No. 87/1921, op. cit.

not to withhold taxes from the government or rent from the landlord; not to prevent the arrest of any of their leaders, etc.[93] These instructions were 'clearly intended to counter the kind of peasant activism that had broken out'.[94] His entire thrust at that time was to influence the peasants to abandon their struggle against the *zamindars*. That he was influenced more by the landlords' interest than the question of the peasants' is apparent from what he wrote: 'The *Kisan* movement must be confined to the improvement of the status of the *kisans* and the betterment of the relations between them and the *zamindars*. The *kisans must be advised scrupulously to abide* by their agreement with the zamindars, whether such agreement is written or inferred from custom.'[95]

The *zamindars* were the creation of the British regime and the agreements between them and their tenants were arbitrary agreements, forced upon the tenants through imperial policies under the imperial bayonets and courts. Gandhi was asking the peasants to abide by these agreements. However, in looking upon the relations between the oppressors and the oppressed from a 'neutral' stance, Gandhi was not taking into account the humiliation and exploitation involved in the oppressor–oppressed relationship. Given the consciousness of the peasantry towards the oppressive role of the landlords, it was irrational to imagine that the peasants could work for their betterment by maintaining friendly relations with *zamindars*.

Gandhi was critical about 'lootings' and burnings by the peasants whereas he himself 'lighted the heap of foreign clothing and it burnt on merrily amidst loud noise of crackers and bursting flames' in the presence of thousands near Elphinstone Mills in Bombay.[96] The effect of this act of Gandhi can be well imagined in the countryside as it was natural for the peasants to interpret Gandhi's revolutionary action in their own way and strike at their exploiters. Gandhi was much concerned about peasant violence but he ignored the violence practised by the landlords on their tenants over a long

[93] *Young India*, 9 March 1921; *Independent*, 16 February 1921.

[94] Pandey, op. cit., p. 154.

[95] *Young India*, 18 May 1922, emphasis added.

[96] *Bombay Chronicle*, 10 October 1921.

span of time. The peasants understood Gandhian non-violence to mean only refraining from the use of violence against human life; the looting and burning of *taluqdari* godowns was not regarded as a violent action by the peasants.[97] No landlord or his agent was killed or injured during the 'crowd action' in Oudh. Thus, as far as the peasants' interpretation of non-violence was concerned, they were perfectly non-violent. As there were no laws to check high prices, ejectment, collection of illegal cesses[98] and humiliation, the peasants acted on their own. They could have plundered the *banias* even without warning them to reduce prices, had their motive been only sheer loot. But they did ask them to reduce prices and only when requests were turned down did the peasants resort to direct forms of action. In fact, their acts were the popular measures to check the triple oppression by the British, the landlords and the merchants.

CONCLUSION

Gandhi wanted to cover up the inherent contradictions in the rural socio-economic set-up in the interests of forging a multi-class alliance against imperialism and this he consistently attempted, shifting his argument to suit the occasion. Where the peasants were prepared to act in perfect non-violent ways to carry out the no-rent campaign, he brought in other issues:

> It is therefore not enough that the peasantry remain non-violent. Non-violence is certainly nine-tenths of the battle, but it is not all. The peasantry may remain non-violent but may not treat untouchables as their brethren . . . they may not have learnt the economic and the moral value of *charkha* and the *khaddar*. If they have not they cannot win *swaraj*. . . . They must be taught to know that the practice of these national virtues means *swaraj*.[99]

While preaching the social upliftment of the untouchables Gandhi did not take into account their economic status in the countryside.

[97] Interview, Anjani Kumar Tewari, Rai Bareilly.

[98] See Kapil Kumar, 'Peasant Exploitation: A Study of Taluqdari Extortions in Oudh, 1886–1922', paper presented at a seminar on Economic and Social Change in North India, September 1981, Kurukshetra University.

[99] *Young India*, 26 January 1922.

The majority among the agricultural labourers came from the 'untouchables' and the 'lower castes' but nothing was offered to ameliorate their economic condition. Moreover, in Oudh villages the 'low castes' had to pay a higher rent than the 'high castes' to their landlords,[100] but no Congressman, not even Gandhi, ever raised the demand that the 'low caste' tenants should be treated on par with 'high caste' tenants as far as rent collections were concerned.

The local Congress leaders made all sorts of promises to the peasants in order to mobilize them behind the non-cooperation movement. For example, Pandit Bishamber Nath Bajpai declared at Maharajganj that 'a day will come when the peasants will rule the whole world'. He also preached social boycott of *tehsil chaprasis* (peons) who troubled peasants for *rasad* (forced supplies).[101] Pandit Jagannath advocated 'non-cooperation with *taluqdars* and government officials'. All this was contrary to Gandhi's instructions. The radical rural intelligentsia, often represented in the form of *babas* and *faqirs*, had much to offer under the name of Gandhi. Gandhi's popularity rested in his 'peasant image' which was projected by the local press, and rumour added to its colour. Gandhi, to the peasants of Oudh, was a symbol which represented justice, a liberator who would undo their wrongs; everything which was unjust, cruel and oppressive was fought under his name. The peasants had their own interpretation of the Gandhian message in relation to their grievances. It was during the Kisan Sabha and Aika movements that the Congress established itself in the Oudh countryside. The slogan of '*swaraj* in a year' created a widespread awakening. This further deepened the anti-imperialist feelings among the peasants who shed their fear to challenge the authority of the British and the oppressive social forces. Viewed politically, the *purna swarajya* (complete independence) came on 15 August 1947. But the crucial question remains: how far were the peasants' hopes and belief that *swaraj* would liberate them, fulfilled?

[100] Sitapur Settlement Report, 1899, p. 8; Fyzabad Settlement Report, 1899, p. 11; V.N. Mehta Report on Agrarian Disturbances in Partapgarh, F. No. 753/1920, Revenue-A, UPSA.

[101] S.R. Mayers to A.G. Sherreff, 25 February 1921, F. No. 50/192, op. cit.

ANNEXURE I*

*SUBALTERN STUDIES III**—Kapil Kumar**: Shahid Amin's essay, 'Gandhi as Mahatma: Gorakhpur District, Eastern UP, 1921–22', the first in Volume III of Subaltern Studies, is a product of meticulous research, and at the same time a self-contradictory exercise. Amin makes it clear that his concern is not with 'analysing the attributes of his [Gandhi's] charisma but with how this registered in peasant consciousness' (p. 2). This, according to him, is a perspective which is 'somewhat different from the view usually taken of this grand subject' (p. 2), i.e. the relationship between peasants and Gandhi. The aim of the exercise, Amin tells us, is a 'limited one of taking a close look at peasant perceptions of Gandhi by focussing on the trail of stories . . .' (p. 2). The two main issues discussed are the 'location of the Mahatma image within the existing patterns of popular beliefs and the way it informed direct action, often at variance with the standard interpretations of the Congress creed' (p. 2). Gandhi's popularity rested on his 'peasant image' which had been projected by the press, intelligentsia and the dominant social groups during and after the Champaran episode. It was not what he had done in South Africa that was registered in peasant consciousness but his role as a leader who took up the peasants' cause and talked about their grievances and exploitation. Let us begin by examining how peasant consciousness registered the image of the Mahatma. Both perceptions and popular beliefs emerge, exist and operate within specific social and economic relationships. And these popular perceptions and beliefs are also influenced by the class positions and interests of the dominant classes who play a vital role in their emergence, propagation and transmission. This is precisely where Amin is not only ambiguous, but his search for a 'somewhat different perspective' takes him away from social reality and what has been claimed as subaltern history. Amin laboriously links the Mahatma's image with rumour and existing popular beliefs but he fails to delineate the links between the image, the rumours, the agrarian structure and political action. After all, rumours are not supra-historical.

When the peasants of Gorakhpur believed in rumours about Gandhi's

* Review of Ranajit Guha (ed.), *Subaltern Studies III*, New Delhi, 1984, in *Social Scientist*, Vol. 16, No. 3, op. cit.

** Reader in History, Department of Humanities and Social Sciences, Indira Gandhi National Open University, New Delhi.

pratap was it just because these were along the lines of popular beliefs? Amin has cited from other regions in this regard. Whether they 'were the product of popular imagination' or 'very consciously spread by the local agitators', the rumours had gained currency in relation to the exploitative agrarian structure in Champaran (p. 6). The exploited peasants saw hope in Gandhi. They perceived and interpreted him in relation to their own economic and social problems. This took place within the pattern of existing popular beliefs, which very often provided the peasant an ideological justification to revolt in the absence of other alternatives. It is not surprising that in many peasant movements in India *babas*, *faqirs* or *sadhus* played a prominent role. We do get evidence of the links between rumours about Gandhi's *pratap* and peasant exploitation in areas of Gujarat, Rajputana, Andhra, as well as the neighbouring region of Oudh. These links were there in Gorakhpur as open 'letters appeared in the columns of *Swadesh* highlighting the oppression suffered by peasants in the bigger zamindaris and challenging the presumption of the rajas to be the natural spokesmen of their praja' (p. 14). Amin informs us: The editor of *Swadesh*, who had himself sought to inculcate an attitude of devotion in the district towards the Mahatma, had thus no hesitation in printing rumours about the latter's *pratap*. It was only when these appeared to instigate dangerous beliefs and actions, such as those concerning demands for the abolition of zamindari, reduction of rents or enforcement of just price at the bazaars, that the journal came out with prompt disclaimers' (p. 50; emphasis added). However, what the editor of *Swadesh* did is repeated by Amin when he ignores the socio-historical basis of the rumours, and writes: 'People in the Gorakhpur countryside believed in these not out of any unquestioning trust in the weekly newspaper but because they accorded with existing beliefs about marvels and miracles, about right and wrong' (p. 48; emphasis added). *Swadesh*, we should add, had a definite motive in propagating such stories and giving respectability to them. For, in the case of a large number of rumours cited, the person reporting the happenings was a 'gentleman', a 'special correspondent', a 'respected person', a 'vakil saheb', etc. But *Swadesh* was critical of a zamindar only when he was likely to be an obstacle to the peasants desiring to have Gandhi *darshan* (p. 24). Amin successfully demonstrates the efforts of the 'elite' to mobilize the peasants behind them. However, a generalization that he makes is not a true representation of reality: 'The Brahman thief of Rudrapur village is representative not just of the ordinary village sceptic but of high-caste opposition to the Gandhian creed' (p. 31; emphasis added). Dashrath Dwivedi, the editor of *Swadesh*, Gauri Shanker Misra, etc., were all brahmins. Consequently, this general observation is erroneous and misleading. Another question that comes up after reading Amin's contribution is, which sections of the peasantry responded to the rumours? Very often popular beliefs are interpreted by different sections in relation to their day-to-day life. It is possible, and it has happened in history, that the same popular belief has been perceived differently by different social groups to justify or oppose the existing social order. The Peasant War in Germany is one example; Christopher Hill's position regarding three Gods in the English Revolution is another. While examining the role of rumour one has to keep this in mind as well. Interestingly, the government attributed the violence at Chauri Chaura to the propaganda of 'non-cooperators' and the stories about Gandhi. Amin starts his paper by citing Dixit, the Magistrate, Chauri Chaura Trials, who talked of many 'miracles' taking place previous to the 'riot'. After listing these miracles in detail Amin's analysis supports the official version. For example, while referring to the punishments meted out by the 'Gandhi Panchayats' of the early 1920s he writes: However, in the spring of 1921 when all was charged with magic, any mental or physical affliction (***kasht***) suffered by persons found guilty of violating panchayat decisions adopted in Gorakhpur villages in the Mahatma's name was often perceived as evidence of Gandhi's extraordinary powers, indeed as something providential and supernatural rather than as a form of chastisement devised by a human agency (p. 9; emphasis added). What needs to be stressed is that not a single 'miracle', 'magic' or rumour listed by Amin is even remotely related to mass initiative or popular action at Chauri Chaura. *Swadesh* cited these happenings, projecting and advocating change through the *pratap* or supernatural powers of the Mahatma, away from the intervention of the popular masses. Yet policemen were the targets of peasant violence at Chauri Chaura. The explanation for this lies not just in the paradox that there 'was no single authorized version of the Mahatma' or the ideas of the peasantry about Gandhi which were 'often at variance with those of the local Congress–Khilafat' leaders. What needs to be also stressed is that the police station was a symbol of peasants' exploitation at the hands of the British and their zamindar allies. The peasants were not fools that they believed in the *pratap* of the Mahatma and the rumours about it and therefore 'attacked' the thana. They had specific grievances against the police who, along with the zamindars, were the two main leverages of the power and control apparatus of the British Empire in the countryside. Amin's work remains incomplete without any reference to these complexities. Moreover, there was indeed one image of the Mahatma that was registered in peasant consciousness during this period: that the Mahatma was a symbol with which to oppose the oppressor, whoever it was. Everything that was unjust, cruel and oppressive was fought in his name.

CHAPTER 6

Congress–Peasant Relationship in the Late 1930s*

Speaking from the Congress Presidential Chair in 1936 Jawaharlal Nehru lauded the role of the masses, especially the peasantry, in the 'direct action struggles' of the Congress.[1] He, however, admitted that 'our policies and ideas are governed far more by . . . middle class outlook than by a consideration of the needs of the great majority of population'.[2] He dubbed the middleclass leadership as a 'two faced' one which 'is bound to injure the cause and to hold back when a forward move is called for'.[3] Nehru's analysis of the leadership of his own class and organization *vis-à-vis* the peasant masses and their struggles was revealing. The Congress had no doubt deepened the anti-imperialist feelings amongst the peasants and drew them into the national movement to win swaraj. Yet, at the same time the Congress and its leadership exploited the peasants' support to secure political independence oblivious of the economic aspect of swaraj and the demands of the peasantry. The *Amrita Bazar Patrika* rightly noted that the question of economic independence 'has been studied mainly from the point of view of the middle classes, and it was often forgotten that the masses might have a say in the matter which, perhaps, would not be palatable to their social superiors'.[4]

* The paper was earlier published in D.N. Panigrahi (ed.), *Economy, Society and Polity in Modern India*, Delhi, 1982

[1] Report of the 49th Session of the Indians National Congress, Lucknow, 1936 (hereafter Congress Report), p. 16.

[2] Ibid. 'They (Congress leaders) ask the masses for support, but seldom ask them for their opinion to set about enquiring what ails them'. Jawaharlal Nehru, *An Autobiography* (Delhi, 1962), p. 577.

[3] Congress Report, p. 16. Nehru's politics, in his own words was of 'his class, the bourgeoisie'. Nehru, ibid., p. 48.

[4] *Amrita Bazar Patrika*, Calcutta, 10 December 1936.

The 'social superiors' of the Congress did not attack the root cause of exploitation in rural India. The constructive programme, although important politically, was a failure on social and economic fronts.[5] Its major function was of 'tension management'[6] or 'providing an outlet to the heat generated by class tension and antagonisms'.[7] Nehru admitted that to 'talk of improving these staggering conditions (peasants' condition) by philanthropy or local efforts are a mockery of the peasant and his misery'.[8] The peasant response to the national movement was of a more radical character which in effect meant the implementation of the 'theory of Swaraj' propounded by the Congress leadership.[9] However the growth of peasant movement was arrested by the nationalist leaders and their role in almost every peasant uprising remained ambiguous.[10] A major cause of the withdrawal of the two mass movements (1920–22 and 1930–2) had been the fear of no-rent campaigns which meant adding anti-feudal struggle to anti-colonial struggle.[11] Sahajanand Saraswati, who had come into politics by a conventional

[5] David Hardiman, 'Peasant Agitations in Kheda District, Gujarat, 1917–34', unpublished Ph.D. thesis, University of Sussex, 1975, p. 219, Nehru Memorial Museum & Library (hereafter cited as NMML).

[6] D.N. Dhanagre, *Agrarian Movements and Gandhian Politics* (Agra, 1975), p. 63.

[7] S.K. Mittal and Kapil Kumar, 'Anti-Feudal and Anti-Colonial Struggles of the Oudh Peasantry in Early 1920s', *Social Scientist*, No. 96, July 1980, p. 41.

[8] Nehru, op. cit., p. 590.

[9] Kapil Kumar, *Peasants in Revolt: Tanants, Landlords, Congress and the Raj in Oudh, 1886–1922* (Delhi, 1984), pp. 146, 152, 208.

[10] Ibid., p. 282. Stephen Henninghnam, 'Agrarian Relations in North Bihar: Peasant Protest and the Darbhanga Raj, 1919–20', *Indian Economic and Social History Review*, Vol. XVI, No. 1, January–March 1979, pp. 74–5. Biswamoy Pati, 'Peasant Tribals and the National Movement in Orissa 1921–36', unpublished M. Phil. thesis, University of Delhi, 1980.

[11] Mittal and Kumar, op. cit., p. 39. Pati observes 'the legacy of these two movements (Non-Cooperation movement and Civil Disobedience movement) pitted the exploited classes not only in a bitter struggle against colonialism but also feudalism in spite of Provinicial Congress Committee's conscious attempt to dilute, disrupt and divert the anti-feudal dimension'. Pati, op. cit., p. 93.

route, under Gandhian influence,[12] stated that the concept of swaraj not only meant end of foreign rule but the establishment of 'own rule' for some rule had to come after the end of alien rule else 'anarchy will take its place'.[13] The answer that it will be the government of Indians was, according to him, not workable

> as the Indians were divided into 'zamindars, *kisans,* capitalists and mazdurs, etc.—classes with mutual contradictions. Which class will form the government? Zamindars or capitalists? The difference between that government and the alien government shall be in name only. In reality it will be the same. The loot of *kisans* and mazdurs would continue unabated. The difference will be that the present loot goes to Lancashire, Manchester or England and the same will then go to Bombay, Ahmedabad, Kanpur, Chattari and Darbhanga.[14]

It must be remembered here that the modern taluqdars and zamindars had been the creation of British imperialism. Brought up in the 'imperialist cradle' they were the bulwarks of the Raj. Despite their hostility to and reservations about the national movement, the Congress had assured them of their rights and status.

Most of the kisan sabhas were initially launched in their areas to bring about mutual harmony between the oppressors and the oppressed. Soon the peasant leaders got disillusioned with the Congress methods which sought to cover up inherent contradictions in the rural socio-economic set-up. They now turned hostile to the Zamindari system and carried forward the kisan struggles. At the same time they supported the political programme of the Congress. The various kisan sabhas, hitherto disparate and unconnected, came to be linked together in 1936 when an All India Kisan Congress was formed at Lucknow. It aimed at securing 'complete freedom from economic exploitation and the achievement of full economic and political power for the peasants and workers

[12] Walter Hauser, 'Bihar Provincial Kisan Sabha', unpublished Ph.D. thesis, University of Chicago, 1961, p. 181, NMML.

[13] Sahajanand, *Kisan Sabha Ke Sansmaran,* Patna, 1947, p. 39.

[14] Ibid., Nehru lectured on 19 May 1936 at Matunga, Bombay, 'If political freedom means the control of the country by the same group which is now cooperating with the British Government, it would not mean any good to the masses. It must be the freedom of the masses', *Bombay Chronicle,* 20 May 1936.

and all other exploited classes'.[15] This formation was not without differences. The Congress Socialist and the Andhra kisan leaders firmly advocated its formation while the Bihar kisan leader Sahajanand had his reservations. He, in fact, wanted first to build up strong peasant movements in different provinces and then to link them together. He wanted the movement to grow from below rather than superimpose it from the top. He feared that in the absence of trained kisan workers there was every possibility of the All India organization falling into hands of 'undesirable leaders'.[16] But the Congress Socialists decided at Meerut to go ahead with idea.

The formation of the AIKC was initially welcomed by the Congress whose leadership was struggling hard to end its 'divorce from the people'.[17] The Congress president put forward the idea to encourage peasant unions so that: the day to day struggle of the masses might be carried on the basis of their 'economic demands and other grievances'.[18] He had advised Sahajanand, the president of the first AIKC 'to keep the sabha separate from the Congress'.[19] He was sure that the Congress in its present form could not wholly function as a peasant organization.[20] The Congress according to Nehru, was 'drawing up a programme of establishing contact with them [peasants] but that would not lead them to their goal unless they were united and well organized', thus they should 'stand on their own legs and form kisan sabhas in every village'.[21] Gandhi also wanted 'to keep the kisan alive' in order to 'make India our own'.[22] Despite the declarations of the Congress leaders a resolution to secure direct representation for workers and peasants through

[15] All India Kisan Manifesto; N.N. Mitra (ed.), *Indian Annual Register*, Vol. 2, 1936, p. 293.

[16] *Indian Nation*, 16 October 1935; N.G. Ranga, *Fight for Freedom* (New Delhi, 1968), p. 201; 'The Origin and Growth of Kisan Movement in India' (hereafter OGKMI), Roll No. 1, Sahajanand Papers, NMML.

[17] *AICC Proceedings*, 1936, p. 17.

[18] Ibid., p. 34.

[19] OGKMI.

[20] Congress Report, p. 34.

[21] *Bombay Chronicle*, 16 April 1936.

[22] Ibid.

their organizations in the Congress fell by 16 to 35 votes in the Subjects Committee at Lucknow.[23] N.G. Ranga opined that the Congress efforts failed to meet the minimum demands of the peasants.[24] Sahajanand wrote:

> They do not want to confront the real issues before the kisans though they are eager to have them behind the national movement. To them a kisan who is always ready to go to jail at their bid, who wears *khadi* and votes for their Congress candidates in the election without murmuring and thinking in terms of his class interest is more desirable than a militant one. They do not know in their own minds so far as the place of the kisans in their conception of *swaraj* that is to be.[25]

However, under the kisan pressure, the Congress had to instruct its provincial units to conduct agrarian enquiries and submit their findings to the AICC so as to facilitate the formation of an all India agrarian programme.

Very few PCs followed that Lucknow resolution regarding agrarian enquiry and Bihar PCC was one of them, Rajendra Prasad had requested Sahajanand to remain out of the enquiry committee as he wanted the report to be unanimous. Sahajanand's inclusion in the committee, Rajendra Babu feared, would lead the government and the landlords to decry the report as if it were a report of the Kisan Sabha.[26] Sahajanand was told that he would be given ample opportunity to go through the report and discuss it threadbare before its publication.[27] The Committee toured many villages but Rajendra Prasad was more keen to listen to zamindari grievances,[28] and, while conducting the enquiry, he would often visit his capitalist friends and Rai Bahadurs.[29] Interrupting the enquiry he rushed to

[23] *Amrita Bazar Patrika*, 11 April 1936. The Kisan Sabhaites and Congress Socialists had opposed the Council entry programme at Lucknow but the Rightists had their way. *AICC Proceedings* 1936, pp. 77–9.

[24] *Bombay Chronicle*, 18 April 1936.

[25] *Congress Socialist*, 26 December 1936.

[26] Sahajanand, *Mera Jivan Sangharsh*, Patna, 1952, p. 470.

[27] Ibid.

[28] *Behar Herald*, 10 June 1936.

[29] He visited the factory of Rai Bahadur Thakur Das at Hindpuri (Patna). Ibid., 17 June 1936.

attend the Agarwal Social Conference at Calcutta with 'the hope of getting a substantial contribution to the election fund' from Dalmia who presided over the Conference.[30] The Congress elite badly needed money for elections and the peasant grievances were relegated into background.

III

The Bihar Congress leaders were annoyed when Sahajanand made a factual statement in the Subjects Committee at Faizpur that in spite of an agrarian enquiry no report had been prepared by the Bihar Pradesh Congress Committee (BPCC); nor were any recommendations made regarding the peasants.[31] He gave reasons for the suppression of committee's findings in his autobiography. He charged that in case the report had been presented it would have been nothing else but to admit the exploitative character of the zamindars and as the BPCC leadership was pro-zamindari it was reluctant to expose their fellow brothers. Moreover, if any recommendations were to be made they were bound to be practised during the ministry period and the BPCC never wanted to bind itself to any promises regarding the agrarian question.[32]

Sahajanand raised his voice in the Subjects Committee to ask 'if any agrarian programme had been chalked out in accordance with the Lucknow resolution'.[33] Welcoming his query Nehru revealed that only five out of the 20 PCCs had sent their reports.[34] Ranga wanted to know 'what action was being taken by the Working Committee to see that the reports from the different provinces regarding the agrarian programme were received in time as certain provincial committees had failed to submit reports for some reasons

[30] F. No. 18/7/1936, Home Political, National Archives of India (hereafter cited as NAI). By December Dalmia had paid Rs. 10,000 of the Rs. 27,000 promised in spite of his differences with Rajendra Prasad over the personnel of certain Congress candidates. F. No. 18/7/1936, ibid.

[31] Sahajanand, *Mera Jivan Sangharsh*, p. 470.

[32] Ibid., pp. 476–7. A similar enquiry had been conducted in 1930 but the report had not been published. Ibid., p. 476.

[33] *The Hindustan Times*, 26 December 1936.

[34] Ibid.

of their own?[35] The pro-peasant Nehru retaliated, if Ranga was making 'insinuations he should bring forward a vote of censure', and gave him half a minute to move it.[36] Ranga termed it 'dictatorial' to which Nehru further sought explanation.[37]

The Congress adopted the famous agrarian programme at Faizpur. Considered as a progressive document at that time[38] the outlined programme included 50 per cent reduction in rent and revenue; exemption of uneconomic holdings from rent and land tax; taxation on agricultural income; abolishment of feudal levies and forced labour; consolidation of holdings and cooperative farming; wiping out arrears of rent; modification of ejectment laws; declaration of moratorium for rural debts and recognition of peasant unions, etc. The resolution was adopted 'pending to the framing of an all India agrarian programme' which remained pending and was never taken up. Govind Ballabh Pant, the mover of the resolution had requested the house to 'regard his proposals as a temporary solution to meet pressing needs, pending a final effective solution of the vast and complicated question later'.[39] Amendments were moved to add the words 'pending to the formation of an all India agrarian programme in consultation with the AIKS' or the addition of a fresh para that 'the programme outlined was a temporary one'.[40] But they were withdrawn on verbal assurances that the final programme would be placed before the AICC, thus it could not be brought on paper that it was merely a temporary programme. The programme did not attack the root cause of peasant exploitation —the zamindari and taluqdari systems and the amendment, to introduce the declaration of abolishing these systems at the earliest, in the programme also went unheard.[41] Nehru clarified that though

[35] Ibid.

[36] Ibid.

[37] Ranga writes that he replied, 'Please remember you can't be dictatorial, I must have sufficient time to formulate my amendment', and 'that brought him [Nehru] down to earth and made him smile . . . the whole house enjoyed that stimulating clash'. Ranga, op. cit., p. 303.

[38] M.A. Rasul, *A History of the All India Kisan Sabha*, Calcutta, 1974, p. 11.

[39] *The Times of India*, 29 December 1936.

[40] Ibid.

[41] Ibid.

the Lucknow Congress had decided to consult kisan sabhas, such consultations were to be done at provincial levels[42] which meant that the AICC was not supposed to consult the AIKC. This was a clear indication that under the rightist pressure Nehru had 'cooled down' in his advocacy of functional representation for the kisans and workers in the Congress.[43] He also turned down Ranga's demand for an assurance that the resolution would form part of the Congress manifesto and it represented the views of Congressmen in their work.[44] The change in Nehru from Lucknow to Faizpur appeared to be a calculated move on his part, i.e. not to annoy the rightists. Ranga, thus, urged the peasants to 'continue to strive for the development by the Congress of a more satisfactory agrarian programme'.[45]

Thousands of kisans had marched to Faizpur but the arrangements made for them by the organizers were very 'unsatisfactory'.[46] The delegate fee had been raised to Rs. 5 and this time unlike Lucknow there were no free tickets for the kisans.[47] This restricted the participation of peasants as delegates making it clear that the village Congress was not for villagers. The massive kisan participation was described by the *Times of India's* special correspondent as an attempt 'to stampede the Congress and capture power within it to complete its proletarian character and then through it enforce their demand for a reduction in rent and the abolition of zamindari system, etc.', and his assessment that the Congress had 'no desire to yield to the *wild clamour of the left*' was far more correct.[48] Only the Congress Socialist Party supported the kisan cause. Jayaprakash Narayan in his presidential address to the CSP urged for militant work amongst the peasantry in place of 'tinkering with sanitation and lighting of villages'.[49] The Congress leadership had kept itself

[42] Ibid.

[43] *Indian Annual Register*, Vol. II, 1936, p. 283.

[44] *The Times of India*, 29 December 1936. Ranga observed 'Nehru had not shown much progress since Lucknow', *Amrita Bazar Patrika*, 3 January 1937.

[45] *Indian Annual Register*, Vol. II, 1936, p. 283.

[46] F.No. 18/12/1936, Home Political, NAI.

[47] Sahajanand, *Mera Jivan Sangharsh*, pp. 472–3.

[48] *The Times of India*, 29 December 1936.

[49] Ibid., 24 December 1936.

aloof from any firm commitments and whatever little had been resolved about the peasants could be termed as a direct result of kisan pressure. The rightists had conceded this much as a part of their manoeuvre to utilize socialist slogans for their own benefit. They knew that they could very well undo the resolutions whenever they wished and, in fact, they did so when the opportunity to practice the resolutions came.

The second AIKC meeting at Faizpur called upon 'all anti-imperialist forces in the country and especially the kisans and workers to develop their day-to-day struggles against the exploiters, as represented by British government in India, the zamindars and landlords and industrialists and moneylenders'. It urged the masses to smash the slave constitution and '*wrench the political and economic power* from the hands of British imperialism and *its allies in the country*' by their 'own dynamic power'.[50] In contrast the Gandhian leadership was never in favour of attacking the British allies in India and the Congress never resolved to fight the native agents of imperialism. The AIKC demanded the abolition of zamindari system to assure 'a modicum of economic well being to the starving millions of the kisans'.[51] It rejected the new constitution once again but with the Congress deciding to go to polls it lent a supporting hand, and urged the Indian National Congress to see that its representatives in the legislatures 'will not become pawns of imperialism by accepting office'.[52] At the same time the AIKC president, Ranga, issued a warning to the would-be provincial legislators and ministers that within six months of their office entry if they failed to recognize peasant demands, the peasants would be forced to launch a campaign against their 'inactivity and hostility to the kisan cause'.[53] The AIKC also decided not to be dependent on the Congress and instead hold its session separately[54] as the salvation of kisans lay in 'their own organization'.[55]

[50] *Congress Socialist*, 9 January 1936.
[51] Ibid.
[52] *The Hindustan Times*, 27 December 1936.
[53] *The Times of India*, 25 December 1936.
[54] Sahajanand, op. cit., p. 471.
[55] *Amrita Bazar Patrika*, 3 January 1937.

IV

Much before the Faizpur session, the Andhra Peasants had in June 1936, negotiated with the Congress president to select persons suggested by the kisan sabhas as Congress candidates.[56] Nehru was personally of the view that 'he would like very much to have ryot's representatives chosen as Congress candidates'. Yet he clarified that he was 'not directly connected with the selection of candidates'.[57] The political awakening and class consciousness amongst the peasantry was developing at the grass root level. When Nehru was travelling to Mungeli from Wardha on 17 November 1936 one Gajadhar Sahu prostrated on the road in front of Nehru's car to get an assurance that peasants alone would be sent as Congress nominees to the Provincial Assembly as the Congress professed to work for the betterment of kisans. Persuasions failed to move Sahu who wanted Nehru's personal assurance. Nehru got down from his car and expressed resentment. Sahu was forcibly removed by Congress workers and Nehru resumed his journey.[58] As negotiations with Nehru bore no fruits, the Andhra Ryots Association approached the Congress Parliamentary Committee, but the reply 'was even less satisfactory' than Nehru's.[59]

In January 1937 The Andhra Ryots Association urged the Congress candidates to sign a pledge which asked for their support inside and outside the legislatures for peasant's cause and help in radicalizing the Congress attitude towards the peasant demands and needs.[60] Anxious to seek the kisan support a large number of Congress candidates jumped to sign the pledge. Those Congressmen who disliked the development of peasant movement raised the pledge issue in the CPC. The president of the CPC, Sardar Patel, publicly denounced this move on the part of Andhra ryots. All those who had signed the pledge were threatened with disciplinary

[56] *Indian Annual Register*, Vol. II, 1936, p. 285.

[57] Ibid.

[58] *Bombay Chronicle*, 18 November 1936.

[59] *Indian Annual Register*, Vol. II, 1936, p. 285.

[60] Ibid., p. 286.

action unless they withdrew their signatures.[61] Same was to be the fate of Ranga if the pledge was not withdrawn. The Secretary of the Andhra Ryots Association asked Patel to take action not only against Ranga but the whole of Andhra Kisan Sabha which had passed the pledge resolutions.[62] The AIKS stood solidly behind Ranga. Ranga never wanted to put the peasants' interests above those of the nation[63] but wanted a say for the peasants in the nationalist politics. Patel's opposition to Ranga and the Kisan Sabha was due to the very fact that the former's 'personal opponent' and his 'victim' Indulal Yagnik had been welcomed by the latter in the Kisan Sabha.[64] As the Sardar was adamant, Ranga 'withdrew the pledge and released the Congress candidates from it in order not to divert the attention of the peasants from their duty to present a united front to British imperialism'[65] and in the 'general interests of the Congress'.[66] However, as soon as the elections were over Ranga took up the issue with the Congress president urging that 'in future Congress authorities would learn to deal with the kisan committees more honourably, becomingly and considerately'.[67] The 'Socialist' Nehru felt that it 'was not a very wise move' on Ranga's part to issue the pledge but recognized his right to advocate peasant demands which should be in 'no way be conflicting to the Congress demands'.[68] It

[61] *Amrita Bazar Patrika*, 28 January 1937.

[62] Ibid.

[63] Ibid.

[64] Ranga, *Fight for Freedom*, p. 305. The relations between Patel and Yagnik had been strained since late 1921. Yagnik wanted to help the Bhil peasants from the Tilak Swaraj Fund as the harvests had failed. Patel, the president of the Gujarat Pradesh Congress Committee wanted to give little. On Gandhi's intervention Yagnik had his way but soon Yagnik resigned as secretary of the Gujarat Pradesh Congress Committee, hoping for Gandhi's intervention. But Gandhi 'had chosen the hard headed Vallabhbhai to lead his organization, not the radical idealist, Indulal'. Hardiman, op. cit., p. 197.

[65] *Indian Annual Register*, Vol. II, 1936, p. 286.

[66] S. Gopal (ed.), *Selected Works of Jawaharlal Nehru*, Vol. 8 (Delhi, 1976), p. 38.

[67] *Indian Annual Register*, Vol. II, 1936, p. 286.

[68] Nehru to Ranga, 5 March 1937, F. No. P-3w/1937, AICC Papers, NMML.

is worth noting that the pledge 'was never to be pitched against Congress discipline'.[69] Nehru asked Ranga to drop the controversy who after consulting his AIKS friends bowed down. Nehru's role in this controversy was not at all surprising. His socialist ideas faded away when the time to practice them arrived. He avoided giving firm support to the so-called 'left' in the Congress, especially where he had to give rulings. He advocated the growth of an independent peasant movement but 'he did not come to the rescue of AIKC'.[70]

The Congress success in elections depended much on the peasant support[71] and the Kisan Sabha, in spite of the former's reluctance to stand kisan candidates, supported its candidates. Sahajanand who was also a member of the Bihar PCC's Working Committee which had to select Congress candidates, wrote:

> When the Provincial Working Committee started selecting Congress nominees I witnessed an amazing scene. I could not know on what principles the candidates were being nominated. At places real Congressmen who had been to jails and thus suffered were completely ignored while big landlords and their associates . . . were nominated. At places persons famous for their *zulum* (tyranny) among peasants were nominated. At certain places the big leaders were trying hard to nominate such persons who had attended the Governors court in the past and were even doing so now.[72]

Sahajanand also ridiculed the caste approach for selecting Congress nominees.[73] He had built his own selection criteria in his mind. Firstly, those Congressmen who had made sacrifices by going to jail, secondly those who were poor or the well wishers of the poor,

[69] Ranga, op. cit., p. 303.

[70] Ibid.

[71] The franchise qualifications for peasants varied from province to province. For example in Bombay Presidency, it was Rs. 8 as land revenue per annum, in the Punjab Rs. 5 land revenue p.a. UP Rs. 10 p.a., as rent and Rs. 5 p.a. as land revenue, etc. See *Indian Franchise Committee Report*, 1932, Vol. I. The recommendations of the report were accepted with a minor change here and there.

[72] Sahajanand, op. cit., p. 479. In the UP also the Congress was relying on zamindari support in many districts. *Pioneer*, 1 and 6 January 1937.

[73] Sahajanand, op. cit., p. 479.

and thirdly, who were from the Kisan Sabha. If all the three merits were not there he would discard the last one and in the absence of second one also he could agree at the first one only.[74] This signified his regard for the Congress organization. But soon he reached his 'breaking point' and resigned from the Working Committee on the ground that he could not owe responsibility to the selection of such (landlords, opportunists and pro-British) nominees.[75] Rajendra Prasad pleaded with him to withdraw his resignation as it might have ill effects on the Congress and on this plea Sahajanand conceded.[76]

The kisan sabhas propagated vigorously for the victory of Congress candidates putting aside their class character. Sahajanand himself went to seek peasant votes for those very zamindars against whom he had made the peasants revolt as they had been taken as Congress candidates. The cautious peasantry did not spare him for this. He was confronted with questions like 'why was he now advocating to vote for these *jallads* (executors)? He argued that the Kisan Sabha held the same view yet it was the question of support to the Congress which was a higher body than the Kisan Sabha.[77] In Andhra Pradesh and Gujarat, Ranga and Yagnik organized vast peasant marches in the countryside to canvass for Congress candidates. Ranga, however, knew that their contribution to the Congress success in Andhra 'may not be acknowledged by the Congress high Gods'.[78] 'The kisan propagators crystallized the issue of 'kisan *versus* the zamindars' and the 'poor *versus* the rich' in these elections.[79] A popular election song in the Bihar countryside was '*Magar kothri mein badal jayenge*' (we shall change at the polling booth) and it was sung by those who were being forced by non-Congress candidates to vote for them.[80]

[74] Ibid., p. 480.

[75] Ibid.

[76] Ibid., p. 481.

[77] Ibid., He was attacked by zamindari agents with *lathis* at Harnaut in Patna district while addressing a Congress election meeting, *Amrita Bazar Patrika*, 30 November 1936.

[78] *Congress Socialist*, 20 February 1937.

[79] Ibid.

[80] Sahajanand, op. cit., p. 483.

The peasant vote had become so vital that even communal organizations like the Hindu Maha Sabha and the Muslim League tried to lure the kisans by declaring their readiness to work for the peasant cause.[81] The Krishak Proja Party could succeed in Bengal only after advocating a fairly moderate economic programme[82] in comparison to Congress which was dominated by richer landholding classes.[83] Both in Bihar and the UP, the Congress victory in lower houses rested on peasant support whereas the Congress lost in upper houses. It should be remembered that the electorate for the upper houses consisted of *zamindars*, *mahajans* and the privileged classes of the Indian society while for the lower houses the poor had an opportunity to display their feelings. The unprecedented peasant support to the Congress was much due to the Faizpur Resolution, which 'however vague and ill-defined appealed directly to the economic interests of peasant masses'.[84] Yagnik described the peasants as 'the repositories of the biggest political power in the country' on whose 'broad shoulders ministers must rise and rest in power'.[85] Sahajanand was convinced from his election experience that 'none can check the class struggle of the peasantry and whoever dares do it, is bound to be annihilated and drowned in the water whose depth cannot be fathomed'.[86] The peasantry it was apparent was prepared to carry the anti-imperialist struggle to any length. The elections had once again demonstrated the landlords alliance with imperialism and those zamindars who had supported the Congress had no doubt done so to safeguard their own interests in case of Congress victory[87] and they were the prime supporters of office acceptance.[88]

[81] *Indian Annual Register*, Vol. II, 1936, p. 284.

[82] Ibid.

[83] *Congress Socialist*, 20 February 1937.

[84] Ibid.

[85] F.No. 15, Indulal Yagnik Papers, NMML.

[86] *Congress Socialist*, 20 February 1937.

[87] Nehru observed 'The upper middle classes support the national movement with the hope that it will benefit them and they will continue to enjoy what privileges they have', *Bombay Chronicle*, 20 May 1936.

[88] *Congress Socialist*, 20 February 1937.

VI

The great *tamasha* (show)[89] at Delhi decided in favour of office acceptance to the chagrin of the AIKS. The leading Indian capitalist G.D. Birla had urged Gandhi to decide in favour of office acceptance.[90] He informed Lord Zetland about Bapu's statement that 'office acceptance was an attempt to avoid bloody revolution on the one hand and mass civil disobedience on the other'.[91] A vocal argument in favour of forming ministries was to enable the Congress to bring succour to peasants and workers through legislation.[92] Sahajanand believed that 'the leaders and their friends' felt exhausted and were 'trying to escape on the pretext of peasants' as this was 'an easy excuse'.[93] A joint statement issued by Ranga, Yagnik and B.P.L. Bedi described the acceptance of office as a retreat from the basic Congress policy of non-cooperation with imperialism.[94] The immediate prize which the peasantry got from the Congress at Delhi was the dropping out of the demand for moratorium, a demand which had been a part of Congress resolutions at Lucknow and Faizpur and the Congress election manifesto.[95] On the other hand, the interim ministries of the six Congress majority provinces 'hastened to try to steal the wind behind the Congress sails and the thunder of Kisan Sabha' by proclaiming comprehensive schemes of rural upliftment and redress[96] as the peasant question had become

[89] Nehru described the convention of Congress legislators held at Delhi in March 1937 as a *tamasha*. Nehru to Padmaja Naidu, 19 February 1937, S. Gopal (ed.), *Selected Works of Jawaharlal Nehru*, Vol. 13 (Delhi, 1980), p. 670.

[90] 'My vanity tickles me to believe that perhaps my letters might have made some contribution in influencing Bapu's mind' G.D. Birla to Mahadev Desai, 7 July 1937, G.D. Birla, *Bapu: A Unique Association*, Vol. III (Bombay, 1977), p. 1.

[91] G.D. Birla to Mahadev Desai, 27 July 1937, ibid., p. 29 (emphasis added).

[92] Sahajanand, op. cit., p. 484.

[93] Ibid.

[94] *Congress Socialist*, 3 April 1937.

[95] Ibid.

[96] *Indian Annual Register*, Vol. II, 1937, p. 386.

a live issue in the country's politics. But there was big hiatus between theory and practice.

The AIKC at Niyamatpur placed before the Congress ministries the immediate peasant demands. These included, reduction in rent and revenue by 50 per cent and exemption of uneconomic holdings from the same; declaration of moratorium to check transfer of lands to *mahajans*; abolition of the Criminal Tribes Act; abolition of landlordism; protection to agricultural labourers, etc.[97] It welcomed the Congress president's 'spirit of cordial sympathy' towards the kisan movement and assured the Congress of its support in any struggle to be waged against the Government of India 'to effect drastic economies'.[98] The kisan conference felt that kisan sabhas should be established everywhere to 'Carry on their day-to-day struggle against government, landlords, moneylenders and all other exploiting classes not only for the economic amelioration but also for developing and intensifying the fight against *foreign imperialism* and its *Indian allies*'.[99]

Most of the provincial Congress Committees had refrained from declaring in any clear terms their posture towards the zamindari and *sahukari* systems. Only the Orissa PCC under the peasant pressure had assured to abolish the zamindari system[100] and later on the Bihar PCC passed a similar resolution.[101] In spite of these resolutions the future was to be entirely different. Soon the Congress under the guidance of Rajendra Prasad was to embrace the zamindars. The AIKS gave a call to celebrate 1 September as the 'Kisan Day' to remind the ministers of their promises and the Faizpur Programme.[102] The day was vigorously celebrated all over India. Yet the 'kisan masses' had by now become 'kisan mobs' for the ministers.[103] Rafi Ahmed Kidwai, the Revenue Minister of the UP declared:

[97] Rasul, op. cit., p. 14; *Indian Annual Register*, Vol. II, 1937, p. 387; *Congress Socialist*, 24 July 1937.

[98] Rasul, op. cit., p. 15.

[99] *Congress Socialist*, 24 July 1937 (emphasis added).

[100] Ibid., 6 March 1937.

[101] Ibid., 17 July 1937. The clause 'with proper compensation to zamindars', was deleted. Ibid.

[102] Ibid., 21 August 1937.

[103] Sahajanand, op. cit., p. 489.

The Congress government would either be forced to adopt coercive measures to get out of office if the peasants did not abide by the laws in force today . . . it would be too difficult for the Congress to adopt coercive measures and therefore only alternative left was resignation.[104]

The Congress minister was thus impressing upon the peasants to follow the colonial laws instead of inviting the Congress to repeal them. G.B. Pant the Prime Minister of UP urged the peasants not to give an opportunity to Congress opponents to say that 'the kisans listen to Congress only when the latter decides to do things which might be of benefit to them, but when its decisions do not benefit them they don't listen to it', thus they should pay rents.[105] The UPCC warned the peasants that failure to pay rents would result in ejectments.[106] Friendly criticism of ministers, too, was not tolerated and whoever indulged in it was treated 'as an enemy'. Every question which turned up was regarded as an issue on which the 'ministry's *izzat*' (honour) was at stake.[107] M.L. Dantwala analysed the ministers' attitude thus:

. . . the Congress ministers on their part are confident that if anything is wrong the 'loyal' civil servants would surely draw their attention to it. The good earth is beautiful, crops are good, the civil servants are loyal, and all is well in India. Let us therefore read the *Harijan* and leave the rest to Gandhi.[108]

In Bihar a large number of Congress office-bearers were zamindars and the ministerial change had no impact on their status. Rather, now they acted more freely.[109] Sahajanand told the Bihar ministry that 'sweet words and fine phraseologies won't bring them (kisans) bread and land' and 'something material and concrete' was badly needed.[110] He gave a call to the peasants for holding a peaceful

[104] At Partapgarh on 20 December 1937. *Modern Review*, January 1938, p. 119.

[105] *The Hindustan Times*, 1 January 1938.

[106] *Amrita Bazar Patrika*, 2 January 1938.

[107] *Bombay Sentinel*, 28 October 1937.

[108] *Congress Socialist*, 9 October 1937.

[109] *Janta*, 9 December 1937.

[110] *Congress Socialist*, 30 October 1937.

demonstration in front of the Assembly to press their demands. Similar calls were made in Gujarat and Maharashtra. As a response more than a lakh peasants attended a rally at Patna on 26 November 1937 and demanded, abolition of zamindari; 50 per cent reduction in rent, cancellation of debts and high prices for agricultural products.[111] The slogans '*Zamindari Pratha Khatam ho*' (end to the zamindari system) and '*Punjiwad Ka Nash ho*' (down with capitalism) rent the sky. Sahajanand pointed out that the kisans and *mazdurs* were the 'real masters of the soil' yet the 'dogs of the rich were far more comfortable than the infants of the labourers'. 'The zamindars', he argued 'had no right to realize rents unless the condition of the kisans was ameliorated'.[112] There was nothing new in his advocacy of the peasants cause as charged by many Congressmen that since the advent of Congress ministry he had gathered 'an army of dissatisfied and disgruntled persons who made no secret of their craving for the blood of the Congress leaders'.[113] Long before the Congress decision to fight elections he had stressed:

> I come to hold a Kisan Sabha so that your dead tongues may find a voice and say to the zamindars this much—later the rent, only first let the producer have something to eat, dry bread, a hut, clothes, medicine and education for children.[114]

The executive of the Champaran District Congress Committee issued a *fatwa* (declaration) asking Sahajanand, the president of the Bihar Kisan Sabha and a member of the Bihar PCC Working Committee, not to visit the district. The local Congress workers were threatened with disciplinary action if they were to attend any meeting addressed by Sahajanand.[115] The DCCs of Saran and

[111] Ibid., 11 December 1937.

[112] *Search Light*, 9 November 1937.

[113] Ibid., 6 January 1938; *The Hindustan Times*, 12 January 1938.

[114] F. No. 16/1935, GBO, SCRO Patna, cited by Walter Hauser, op. cit., p. 96.

[115] *Congress Socialist*, 11 December 1937. The President of the Champaran District Congress Committee Bipan Behari Verma was also a member of the All India Congress Committee and Secretary of Bihar Pradesh Congress Committee. A zamindar, he took *begar* (forced labour) and *nazarana* (extra premiums) and confiscated tenant holdings in his estate. *Janta*, 30 June 1938.

Monghyr followed suit. It was a unique incident that lower level organizational bodies had banned the entry of a person who was member of their higher organizational body. Their action was soon endorsed by the Bihar PCC. It took no notice of the Bihar Kisan Sabha resolution that 'any attempt to weaken the Kisan Sabha by Congressmen or to the building up of mass action for the overthrow of British imperialism'.[116]

Another shock awaited the Bihar peasantry. Completely ignoring the Kisan Sabha, the BPCC concluded a pact with zamindars regarding amendment of tenancy laws.[117] The whole deal had been supervised by Patel, Maulana Azad and Rajendra Prasad. The Congress had adhered to the imperialist policy of confiding in landlords. Mahadev Desai described this as a zamindar–kisan agreement which demonstrated the capability of the Congress to represent and safeguard the interests of both.[118] The BPCC banned the participation of Congressmen in Kisan Sabha[119] and it came at a time when the Congress zamindar pact had been signed.[120] It gave rise to suspicion whether the pact carried some secret provision of an assurance by Congressmen of withdrawing Congress support to kisan sabhas. It was declared at the landholders' meeting in Patna that, 'for the sake of zamindars the kisan movement was being suppressed by the Congress' and 'the Congress had no alternative but to compromise with the zamindars,' only 'the question was whether the right-wingers remained in the office or not'.[121] The Deputy Speaker of the Orissa Legislative Assembly and a prominent member of the Gandhi Seva Sangh, Nand Kishore Das, congratulated Rajendra Prasad for taking a bold stand against the Kisan Sabha. He thanked him for showing the way to the Orissa

[116] Awdeshwar Prasad Sinha to Indulal Yagnik, 1 December 1937, Yagnik Papers.

[117] *Congress Socialist*, 22 January 1938. *Indian Annual Register*, Vol. II, p. 388.

[118] *Harijan*, 25 December 1937.

[119] Ibid.

[120] *Leader*, 18 December 1937.

[121] *The Hindustan Times*, 6 January 1938.

Committee to deal with the kisan problem and asserted 'may you be the saviour of Orissa as you have been of Bihar'.[122] In Bombay two Congress MLAs issued hand-bills denouncing the formation of separate Kisan Sabhas and warned peasants against joining them.[123] All this was in contravention to the Faizpur resolution but the protests of Kisan Sabha leaders were of no avail. This also exhibited that Congress resolutions had no impact on the Rightist members of the organization. The authenticity of a separate class organization for the kisans was challenged by those who had recognized the class organization of zamindars. Mahadev Desai advocated:

> If a Kisan Sabha sets up internal feud as between Kisans and Zamindars it harms the Congress cause. The Congress knows best how to deal with the different elements composing the nation . . . it is for the Congress to lay down the policies, *not for individuals or for groups* to dictate them by a threat or show of force.[124]

Perhaps Desai forgot that whether inside or outside the Congress, it was an individual, i.e. Gandhi who laid the Congress policies. Sahajanand had earlier stressed on the need of a separate kisan organization which saw politics 'through the economic problems of kisans'. He agreed with the view expressed by the *Advance* that in case class organizations went under the control of designing men 'who hope to thrive by acting as agents of British imperialism' these organizations might embarrass the Congress, but argued that if the Congress passed into the hands of such persons, what would be the fate of the entire masses of the country? He believed that the congress contained such 'germs' in the form of zamindars and capitalists and as the Congress creed and programme were prepared with a view not to antagonize the British allies in India, it was easy for these germs to spread infection.[125]

The contradictions with the Congress over the kisan issue became quite apparent. The Congress President found nothing objection-

[122] *Amrita Bazar Patrika*, 14 January 1938.

[123] *Congress Socialist*, 11 December 1937.

[124] *Harijan*, 25 December 1937.

[125] *Congress Socialist*, 5 June 1938.

able in the slogan '*Kisan Raj Kayem ho*' (Peasant Rule should be established) but the slogan had been deplored by the Bihar PCC and the right-wingers. Nehru had to admit the upper class domination of the Congress in Bihar.[126] He maintained his stand of strengthening the Kisan Sabhas with the reservation that they should not come in opposition to the Congress. The kisans were described by him as the 'life of the country' and swaraj meant 'the end of peasant grievance'.[127] But his phrases were redundant as they had no practical value. He avoided becoming a party to the kisan controversy against the right wing Congress leadership. When the Secretary of Madhubani Town Congress Committee sought his advice as to the participation of Congressmen in the Kisan Sabha activity, he told him to seek the advice of local Bihar leaders[128] who were obviously to give a negative verdict. At the same time he repented, 'It was a mistake to think that the ministers would bring about an improvement in the conditions of the kisans' and opined that 'the people themselves should work for the improvements of their lot'.[129]

Sahajanand was now the target of rightist attacks. Their followers greeted him with slogans of 'go back *swami*' and attempted in vain to break up his meetings. He was referred to as a 'political turn coat' who was 'over anxious for leadership'[130] and was 'being paid by the British to defame the ministry'.[131] Another prominent Bihar kisan leader Ramnandan Misra was alleged to have been financed by 'Stalin, Sir Ganesh and Maharaja of Darbhanga'.[132] Sahajanand was charged with preaching violence and class war through his '*Danda* cult' and raising the slogan '*Malguzari kaise loge danda hamara zindabad*' (how will you take revenue long live our stick).[133] Rajendra Prasad believed that a 'violent atmosphere' prevailed in

[126] *Indian Nation*, 29 December 1937.

[127] *Sangharsh*, 3 January 1938.

[128] F.No. G-39/1938, AICC Papers, NMML.

[129] *Leader*, 23 December 1937.

[130] *Search Light*, 1 December 1937.

[131] Ramnandan Misra to Rajendra Prasad, 17 January 1938, File No. G-98/1937, AICC Papers, NMML.

[132] Ibid.

[133] *The Hindustan Times*, 14 January 1938.

many parts of Bihar by the preaching of *danda* cult.[134] This campaign, it was alleged, had 'produced such an atmosphere of violence in the countryside that an explosion may occur at any moment' and 'as the government of the country' the Congress was 'bound to suppress all activity likely to lead to a breach of peace'.[135]

Sahajanand resigned from the Working Committee of the BPCC. He listed a number of reasons for his resignation in a letter to Rajendra Prasad: (i) When he and the Kisan Sabha were 'hanged' by the Working Committee though a member, he was not invited to attend the meeting, nor was the Kisan Sabha given an opportunity to argue its case. (ii) He opposed the Congress–Zamindar Pact and did not want to be a party to it by remaining in the working Committee. (iii) The Working Committee had fixed 6 annas per maund as the procurement price for sugar cane but the ministry slided to 5 annas which was incomprehensible to them. He felt that he could 'serve the Congress better by remaining outside the committee' which did not want him.[136] His resignation was termed 'dangerous' by Mahadev Desai as he had not retired from the Congress organization too.[137] Sahajanand stressed:

> Kisan demonstrations and movement does [*sic*] not mean lack of faith in ministries. But so long there is pain in our stomach we shall raise a cry no matter our own beloved son, brother, or father may be treating us as a doctor.[138]

He described as utterly false the allegation of preaching *danda* cult during the Congress ministry, encouraged by the thought that he won't be sent to jail. On the contrary he asserted that he had used much milder language than before.[139] The opponents of the kisan movement had charged him of preaching violence in 1936 also but a government report described it as a piece of pro-landlord propaganda as he had only said 'if *zamindari amala* [agent] and other unauthorized persons used violence on the raiyats, the

[134] *Harijan*, 22 January 1938.
[135] *The Hindustan Times*, 14 January 1938.
[136] Ibid., 5 January 1938.
[137] *Harijan*, 29 January 1938.
[138] *Sangharsh*, 10 January 1938.
[139] *The Hindustan Times*, 5 January 1938.

latter could retaliate in kind'.[140] This he maintained still: 'I have always exhorted them to muster strong in self defence and tell the oppressors accordingly to stop their oppressions, otherwise the result would prove disastrous.'[141]

He asked how his preaching of self-defence was a violation of Congress principles? He cited Gandhi's words in favour of his argument that 'violence is better than cowardice' and 'whilst your women are dishonoured, you should offer physical resistance to them [oppressors]'[142] Sahajanand questioned:

> Should I tell the kisans that they must keep mum even if the mad dog bites them and snatches away the piece of bread which they want to eat? Should they be asked to remain quiet when *badmashes* [rougues] enter their houses, loot them, and insult their wives and sisters? I maintain that unless the oppressors realize that they will receive *dandas* if they cross a certain limit, they would not abstain from their action.[143]

Mahadev Desai challenged him for citing Gandhi on the use of violence but Desai's case was weak as he himself cited Gandhi:

> *Dharma* never teaches cowardice and supine submission to tyranny; *Dharma* teaches us to meet the oppressor bravely and defy him to do his worst. . . . But *Dharma* does not mean flying away from injustice and oppression. . . . If you cannot show the highest heroism, you can certainly show that you are not cowards by *dealing a blow* for blow.[144]

Desai remained blind towards zamindari tyranny and opposed peasant resistance. As the 'chief capitalist agent' in the Congress he was supposed to be tough and safeguard rightist interests.[145] He argued in favour of the zamindari system and described the legitimate interests of the zamindars as a 'commission for the use of their intelligence in wisely directing the energies of their ten-

[140] F.No. 18/1/1936, Home Political, NAI; also see Walter Hauser, op. cit., pp. 89, 96.

[141] *Harijan*, 29 January 1938.

[142] Ibid.

[143] Ibid.

[144] Ibid. (emphasis added).

[145] This assumption is based on reading the correspondence between G.D. Birla and Mahadev Desai. G.D. Birla, No. 90.

ants'.[146] Gandhi wanted the zamindari system to be mended rather than being ended. He did not want the zamindars to be pushed out for 'the man who supplies brains and metal is as much a tiller as the one who labours with his hands'. He wanted to utilize their services for the nation.[147] This seemed utopian for how much intelligent were the zamindars and how they bled their peasantry was well known. The AIKS repudiated the Gandhian theory of class collaboration and maintained that the kisans were bound to take self-defensive measure so long as the class conflict persists owing to the exploitation practised by the landlords.[148]

Sahajanand wanted to 'create a situation wherein the zamindars, his officers and *sipahis* [soldiers] will not dare to harass and terrorise the tenants'.[149] It was a matter of great satisfaction to him that his teaching was having the desired effect of striking terror in the hearts of oppressive zamindars.[150] Ranga deplored the call of asking the Indian kisans to give up their traditional *danda*.[151] It is worth mentioning that at all the Congress sessions where songs in praise of non-violence used to be sung the Congress volunteers, not only men but women also, paraded with *dandas* and gave *dandasalami* (salute). Why this use of *danda* at the Congress sessions? Nobody dare asked. Gandhi agreed with Birla that 'anarchy in the Congress seems to be on the increase'[152] and as he had already stated, he was prepared to 'strain every nerve' to prevent a class war.[153]

[146] *Harijan*, 25 December 1937.

[147] Ibid., 23 April 1938. However, in 1942 Gandhi said as regards to the lot of peasantry in free India, 'The peasants would take the land' and 'we would tell them to take it. They would take it', He described it 'fiscally impossible', to compensate the landlords. See Louis Fischer, *A Week with Gandhi* (Bombay, 1944), p. 43.

[148] *Indian Annual Register, 1938*, Vol. I, p. 350.

[149] *Congress Socialist*, 12 March 1938.

[150] *Search Light*, 19 January 1938.

[151] *Indian Annual Register*, 1938, Vol. I, p. 349.

[152] Gandhi to Birla, 26 March 1938, *Collected Works of Mahatma Gandhi*, Vol. LXVII (Delhi, 1978), p. 283.

[153] Gandhi to Agatha Harrison, 30 April 1936, in B.G. Kunte (ed.), *Source Material for a History of the Freedom Movement in India*, Vol. III, Part VII: *1934–45* (Bombay, 1975), p. 533.

The Kisan Sabha had to face a number of problems for the Haripura Congress session. The elections of Congress delegates for the session were marked with clashes in Bihar. Two AICC members, 14 BPCC members, one MLA and 40 members of the Darbhanga DCC complained that the kisan members of the Congress were not allowed to vote; *lathis* were freely used to stop them and elephants were let loose on kisan voters.[154] The kisan sabhaites supported Subhas Bose's candidature who in his Presidential address to the Congress mentioning about class organizations, said:

> My own view is that we cannot abolish such organizations by ignoring or condemning them. They exist as objective facts. . . . It should be manifest that there is a *historical necessity* behind them. . . . I am afraid that whether we like it or not, we have to reconcile ourselves to their existence.[155]

Patel, however, warned the 'leftists' that the Congress having tolerated them for two years was 'now determined' not to tolerate them.[156] He banned the kisan rally and conference at Vithalnagar[157] but the kisans staged a demonstration before the Subjects Committee *pandal* (huge tent) with red flags in their hands.[158] Their meeting 'had to be carried on without light for most of the time in that great city of million lights'.[159]

The Haripura resolution on kisan sabhas though recognized their independent existence but warned that the Congress 'cannot countenance any of the activities of those Congressmen who as members of the Kisan Sabha help in creating an atmosphere alien to Congress principles and activities'.[160] The *Hindustan Times* described this part of the resolution as an open challenge and threat to the kisan sabhaites,[161] and it was not at all an oral resolution. A month later Patel denounced the separate class identity of the kisan organization

[154] *Janta*, 6 January 1938. Yagnik Papers.
[155] *The Hindustan Times*, 20 February 1938.
[156] Ibid., 21 February 1938.
[157] *Indian Annual Register*, Vol. II, 1937, p. 388.
[158] *The Hindustan Times*, 19 February 1938.
[159] *Indian Annual Register*, Vol. II, 1937, p. 388.
[160] F.No. 42/1936, AICC Papers, NMML.
[161] *The Hindustan Times*, 1 March 1938.

where as he proposed to organize a labour union under the Gandhi Seva Sangh in opposition to the All India Trade Union Congress as the latter preached class war.[162] Thus, he was denouncing class organizations on the one hand and advocating building a rival class organization on the other. This signifies the rightist intentions to utilize class organizations for their own benefits, failing which they were to be suppressed. Nehru, too, now scoffed at the idea of holding kisan demonstration in front of Council chamber at Lucknow.[163]

The Peasant movement was once again emerging on a militant scale in UP. In Baharaich tenants had looted the *thekedars* (contractors) paddy godowns[164] and in Unao the social boycott of zamindars was so complete that they could not even obtain barber services.[165] In Bihar 77 clashes between tenants and zamindars occurred in the course of five months and ten lives were lost.[166] The Bihar Premier exempted the Kisan Sabha from the charge of being responsible for the agrarian trouble and described high rents as the cause of trouble.[167] He talked of immediate relief to the tenant but under his very nose Gurkha armed force was used to crush the tenants.[168] At many places kisans holdings were attached and notices under Section 144 were served on kisans. The Kisan Sabha leaders personally came to defy such orders and ploughed the attached lands themselves. They not only organized the tenants but their women folk also.[169] Sahajanand accused the Congress ministers of adopting the jargon of constitutionalism and forgetting the direct action struggles.[170]

The AIKS session at Comilla once again stressed the necessity of separate kisan organization. Sahajanand advocated that it was

[162] Ibid., 30 March 1938.
[163] *Bombay Chronicle*, 15 March 1938.
[164] *The Hindustan Times*, 15 January 1938.
[165] Ibid.
[166] Ibid., 25 March 1938.
[167] Ibid.
[168] *Bombay Sentinel*, 2 July 1938.
[169] *Janta*, 29 December 1938.
[170] *Sangharsh*, 22 August 1938.

'dangerous' to agree that the Congress was a kisan organization because 95 per cent of its members were kisans. 'Such reasoning', he felt, 'would lead to the fallacious view that the Congress is a Hindu organization because an overwhelming majority of its membership is Hindu.' He did not want the Congress to be a kisan organization in name only but, if ever, to be so in ideology.[171] The AIKS justified the use of Red flag and assured that it was not in opposition to the Tricolour, nor did it mean any insult to it. The Red flag represented the cause of the oppressed and thus the Kisan Sabha favoured it. The Muslim League and the Krishak Proja Party tried their best to sabotage this session which was held in a predominantly Muslim district. Religious slogans were raised to check the participation of Muslim peasantry and even assaults were made.[172] But the massive participation of Muslim peasants demonstrated that class solidarity could cut across communal lines if the class interests were genuinely represented.[173] Sahajanand lectured: 'Bread was greater than God'.[174] The AIKS declared its aim to achieve agrarian revolution and assured the Congress of its support in the anti-imperialist struggle. The Kisan Sabha opposed the War Bill and urged the peasants to refuse recruitment in the army.[175]

In spite of the all out support to the national movement by the Kisan Sabha, its conflict with the Congress was on the increase, kisans were induced not to attend Kisan Sabha meetings. In Bihar the local protégés of the rightist leadership preached that 'this Sahajanand was not the same person who visited last year but an impostor who was the enemy of the Congress'. In many villages it was falsely propagated that kisans' meetings could not be held as Sahajanand had met with an accident and his legs were broken. At Saran 'radio-fitted' government cars meant for prohibition propaganda were utilized for anti-Sahajanand campaign.[176] However, the

[171] Rasaul, op. cit., p. 30.

[172] Ibid., p. 38.

[173] *Indian Annual Register*, Vol. I, 1938, p. 349.

[174] Sahajanand, *Mera Jivan Sangharsh*, p. 528.

[175] Kisan *Bulletin*, 4 September 1938.

[176] *Hitavada*, 18 August 1938.

pro-kisan Congress members in the Bihar Assembly 'unfurled the banner of revolt' by either voting against or abstaining from government amendments on Tenancy law despite a distinct party mandate.[177] At the Delhi AICC in September 1938, Bhulabhai Desai, moving the Civil Liberties resolution made it clear that it was directed against the kisan sabhas. The Congress Socialists walked out when the rightist majority passed it.[178] Ranga maintained that the kisans would stick to the Congress unless they were driven out by the rightists.[179]

Mahatma Gandhi who led the great Dandi March was against peasant marches. Condemning indiscipline among Congressmen he said: 'Kisans of Bihar are supposed to be Congressmen. Their leaders are Congressmen. Bihar ministers live in perpetual dread of risings and kisan marches.'[180]

In the present condition of the Congress he saw 'nothing but *anarchy and red ruin* in front of the country'.[181] He inclined to bring those Congressmen 'under rigid discipline' who did the 'greatest mischief' in the villages[182] and these Congressmen were no one else but kisan sabhaites. The All India Landholders Federation had condemned those who were 'attempting to make Russia of India' and resolved to extend their utmost cooperation to those who disapproved of revolutionary methods.[183] Nehru now felt that he had been 'unnecessarily hard on Congress ministers',[184] and the acceptance of office had resulted in a 'lot of good' to the peasants.[185] Thus he contradicted his earlier statement about ministers. When the Viceroy complained against Shibban Lal Saxena, a Congress MLA from Gorakhpur, Nehru replied:

177 Ibid., p. 38.

178 *Indian Annual Register*, Vol. I, 1938, p. 357.

179 Ibid.

180 *Harijan*, 28 January 1939.

181 Ibid.

182 Ibid., 29 April 1939.

183 *Amrita Bazar Patrika*, 12 December 1939.

184 Nehru, op. cit., p. 604.

185 *Leader*, 2 January 1939.

I must confess that he is crude of speech and occasionally his tongue runs away with him when he discusses the plight of the peasantry. *We have warned him privately several times* and our advice *has had effect on him.*[186]

The AIKS was concerned not only with the middle or poor peasant but was equally vocal for the rural proletariat. It felt that there was hardly a line of demarcation between these peasant categories, i.e. poor peasants and agricultural labourers. It declared the low standard of rural wages, primitive conditions of work, social repression of agricultural labourers, so-called Harijans and other suppressed classes as 'inhuman and unbecoming to any civilized society'.[187]

It resolved to organize agricultural labourers into their unions to fight against the chains of slavery. Sahajanand described the agricultural labourer as kisan in true sense of the term 'who had no actual share in the absolute possession of the land' he cultivated,[188] He regarded the entire socio-economic problem revolving itself into a kisan problem as a significant proportion of the urban proletariat consists of those who migrated in search of some relief from the suffering confronted in rural India and they kept changing from fields to mills and vice versa.[189] The labourers were asked to demand living wages or give an ultimatum to refuse to work which would wreck the entire economic machinery of the nation.[190] The peasants were asked to live in harmony with the agricultural labourers and the latter were urged to make a united front with the farmer. The Bihar Assembly rejected a proposal to form an enquiry committee to go into the conditions of *khet majdurs* (agricultural labourers) with the Congressmen voting for the rejection.[191] Was it that as the agricultural labourers had no electoral rights, their conditions should not be probed by the elected elite?

[186] Nehru to Linlithgow, 6 October 1939. J. Nehru Papers Correspondence Vol. 42, S. No. 2704, NMML (emphasis added). Nehru had described Saxena as 'one of our most honest and hardest working members'. Ibid.

[187] *Congress Socialist*, 9 January 1937.

[188] Ibid., 26 December 1936.

[189] Ibid., also see Hauser, op. cit., p. 18.

[190] *Search Light*, 9 November 1937.

[191] *Janta*, 28 April 1938.

The Congress attitude towards the AIKS was ambivalent. Nehru's theoretical love of socialism goaded him to vocalize peasant issues and the rightists were clever enough to use his utterances for electoral politics. Kisan organizations and their workers were looked down with suspicion and distrust. They were seldom welcomed by ministers.[192] Peasant leadership was never encouraged by Congressmen.[193] All that the Congress wished was to utilize the peasants' energy for take over of power by the dominant social groups.

'The main strength of the Congress lay in the villages and now this alternative leadership in the form of Kisan Sabha of those very villages is for them simply an unthinkable phenomenon and it pains them (Congress leaders) the most' were the words of Sahajanand Saraswati at the end of 1930s.[194]

[192] Acharya Narendra Deva's presidential address at All India Kisan Sabha, Gaya, March 1939, in Brahmanand (ed.), *Towards Socialist Society* (Delhi, 1979), p. 160

[193] See Mittal and Kumar, 'Anti-Feudal and Anti-Colonial Struggles . . .', op. cit., pp. 35–41. Mittal and Kumar 'Baba Ramchandra and Peasant Upsurge in Oudh 1920–1921', *Social Scientist*, No. 71, June 1978, pp. 47–51; Kumar, op. cit., p. 226.

[194] OGKMI.

CHAPTER 7

Peasants, Congress and the Struggle for Freedom: 1917–1939*

From the time the Indian National Congress entered the phase of mass politics by basing its struggle on mass action and till the coming of independence *along with partition* (we emphasize this as the nationalist and neo-nationalist historians tend to ignore this tragic fact of history while glorifying the role of the Congress) one crucial question which bothered the British was: What would be the attitude of the Congress towards the agrarian issues, particularly the no-rent demand of the peasantry? Official literature reveals—concern over this issue as it was the peasantry which provided the bulk of manpower for the Congress in the course of freedom struggle. In recent years peasant movements have drawn considerable attention from scholars and we have a good number of micro-level studies on the subject. Few attempts have been made, however, to study the situation at the macro-level.[1] We believe that neither can be studied in isolation from the other for there was constant interaction between divergent and often antagonistic social forces.

To analyse the attitude of the INC towards the peasants and vice versa we have to take into account the various roles of the Congress; the Congress as an organized political party; as a platform; in the course of active struggles (i.e. the mass movements phase) and while in power (ministry period).

Equally important is to examine the status of peasant leadership

*This paper was earlier published in Kapil Kumar (ed.), *Congress and Classes* (Delhi, 1988). The author is thankful to the Nehru Memorial Museum & Library, New Delhi for granting a fellowship which helped him in collecting material on 'Congress-Peasant Relationship 1917–39'.

[1] For example see D.N. Dhanagare, *Peasant Movements in India, 1920–50* (Delhi, 1983); A.R. Desai (ed.), *Peasant Struggles in India* (Bombay, 1979).

within the organizational hierarchy of the Congress from the village to the national level; peasants' perception of the Congress and its leadership; and finally their reaction to the policies and programmes of the Congress.

We are aware of the problems and limitations that are here in any study of the all India situation in this regard—a situation full of complexities produced primarily by regional variations in agrarian structures and relations as also by differentiation within the peasant as well as landlord categories. In spite of this we believe that as far as the oppressive apparatus of the Raj and the attitude of its allies are concerned, the general situation remained virtually the same in all the regions with only marginal variations. The same, moreover, could be said about the attitude of the Congress towards the peasants and landlords. The issues taken up in this study will illustrate this.

I

'Swaraj depends on the agriculturists', Gandhi told the merchants at Calcutta while launching his first massive movement against the British in 1920. He stressed that if the peasants 'do not help' swaraj 'cannot be attained' and that if 'they cooperated with the government, then all your virtues will not help in winning swaraj'.[2] This was the period when the Congress took notice of the peasantry as a force to combat the British authority and this change in the policy was brought about by Gandhi. But in this regard some crucial facts have to be accounted for. The initiative was not taken by the Congress to reach the peasant. Gandhi, it may be noted, had deliberately kept the Congress away at Champaran even though the Congress 'was practically unknown in these parts'.[3] The struggles of the peasantry against the British date back to the efforts of the latter to establish their supremacy in the countryside, and this was much before the advent of the initiatives of the educated middle class in the freedom struggle. Different regions in the country

[2] *The Collected Works of Mahatma Gandhi* (*CWMG*), Vol. XIX, p. 281.

[3] M.K. Gandhi, *An Autobiography or The Story of My Experiments with Truth* (Ahmedabad, 1969), p. 411.

witnessed various peasant uprisings.[4] Despite their limitations and shortcomings these uprisings demonstrate that anti-British sentiment was present in the peasant mind long before and independently of the efforts of the Congressmen. Before the Congress was called in or at a later stage when it moved in, some levels of organization and leadership did exist amongst the peasants in different regions. Whatever may be their form but they were certainly based on an understanding against the oppressor—whosoever it may be. The local peasant leaders banged at the Congress doors in search of some support for the oppressed peasantry. One can cite here the journeys taken by Raj Kumar Sukul to the Congress sessions, Baba Ram Chandra's march to Allahabad and Swami Vidyananda's presence at the Amritsar Congress (1919) along with a large number of peasant delegates. In spite of objections to the exemption of delegate fees for peasants, their representation went up considerably at the Delhi and Amritsar sessions and Motilal Nehru was 'glad to see' them in their hundreds.[5]

The constant banging of the Congress doors by the peasants on the one hand and the need to enlist the peasants' support; for the national movement—as visualized by the Congress—on the other, ultimately brought an almost reluctant Congress leadership to the countryside. Once the Congress moved in, it emerged as a strong political force in the countryside. No single reason can account for this grand success of the Congress. If rumour created myths about Gandhi, peasants believed them not because they were fools but because they had their own perception of him and his programme.[6] Gandhi, to the peasants, had become a symbol to oppose the oppressor and now the peasants looked upon him and the Congress to ameliorate their lot. They related his or the preachings of the Congress to their own economic and social grievances and acted on their own.

[4] See Kathleen Gough, 'Indian Peasant Uprisings', *Economic and Political Weekly*, special number, August 1974.

[5] *Congress Presidential Addresses 1911–34* (Madras, 1934), p. 467.

[6] See Kapil Kumar, 'Peasants' Perception of Gandhi and his Programme: Oudh, 1920–1922', *Social Scientist*, February 1983.

The Congress policy was to convert the hitherto existing peasant organizations into Congress bodies in the name of discipline. This was an excuse used constantly by the conservative and reactionary elements within the Congress to maintain their hegemony in the organization; to accuse the peasants and workers of breaking it as if discipline was meant for them only; and to use it as a weapon against all those who dared to challenge vested interests within and outside the organization. The Congress line, during the 1920s, was quite vague in relation to the British; but so far as the landlords were concerned, the policy was exemplified, among other examples, by the Bardoli resolutions (1922). One can understand the historical necessity of such a manoeuvre to fight the British. But the question is, was it that straight and simple? Was such a policy pursued only to fight imperialism? Was not there any class element involved in adopting it? Was it not an outcome of the influence of the dominant social groups active within the Congress—groups which were there in the Congress not only for the sake of nationalism but also for safeguarding their vested class interests. As far as the Congress policy towards the peasants was concerned, the reactionary elements (both landlords and capitalists), who never even formed a part of the Congress organization, did influence it at crucial junctures.

One vital question here is: How far were the landlords a constituent of the multi-class alliance of the Indian people against imperialism? It will not be a vague generalization to assert that in the taluqdari or zamindari regions the British Raj was more known through the local landlords than through any of its other leverages. In the imperial language, they were the 'forces of order', 'loyal supporters' and the 'bulwark against the disintegrating forces'.[7] They played a dominant role in strengthening British authority. To quote the Nawab of Chhattari (in 1939):[8] '. . . the greatest of all services the zamindars had rendered was the maintenance of law and order in the rural areas.'

[7] For details see Kapil Kumar, *Peasants in Revolt: Tenants, Landlords Congress and the Raj in Oudh, 1886–1922* (New Delhi, 1984), pp. 4–16, 174–7, 213–15.

[8] Address at the All India Landholders Conference, Lucknow, April 1939, cited *Indian Annual Register*, 1939, Vol. I, p. 392.

The zamindars or taluqdars as a class were never a part of the Congress or of the freedom struggle. Barring a few isolated cases where they supported the Congress in individual capacity, they were mostly on the other side. There were a few uprooted or petty zamindars who did side with the Congress. But they did so more due to their declining economic status which they attributed to the British. In fact I equate these petty landlords with the rich peasants of the raiyatwari regions. Even where a few big landlords supported the Congress, the peasantry in their estates remained exploited. The Kalakankar taluqdari in Oudh can be cited as one such case. The peasants of this state complained to Gandhi that though the taluqdar was a nationalist in appearance they were subjected to *begar*, *rasad*, evictions and all kinds of extortions which were prevalent in other taluqdari estates.[9]

At the time of every movement launched by the Congress the landlords actively aided the British in crushing it.[10] During the elections they fought the Congress tooth and nail through their class organizations like the British India Associations in different regions, National Agriculturist Party, and the Bihar Landholders Association. In some cases they penetrated the Congress ranks and were put forward as Congress candidates (for example, in Bihar Sir C.P.N. Singh's brother won on a Congress ticket in 1937; David Arnold gives similar examples for Madras). The Bihar Kisan Sabha was very vocal against zamindars being accepted as Congress candidates. But ultimately the Kisan Sabha leadership surrendered to the Congress. It did so not because it had altered its policy of fighting landlordism but on the ground that there should be no division within the Congress against the British.[11]

[9] Interview with a number of peasants in Partapgarh district, The V.N. Mehta Report on Agrarian Disturbances in Partapgarh has an appendix about extortions from the peasantry in Kalakankar estate, F. No. 753 (A), 1920, Rev., UP State Archives, Lucknow.

[10] This holds true for practically all the regions and recent research has demonstrated this very well; Gyanendra Pandey and Kapil Kumar on UP, Stephen Henningham on Bihar, Biswamoy Pati on Orissa, David Arnold on Madras, A. Murali on Andhra Pradesh, etc.

[11] Swami Sahajanand Saraswati, *Mera Jivan Sangharsh* (Patna, 1952), p. 481.

The Congress had always assured the landlords' of their rights and privileges. But it was only in the late 1930s that the landlords fully realized the restraining role of the Congress as far as peasant struggles were concerned. It was during the ministry period that a formal relationship was established between the Congress and the landlords. The Congress victory in elections and the increasing influence of the Left among the masses facilitated this direct relationship which the landlords and the Congress right wing sought with each other.

The outcome of this was a Congress zamindar pact in Bihar and similar negotiations in other regions. A revealing feature of this pact is that while questions related to landlords' rights and privileges, along with tenants' position, were discussed and agreed upon, there was no mention of landlords' role in the Indian national movement. The vast literature[12] available on the Congress zamindar negotiations (1937–9) shows that those negotiating on behalf of the Congress (Rajendra Prasad, Sardar Patel, Maulana Azad, etc.) at no stage asked the landlords to support the Congress in the struggle against the British. Realizing that they were acting against the declared policy of the Congress in relation to the kisan sabhas and the agrarian question (Lucknow and Faizpur resolutions);[13] these leaders took precautions to justify their actions. Thus Rajendra Prasad wrote to a prominent landlord of Bihar:[14]

> . . . We had gone to the furthest length possible and had done so *even at the risk of being openly criticized* in the All India Congress Committee of *having gone against* the Congress resolution. I had in anticipation brought the Maulana so

For details see Kapil Kumar, 'Congress-Peasant Relationship in the Late 1930s', in D.N. Panigrahi (ed.), *Economy, Society and Politics in Modern India* (New Delhi, 1985).

[12] For example, Rajendra Prasad Papers (RPP), Linlithgow Papers (LP), and Haig Papers (HP) at the NMML, New Delhi; *Behar Herald*, *Indian Nation*, etc.

[13] For a detailed discussion on kisan sabhas and agrarian issues at the Faizpur session of the Congress, see Kapil Kumar, 'Congress–Peasant Relationship', pp. 235–7.

[14] Rajendra Prasad to Ramdayalu Sinha, 7 December 1937, RPP, NMML, Roll 5 (emphasis added).

that if any question arose in the Working Committee or AICC, I might have a strong supporter by my side.

Prasad enlisted Azad's support because he knew that he 'shall come in for a great deal of criticism from not only the Kisan Sabha but congressmen in general and even perhaps the high command'.[15] Azad was assigned the task of taking Jawaharlal Nehru into confidence. He assured Prasad that there would be 'no difficulty' as far as Nehru was concerned.[16] The green signal from Nehru, to go ahead with zamindars, came when Kriplani wrote on his behalf: 'If you and Maulana Saheb were satisfied it was alright'.[17]

What followed was the process for an agreement during which Prasad pleaded with the landlords that if the Congress proposals were 'unsatisfactory the zamindars should be prepared to propose a better solution' and assured that the 'Government will not fail to give it their utmost consideration'.[18] Patel's advice to Prasad was:[19]

> It is no use trying to improve it (the tenancy bill), if it has to be forced down the throats of unwilling landlords. We shall have to resist the excessive demands of the tenants who have been worked up and expect too much from the Congress ministries.

Who had 'worked up' the peasants? We shall come to this a little later. Be it noted at the moment that it was peasants, and not landlords who needed to be resisted; and that the right wing of the Congress, with the sanction of Nehru, had all the liberty to go back on the election promises made by the Congress.

It was during this period that the Maharaja of Darbhanga, after getting a negative reply about the zamindars being protected as a minority by the British, sought the advice of the Bihar Governor regarding the zamindars joining the Congress. But this was found to be ultimately prejudicial to their interests. It was instead decided

[15] Rajendra Prasad to Maharaja Darbhanga, 20 April 1938, ibid., F-I/A-1938, NAI.

[16] Azad to Prasad, 26 and 28 November 1937, ibid.

[17] Kriplani to Prasad, 29 November 1937, F-I/1937, ibid.

[18] Prasad to Mohd. Ismail, 20 October 1937, NMML, Roll 8.

[19] Patel to Prasad, 4 December 1937, ibid.

to have a strong zamindari organization and through it to influence the Congress.[20] This led to the formation of the All India Landholders Association (AILHA) in April 1939.

Throughout the ministry period the zamindars remained confident that for their sake 'the kisan movement was being suppressed by the Congress' and it was in their interest to 'strengthen the hands of the government in counteracting the mischievous move of the leftist group in the Congress to make Russia of India';[21] that 'the Congress had no alternative but to compromise with the zamindars'; and that the only 'question was whether the right wingers remained in the office or not'.[22] In his presidential address to the AILHA, Maharaja of Darbhanga stressed:[23]

> Most of those who are in power in the Congress organization which runs the government of seven provinces want adjustment and peace . . . we want adjustment because therein *lies our security.* We want peace because *only then we can develop our strength.* For a minority interest like ours it is only desperation that can drive us to fight and I have reasons to believe that so long as the group following the directions of Mahatma Gandhi *rules* in the Congress and the Socialists and Communists are *kept in check* we shall not have to take the extreme step.

The landlords would thus support the Congress right wing – which, too, looked up to them in checking the left, without being obliged to extend this support to the fight against the British. The lone voice raised rather reluctantly by Chandreshwar Prasad Singh, the leader of opposition in Bihar, to fight for freedom found no response at the AILHA conference. But a resolution was passed to form a Committee of Understanding to negotiate with the Congress and the provincial governments with regard to problems of landlords and tenants.[24] Without being a constituent in the multi-class alliance against, the British, the landlords were in alliance with that group within the Congress which stood for the suppression of the kisan movement and the Left.

[20] Hallet to Linlithgow, 17 August 1937, LP, S.No. 113, NMML.

[21] *Hindustan Times*, 6 January 1938.

[22] Ibid.

[23] *Indian Annual Register*, 1939, Vol. I, p. 396 (emphasis added).

[24] Ibid., p. 398.

It cannot be mere coincidence that about this time Gandhi told Guy Wint:[25]

> . . . the agrarian unrest is a much greater danger, but if the Congress retains non-violence it is bound to be disciplined. . . . We who believe in non-violence are trying to cope with it, but we may fail. And yet we are not going the way of China. In China peasants can be soldiers at will, not here in India. In India we cannot make soldiers so easily. But I agree that you have spotted the real danger. However, it, will cease if the Congress can produce real type of workers for the villages.

Gandhi 'did not dread' the labour unrest much 'for factory labourers were not more than 20 lakhs' and they lived 'only in artificial cities'. Discarding the 'psychological importance' of labour unrest and confident that 'those bent on mischief cannot spread red ruin in the villages', Gandhi advised Wint to 'hook his mind to the villages and not the towns'.[26]

These observations by Gandhi came in April 1939, at a time when the Congress was not struggling to find a mass base but was holding power in the provinces. These, it may be noted, were the observations of a leader whom the peasants regarded as their messiah who would effect their emancipation from feudal and colonial exploitation.

What did he mean by 'much greater danger' and 'real danger'? What was his understanding of 'red ruin'? What was his definition of a disciplined peasantry? He was not a leftist and, was opposed to communism. To 'prevent a class war' he was ready to 'strain every nerve'.[27]

What Gandhi, and the Congress right wing, preached amongst the peasants was not 'class-adjustment' or class collaboration with the landlords but submission to them: 'You should bear a little, if the zamindar torments you'; 'If the zamindars harass them I would ask my kisan brethren not to fight with them but adopt a con-

[25] G.D. Birla (ed.), *Bapu: A Unique Association*, Vol. 3, Bombay, 1977, p. 267.

[26] Ibid.

[27] Gandhi to Agatha, 30 April 1936, in B.G. Kunte (ed.), *Source Material for a History of the Freedom Movement in India*, Vol. III, Part VII (Bombay, 1975), p. 533.

ciliatory attitude'; 'They should not quarrel with the zamindar'; 'Kisans must be advised scrupulously to abide by their agreement with the zamindar, whether such agreement is written or inferred from custom'.[28]

The disciplined peasants in Gandhian terminology were those who would not stop services to the landlord; would not even resist the landlord's violence by non-violent methods; would pay rents, however, exorbitant they might be; would not prevent the 'arrest of their leaders and would abide by all government laws; and would go on suffering humiliation and exploitation.[29] The 'legitimate interests' of the landlords were described by Mahadev Desai as a 'commission for the use of their intelligence in wisely directing the energies of their tenants'.[30] Despite acknowledging the 'present terrible inequality' between the landlords and the peasants, Gandhi treated the two at par, his logic being,[31] 'The man who supplies brains and metal is as much a tiller as the one who labours with his hands.' His outcry was always against the actions of peasants against landlords and he remained silent about the violence practised by landlords on their tenants.[32]

The argument of 'class adjustment' in the name of nationalism given in defence of Gandhi's approach, though relevant, fails to explain the situation in totality. There are scholars[33] who refer to Mao and the Chinese experience to justify the policy pursued by the Congress and Gandhi. Indeed, they stress, this policy should have been followed by the Left also. The comparison with Mao and China serves little purpose because conditions in the two countries were quite different. Mao advocated class-adjustment at a time when Japanese imperialism was trying to make in roads in China and the landlords were not the active supporters of imperialism. Even then Mao adopted a cautious approach towards them and

[28] *Young India*, 26 January, 9 March and 18 May 1922.

[29] Ibid., 26 January 1922.

[30] *Harijan*, 25 December 1937.

[31] Ibid., 23 March 1938.

[32] For details see Kapil Kumar, *Peasants in Revolt*, pp. 228–31.

[33] Bipan Chandra, *The Long Term Dynamics of the Indian National Congress* (Presidential Address to the Indian History Congress), Amritsar, 1985.

the aim of agrarian revolution was never forgotten. Moreover, the Chinese Communist Party was talking from a position of strength at this time.[34]

In India the Left was in a weak position and the Congress never had agrarian revolution as its aim—either as a primary or as a secondary goal. Moreover, imperialism was firmly entrenched here having the active support of the landlords. If anything, the experience of 1857 should have militated against any attempt at class adjustment. The people had then made common cause with the princes and landlords in opposing the British. The ultimate result of this struggle was that the princes and landlords not only compromised with imperialism but threw in their lot with the imperial masters. The peasantry was henceforth subjected to the double oppression of feudal lords and the imperialist power.

It was not so much class adjustment as class submission for national unity that Gandhi and the Congress preached amongst the peasants. On many occasions the issue of national unity was set aside. The picketing of landlords' houses by peasants was checked in the name of national unity whereas the picketing of a Muslim's shop was encouraged despite the knowledge that such an act might cause communal disturbance.[35] This leads us to conclude that issues which did not disturb the class character of the Indian society could be taken up at the cost of national unity, but issues involving class conflict had to be suppressed in the name of national unity.

Mushirul Hasan has shown that even during the mass contact phase (1937–9) 'Muslim peasants and underprivileged groups in the countryside, the very sections supposed to be mobilized on a massive scale, were largely ignored'.[36] His study demonstrates how communal minded persons led the district Congress Committees;

[34] See the comments of Sumit Sarkar in Nalini Taneja, 'Seminar Report', *Social Scientist*, August–September 1986, p. 138.

[35] Gyanendra Pandey, *The Ascendancy of the Congress in Uttar Pradesh, 1926–35* (Delhi, 1978), p. 267; Vijay Srivastav, 'Business Pressure Groups in UP', paper presented at a Seminar on 'Role of UP in Freedom Struggle', Lucknow, 16–18 January 1987.

[36] Mushirul Hasan, 'The Muslim Mass Contact Campaign: An Attempt at Political Mobilisation', Occasional Papers, No. XIV, NMML.

Muslims associated with the Congress were not allowed to contest Provincial Congress Committee elections and how the right wingers worked for the defeat of Muslim Congress candidates. Mobilization on economic lines to combat communalism was successfully opposed by the right wing. It is a cruel joke of history that the very leadership which suppressed economic struggles in the name of violence, bloodshed and threat to unity could not avoid these and succumbed to a communal divide of the country.

II

The peasant leaders of the period under study can be broadly categorized as follows:

1. In contrast to the bourgeois-Congress leadership there was in the countryside a traditional leadership represented by *babas*, *sadhus* and *faqirs*. We find one such character active in almost every peasant struggle. Though not peasants themselves, these characters were very much a part of the peasant's world. It was towards them that the peasant looked for solace 'in the world of feudal oppression'. Such leadership did not indulge in double-faced political propaganda. Aware of the social contradictions, this leadership identified itself with the peasants' interests and directed their ideas and aspirations. This leadership employed the religious, cultural and traditional symbols of the society to expose its existing exploitative structure and to foster anti-feudal and anti-British sentiments among the masses.
2. There were leaders (like Motilal Tezawat) who, though belonging to slightly well-off sections (petty merchants), identified themselves with the poor struggling peasants and organized them.
3. When oppression became unbearable leadership emerged from among all sections of the peasants—rich, middle and poor. Raj Kumar Sukul, Amol Sharma, Jhinguri Singh, Sitaram Raju, Brijpal Singh, etc., come in this category.
4. There were leaders, like Indulal Yagnik, Swami Sahajanand Saraswati and N.G. Ranga, who had a professional base but who came to the peasant and remained with him. They stand apart from leaders like Prasad, Kriplani and Patel who claimed

to be peasant leaders due to the association of a name, Champaran or Bardoli, with their political career.

5. There were leaders who felt impelled by their faith in communism and socialism to mobilize the peasants. Prominent among these were Bankim Mukerjee (Bengal), B.P.L. Bedi (Punjab), P. Sundarayya (Andhra), etc. Certain socialists like Acharya Narendra Dev and Jayaprakash Narayan were very vocal on peasant issues.

In fact, what we find is a five-tier peasant leadership: leaders at the grassroots level; those influential in certain regions; peasant leaders taking active part in provincial politics; and those who, following the formation of the All India Kisan Sabha in 1936, were making their presence felt at the national level and also the ones with ideology.

Raj Kumar Sukul is, perhaps, the first name among the local peasant leaders of which we know during a period when the element of mass mobilization was being introduced in the Congress. Formerly a fairly rich peasant but now almost ruined, Raj Kumar 'was filled with a passion to wash away the stain of indigo for the thousands who were suffering as he had suffered'.[37] Having lost faith in official channels, this one time rich but now ruined peasant narrated his people's woes before the Bihar Provincial Conference at Chapra on 6 April 1915, but failed to evoke any response:[38] 'When nothing was done by anyone, then becoming hopeless I went to the Lucknow Congress in December 1916.'

Tilak and Malaviya had no time for the indigo cultivators and Gandhi would give no opinion unless he had seen the situation himself. Gandhi entrusted to Brij Kishore (an advocate) the task to move a resolution and leave him free for the present.[39] The resolution was limited to enquire into the 'strained relations between

[37] Gandhi, op. cit., p. 404.

[38] Statement of Sukul before the Champaran Enquiry Committee, in B.B. Misra (ed.), *Select Documents on Mahatma Gandhi's Movement in Champaran* (Patna, 1963), p. 278.

[39] Gandhi, op. cit., p. 404.

the indigo ryots and European planters in North Bihar and to suggest remedies there for'.[40] This, in the words of Gandhi, made Sukul 'glad' but 'far from satisfied'.[41] Its limited nature apart, the resolution made no mention of the scope, time span or agency of the enquiry.

Sukul had expressed fears about his fate on return to his village:[42] 'I am a ryot of Champaran. I do not know what I shall have to suffer when I go back to Champaran for my coming here and relating the story to you all.'

But he was determined to go ahead in his mission. The Commissioner of Tirhut reported 'recrudescence of trouble as regards the relations of landlord and tenant in Champaran district since the return from Lucknow of one Raj Kumar Sukul'.[43]

This suggests that Sukul attempted to organize the peasants as, in the official language; raiyats were 'being intimidated and forced to join the anti-landlord movement'.[44] The indigo peasants had a history of militant uprisings and, as the official reports show, a movement was already there when Gandhi appeared on the scene to conduct an enquiry.

A fresh quarrel with a planter' and another incident in which the modesty of some women had been violated by the factory people became the immediate reasons for Sukul rushing to Calcutta to fetch Gandhi. This time Lomraj, another cultivator whose daughter's modesty had been violated, was with him. Burning with agony, Lomraj had told Gandhi at Bankipore that 'he would commit suicide' if he refused to come.[45] Gandhi's visit to Champaran and what followed thereafter is well known. Here we are interested in analysing some of Gandhi's impressions and observations about Sukul.

In his autobiography Gandhi wrote: 'Thus this ignorant, un-

[40] D.G. Tendulkar, *Gandhi in Champaran* (Bombay, 1955), p. 24.

[41] Gandhi, op. cit., p. 405.

[42] Misra, op. cit., p. 55.

[43] Ibid.

[44] Ibid.

[45] Ibid., p. 93.

sophisticated but resolute agriculturist captured me'. He hoped that this simple agriculturist 'must have some influence in Patna'. He had come to know Sukul 'a little more on the journey', and by the time they reached Patna Gandhi had no 'illusions left concerning him'. Sukul was 'perfectly innocent of everything'.[46] Another observation we find in a letter written to Maganlal Gandhi on reaching Patna.[47]

> The man who has brought me here doesn't know anything. He has dumped me at some obscure place. . . . If things go on this way I am not likely to see Champaran. So far as I can see my guide can give me no help and I am in no position to find my own way.

Let us examine how ignorant Sukul was and how helpless he was in assisting Gandhi. The man certainly knew his way to Champaran and had toured around. He had given a fairly accurate account of peasant grievances at the Congress session. His statement before the Agrarian Enquiry Committee shows his knowledge and awareness of peasant oppression.[48] The official literature describes him as a 'local agitator'; 'a sender of false reports to Gandhi'; 'an arch enemy of planters'.[49] Unsophisticated and resolute he was, but not ignorant. It was his understanding of the prevailing situation that made him approach the sophisticated leadership for help. His innocence was that he had taken the vakils to be his friends, and here Gandhi rightly observed,[50] 'poor Raj Kumar was more or less a menial to them (advocates). Between such agriculturist clients and their vakils there is a gulf as wide as the Ganges in flood.'

However, in spite of his awareness of the exploitative relationship between the vakils and their peasant clients, Gandhi depended on the vakils for his enquiry in Champaran. We are not going into the details of the Champaran affair. Yet it would not be out of context to note that Gandhi's intervention was only aimed at and confined

[46] Gandhi, op. cit., p. 405.

[47] *CWMG*, Vol. XIII, pp. 360–1.

[48] Statement of Sukul, cited above in fn. 38.

[49] See S.K. Mittal and Krishan Dutt, 'Raj Kumar Sukul and Peasant Upsurge in Champaran', *Social Scientist*, April 1976.

[50] Gandhi, op. cit., p. 405.

to enquire into certain grievances and, if possible, as Indulal Yagnik put it, to have 'a re-adjustment made of the landlords system, more or less in conformity with similar changes and reforms which had been made before by the government itself in response to the tenants riots'.[51] Nothing was done in the name of the Congress and Gandhi even wanted the press to remain away.[52] At this stage he had not much influence in the Congress and had conducted the enquiry as his personal affair. The government feared that 'Gandhi might very easily put the match to fire' as Champaran was 'in a very readily inflammable condition'.[53] But he poured water on the fire, saying that his mission was aimed at 'making peace with honour'.[54] He even told the manager of Bettiah Raj 'that the refusal to pay rent is due to the stupidity of the raiyats who misinterpreted the order passed'.[55] He constantly advised the peasants not to stop services to the planters, not to withhold rents, not to agitate for higher wages and so on; and all this in the name of improving relations between planters and tenants.[56]

This episode brought Gandhi an all-India fame and a pro-peasant image. Conventional historiography describes Champaran as a great personal victory for Gandhi and the peasants. One would not question the positive gains of the compromise. But recent research has shown that objections were raised to the agreement in Champaran by persons whom official documents describe as the 'more turbulent elements'.[57] Also, the peasantry continued to protest as is clear from a series of local campaigns. But now no national or provincial leader appeared on the scene. As Yagnik observed, 'Gandhi really made Champaran safe and quiet and comfortable for government and planters for many years to come'.[58] Leaders like Rajendra Prasad and Kripalani emerged at the national political scene out of

[51] Indulal Yagnik, *Gandhi As I Know Him* (Delhi, 1943), p. 26.
[52] Gandhi, op. cit., pp. 411–12.
[53] Misra, op. cit., p. 56.
[54] Ibid., p. 59.
[55] Ibid.
[56] Gandhi, op. cit., pp. 428–9.
[57] Misra, op. cit., p. 58.
[58] Yagnik, op. cit., p. 26.

the Champaran episode (their role during this period has been over glorified). But what happened to Sukul? No one seems to have heard about him any more.[59] He was lost. Though Gandhi was introducing the element of mass politics in the Congress, he preferred to stick to the inherited leadership structure within the Congress organization—the leadership of vakils, dominant social groups and the 'vocal' sections.

Our observation gets strength from an incident in Rajputana—the treatment which Motilal Tejawat received at the hands of Gandhi. Motilal organized the Bhils in Sirohi state. He described himself as a follower of Gandhi and launched a no-rent campaign.[60] Here again one finds the element of local peasants' perception of Gandhi and the high hopes pinned on him. The Dewan of Sirohi, Rama Kant Malaviya (a relation of Madan Mohan Malaviya) rushed to inform Gandhi that 'great mischief' was being done under his name. Gandhi acted promptly by denouncing the movement and its leadership in *Young India*.[61] Though upholding their right to withhold payment of taxes, Gandhi not only pointed the odds against them but also advised them to 'lay their grievances before the state authorities and never resort to arms'.[62] This was a total negation of the factors which had forced the Bhils to adopt the course of direct action in their struggle against the State and the British. Their pleading to authorities had brought more oppression in place of succour.

Gandhi sent Manilal Kothari to enquire 'all sorts of complaints against Motilal'. Kothari did this with the 'permission and help' of the state authorities and received full cooperation from them.[63]

[59] Mittal and Dutt, op. cit. It has been rightly pointed out that the Bihar Congress was content with 'providing space in the nationalist media for criticism of planters', and the focus was on the 'planters as Europeans and exploiters, rather than on the structure of landholding', Stephen Henningham, *Peasant Movements in Colonial India: North Bihar 1917–42* (Canberra, 1982), p. 68.

[60] *Young India*, 2 February 1922.

[61] Ibid.

[62] Ibid.

[63] *CWMG*, Vol. XXII, p. 477.

In a letter to Gandhi, Motilal explained his position, but the former's reaction was:[64]

> This letter betrays ignorance about some matters. The British have nothing to do with this issue and the matter ought to have been brought to the notice of the states concerned in a proper manner.

What did Gandhi mean by 'a proper manner?' Petitioning? But that had already failed. It may be pertinent at this juncture to note his views on the emerging anti-British sentiment among the people of princely states.[65]

> We may not, in Indian states, make any comments about the British empire, and refrain from putting them in an awkward position. . . . It may be necessary in British India to condemn British rule, but there should be no need at all to do so in Indian states.

When Gandhi was informed that Motilal was making efforts to introduce prohibition and stop flesh eating and gambling among the Bhils, he acknowledged that these 'activities have brought about an awakening among the Bhils'.[66] This indicates that Gandhi's understanding of awakening was confined to social ills. Awareness of economic exploitation had no scope in it. Gandhi commented that 'there would have been no ground for criticism if he (Motilal) had stayed at one place so that the Bhils could come and meet him instead of roaming around accompanied by groups of them'.[67] Such was the advice of a leader who had the reputation of moving about the countryside listening to peasants' grievances.

Motilal and the Bhils assured Kothari of their peaceful intentions. But the state authorities, with the help of British troops, resorted to crush the Bhils, many of whom were killed in incidents of firing by the troops. There was no condemnation of the violence perpetrated by the state; all that Gandhi had to say was:[68]

[64] Ibid.
[65] Ibid., Vol. XX, p. 477.
[66] *Young India*, 2 March 1922.
[67] *CWMG*, Vol. XXII, p. 476.
[68] *Young India*, 2 March 1922.

I do not know the full details nor do I know the reasons for the action. I can only hope that they will settle the Bhil complaints by appointing an arbitration court and promise free pardon to Motilal if he comes out of the hills and surrenders himself.

Gandhi's concern was to divert the Bhils from the path of economic struggle to social reform:[69]

The Bhils have been long neglected by the states and reformers. If they are given a helping hand, they can become the pride of India. All they need is the spinning wheel in their homes and schools in which their children can receive simple education.

One can go on adding cases like that of Motilal Tejawat. The actions of Sitaram Raju were condemned by the Congress in Andhra Pradesh. But once he died, his name was utilized for mobilizing the people behind the Congress.[70] Swami Vidyanand tried his best to get Congress's support for the oppressed peasants of Darbhanga Raj in Bihar. He kept knocking at the Congress doors, failed to evoke any response and, ultimately started his own movement. The Congress condemned the movement and the Raja crushed it with a heavy hand.[71] The Congress leadership openly preached against the Aika movement in Oudh and condemned Madari Pasi.[72] Motilal Nehru went to the extent of detaining Baba Ram Chandra in Anand Bhawan to establish his own control over the Oudh peasants.[73] Ram Chandra devoted his life to the peasants' cause, remained a staunch supporter of the Congress and a great admirer of Gandhi and Jawaharlal Nehru.[74] His sin was that he criticized the double-faced local and provincial leaders who worked in alliance with the landlords in dealing with the peasants. Jawaharlal, after acknowledging Ram Chandra's role during the 1920–1 movement,

[69] Ibid. I am thankful to Hari Sen (Ramjas College, Delhi) discussion with whom on Motilal enlightened me more on the subject.

[70] A. Murali, 'Alluri Sitarama Raju and the Manyam Rebellion of 1922–4', *Social Scientist*, April 1984.

[71] Henningham, op. cit., pp. 70, 77, 88–9, 95, 197–8.

[72] Kapil Kumar, *Peasants in Revolt*, pp. 200–3.

[73] Baba Ram Chandra Papers (BRP) Part I, Subject Files (SF) No. 1, NMML.

[74] Ibid.

described him in his Autobiography as a 'very irresponsible and unreliable person'.[75] Ram Chandra pleaded that his only fault was that he spent his energies among the peasants working for their welfare and for the Congress cause whereas the position-hungry Congressmen made all sorts of allegations against him.[76] He pinned his hopes on Gandhi and Jawaharlal for justice to the peasantry which never came.

It was only in the raiyatwari regions of Gujarat that Gandhi went ahead with no-revenue campaigns at Kheda and Bardoli. Here, too, some facts have to be noted: (a) The confrontation was with the British government and no native landlords were involved. (b) The campaigns were not launched under the Congress auspices. (c) They were taken up as experiments by Gandhi. (d) The background for no-revenue campaigns was prepared by ex-revolutionaries, Mohanlal Pandeya and Shankerlal in Kheda and Kunwarji Mehta in Bardoli, (e) The lower sections among the peasants like the *dublas* and *bharaiyas* were ignored and leaders like Indulal Yagnik were pushed aside by Gandhi in the organizational hierarchy of the Congress. Hardiman has demonstrated that no doubt the movements were a success in terms of political mobilization, but in terms of their economic implications for the peasantry, they were a failure.[77]

Mobilization among the peasants was carried on by touching on their economic grievances, the solution to which lay in fighting for and achieving swaraj. The demands put forward by the Congress related to a variety of economic issues. But the peasant was absent from these demands, except by way of reference to reduction in land revenue; and that incidentally, would have affected the raiyatwari regions only. The demands were calculated more to benefit the trading community, capitalists and other dominant sections of the Indian society.[78] On the other hand, the peasants on their own

[75] Nehru, *An Autobiography* (Delhi, 1962), p. 53.

[76] BRP, Speeches and Writing, F. No. 2A.

[77] David Hardiman, *Peasant Nationalists of Gujrat: Kheda District 1917–34* (New Delhi), 1981.

[78] See Sumit Sarkar, 'The Logic of Gandhian Nationalism: Civil Disobedience and the Gandhi–Irwin Pact, 1930–1', *Indian Historical Review*, July 1976.

attached their economic grievances to the political issues, and this alarmed the Congress. The peasant pressure for including the no-rent demand was a contributory factor in the hasty retreat of the Congress struggles in 1922 and 1931.

In Gujarat (in 1931) Gandhi's stand was to assure the peasants that they 'would get their lands (back) at no distant date'. On the issue of land revenue his attitude was ambiguous: 'to pay if they could but if they could not pay they should not be afraid to refuse'.[79] After the withdrawal of the movement the peasants in UP continued to press for their demand of reduction in rent. This disturbed the Congress leadership, and Gandhi wrote to Mohanlal Saxena:[80] 'On your side it's all well, so long as you *hold the kisans* in *check.* But Jawaharlal's presence must now ease the situation. He has no difficulty in dealing with the kisans and restraining them.'

It is worth mentioning here the tactics adopted by Jawaharlal to restrain the peasants. Kalka Prasad, the Secretary of the Rai Bareilly DCC, wanted to peacefully picket the house of a landlord, Umanath Baksh Singh, who had evicted all the tenants who had participated in the Civil Disobedience movement. The demand of the peasants was restoration of holdings and some picketing took place. Jawaharlal suspended Kalka Prasad not only from the post of secretary but from the Congress too. The landlord, who had actively crushed the Congress movement in his estate, was assured by Jawaharlal:[81] 'I am sorry that Kalka Prasad behaved in this manner and put you to trouble. But I hope you realize that Congress *has nothing to do with any such acts.*'

Jawaharlal further wrote to him:[82]

> You will appreciate that this is the fault of some misguided individuals. We propose to take action against them. . . . Meanwhile I shall be glad if you will inform me of any grievance that you might have against the local Congress workers.

[79] *Bombay Chronicle*, 29 April 1931.

[80] Gandhi to Mohanlal Saxena, 15 June 1931, *CWMG*, Vol. XLVI, p. 384.

[81] Nehru to Umanath Baksh Singh, 25 July 1931, AICC Papers, F. No. G-59/1931, NMML.

[82] Nehru to Umanath Baksh Singh, 28 July 1931, ibid.

This was another example of how the lower level pro-peasant leadership within the Congress was a victim of the pro-landlord leadership at the higher levels in the organizational hierarchy of the Congress.

III

During the mid-1930s there was considerable awakening among the peasants, and the formation of the All India Kisan Sabha offered the Left forces an opportunity to mobilize the peasants at an all India level. I have elsewhere discussed this formation and its impact on the Congress which led to the adoption of an agrarian programme at Faizpur.[83] Here I shall analyse only the extent to which the peasants had been 'worked up' (a phrase used by the conservative leadership in relation to the peasants' awakening) by the Congress propaganda itself.

There is ample evidence to indicate that the Congress election propaganda rested on highlighting economic issues in the countryside. Nehru instructed the Congress volunteers that the Faizpur Agrarian Programme had 'great importance' and 'the vast body of our rural electors and others will appreciate it'.[84] He stressed that it should 'find a prominent place in our election campaign, especially in the rural areas'.[85] Canvassing among the Allahabad villagers, he stated.[86]

> There were only two parties in India—those fighting for the cause of the people and the other against it. They (people) had no power to solve the problem of poverty. Only a handful of people were ruling over them. . . . Whether the rulers were Indians or Englishmen, they only knew how to further their ends. . . . The Congress was going to the Councils to keep out Khan Bahadurs, Raja Bahadurs and Nawabs who sided with government.

Sardar Patel told the peasants that it was only the Congress candidate 'who will sooner or later help him out of the morass—of poverty

[83] See Kapil Kumar, 'Congress–Peasant Relationship', pp. 235–6.
[84] *Bombay Sentinel*, 4 January 1937.
[85] Ibid.
[86] *Bombay Chronicle*, 26 January 1937.

into which he is sunk'.[87] The Faizpur programme was coming up to the expectations of the right wing leadership and its allies as the peasant rallied round the Congress. A feeling seemed to gain ground that Congress Raj would replace the British Raj in two months' time. The following example from UP is one out of many which demonstrates why and how the peasant expectations had gone up:[88]

> Congress volunteers are going about with notebooks and asking tenants what their present rent was? The tenant says perhaps Rs. 2 a bigha. The Congress volunteer says: 'That's all right. If you vote for the Congress that will be put down to 4 annas.' He writes it down in his notebook and the unfortunate villager is duly impressed.

An interesting development of such propaganda was that in many CP villages peasants cast their votes in what they thought was 'Gandhibox' believing that Gandhi himself was a candidate.[89] In Bihar 'some of the voters regarded the ballot box as a letterbox for Gandhi and smuggled in petitions addressed to him with their voting papers'.[90]

The Congress victory in elections was attributed by the governors to the name of Gandhi and 'due to wild Congress promises of reduction in rent, canal taxes and chaukidari tax'.[91] In fact the victory was a combination of nationalist feelings with economic issues, with the latter playing a crucial role. The failure of the Congress in Bengal was, besides other factors, related to the pro-landlord stance of the party in comparison to a moderate economic programme offered by the Proja Krishak Party.[92] The Bengal Con-

[87] Ibid. After the elections those peasants who supported the Congress had to further face oppression by zamindars, *Bombay Chronicle*, 19 February 1937; *Sangharsh*, 19 September 1937.

[88] Haig to Linlithgow, 29 October 1936, LP, No. 112.

[89] *Bombay Chronicle*, 13 February 1937.

[90] James Sifton to Linlithgow, 9 February 1937, LP, No. 112.

[91] Ibid.

[92] *Indian Annual Register*; Vol. II, 1936, p. 984. In fact, the peasant vote became so vital during this period that even communal organizations like the Hindu Maha Sabha and the Muslim League tried to lure the peasants by declaring their readiness to work for the peasants' cause. Ibid.

gress, right from the Swarajist days, had pursued a policy favourable to the landlords. This later on became a contributory factor in the emergence of communalism as a dominating leverage of political control.

During the interim ministry period the pro-office acceptance lobby in the Congress utilized the sentiments of the kisans to put pressure for ministry formation. When the Nawab of Chhattari formed his ministry in UP, Congress leaders encouraged peasants not to pay rents. They assured the peasants that all arrears of rent would be remitted when the Congress took office.[93] When the Congress really did so, its first advice to the peasants was 'pay rents immediately' or else 'it would lead to ejectment.'[94] Similarly, in Bihar the work of the Kisan Enquiry Committee was revived as a cover to preach office acceptance. The Governor of Bihar informed the Viceroy:[95] 'It is significant that at all the meetings which they have held they do not pay much attention to the grievances of the tenants . . . but in their speeches refer to the office acceptance question.'

Various studies of peasant mobilization by the Congress reveal that prior to the Non-Cooperation movement the Congress leaders were keen to show that it had a rural following in order to contradict the British propaganda about its limited representative character. They were 'glad' to see peasant delegates at the sessions, but were indifferent to their demands. During the non-cooperation days economic issues were raised to mobilize the peasants. All kinds of promises were made in the name of swaraj, but the thrust was to sidetrack economic issues.[96]

Charkha was offered as the remedy of all ills and Gandhi was the doctor who prescribed this. A similar situation existed during

[93] Quarterly Survey of Political and Constitutional Position in British India No. I, LP, No. 142.

[94] *Amrita Bazar Patrika*, 2 January 1938; *Hindustan Times*, 1 January 1938; the Fortnightly Report read: 'Congressmen generally helpful in Inducing tenants to pay rents', Home Political No. 18/1/19-38, NAI.

[95] Halet to Linlithgow, 10 May 1937, LP, No. 113.

[96] See Kapil Kumar, *Peasants in Revolt*, p. 230.

the days of civil disobedience and the elections of 1931. It is crucial to analyse the Congress attitude towards the peasantry during a period when there was no movement or direct struggle against the British. The period between 1931 and 1939, when the Congress was in power, provides us an opportunity to study this.

IV

Nehru observed in 1931: 'The outstanding problem of India is the peasant problem. All else is secondary.' The coming of Congress ministries, he felt, had given new hope and new life to the peasants whereas the big zamindars and taluqdars were 'organizing to resist this long deferred justice to the peasantry'.[97] He stressed that 'we must remain true to our pledges and give satisfaction and fulfilment to the hopes of the peasantry'.[98] The peasants and the Kisan Sabhas welcomed these public statements of the Congress president and anxiously waited for the implementation of the Faizpur agrarian programme under the Congress ministries. However, the statements of the Congress president and the agrarian programme of the Congress had no impact on the right wing leaders. Once in office this leadership was busy devising ways and means to check the Left in general and the Kisan Sabhas in particular.

In a letter to Rajendra Prasad, Sardar Patel wrote:[99]

> The Kisan Sabha will give much greater trouble in future and my opinion has definitely been against its formation. They are waiting for a time when they could displace us. That is why I have given them no quarters . . . we must fairly and squarely face the situation at Calcutta, a few months later we will not be able to control the situation created by them.

During the Calcutta AICC meeting in October 1931 it was strongly felt by the right wing that they should organize themselves, and Jairamdas Doulatram's suggestion that 'we should not sit down . . .

[97] *AICC Papers*, P-9/1937.

[98] Ibid.

[99] Patel to Prasad, 2 October 1937, *Rajendra Prasad Correspondence and Selected Writings*, Vol. I, Delhi, 1984, p. 103.

any more' was put into active operation.[100] Instructions were issued that all 'orthodox programmewallas' would work in a concerted manner or else there would be 'great difficulty' in future.[101] In clear language Patel wrote to Prasad:[102]

> Bapu is not at all happy. . . . Anyway we may have a fixed struggle at Haripura . . . please see that in selection of delegates, *eliminate all anti-Gandhi elements.* We must no more tolerate the forces of dis-order in the name of united front. They have taken undue advantage of our toleration, but time has come for a definite stand.

Prasad assured Patel: 'I have asked friends in the districts to be vigilant and to organize as suggested by you.'[103] Clearly Gandhi's faithful followers were busy ensuring that the Left did not move up in the organizational hierarchy. Better still if it could be obliged to leave the Congress on its own. How things were made difficult for the pro-peasant Congressmen to function within the Congress we shall discuss a little later.

The British, worried about the 'agrarian danger', encouraged the Congress ministers to act against the Kisan Sabha. The Viceroy asked the Governor of Bihar to 'give a bed time story' to his ministers of how in 'the good old days the Government used to stop nonsense of this sort'.[104] The story must have been told, for the Governor replied with pride:[105] 'My ministers seem to me to realize the danger fully; they are prepared to watch the major kisan leaders and have agreed that their speeches should be reported.'

The ministers were more than willing to oblige. They even 'advocated that the Kisan leaders' correspondence should be intercepted'.[106] The Bihar PCC imposed a ban on the participation of Congressmen in the Kisan Sabha. Patel welcomed this action:[107]

[100] Prasad to Sri Krishna Sinha, 2 December 1937, ibid., p. 131.

[101] Ibid.

[102] Patel to Prasad; 7 December 1931, ibid., p. 141.

[103] Prasad to Patel, 28 November 1937, RPP, Roll 5.

[104] Linlithgow to Hallet, 26 December 1937, LP, No. 110.

[105] Hallet to Linlithgow, 11 November 1937, ibid., No. 113.

[106] Hallet to Linlithgow, 5 December 1937, ibid.

[107] Patel to Prasad, 16 December 1937, RPP, Roll 5.

Personally I feel that such action should have been taken long ago, but better late than never is also a good thing. I hope it is not too late to mend matters and to prevent the enormous mischief that Swami (Sahajanand) is doing.

The Champaran, Saran and Monghyr district Congress Committees instructed Sahajanand—a member of the Bihar PCC and president of the Bihar Kisan Sabha—not to visit their districts. Local Congressmen were threatened with disciplinary actions if they attended his meetings.[108] This ban came at time when the Congress right wing had signed an agreement with zamindars. The two had joined hands to crush the kisan movement. It is significant here to cite Chandreshwar Prasad Singh's letter to Prasad:[109]

I am in entire agreement with your ideas regarding our taking action jointly whenever we find such a course profitable to adopt. I shall be perfectly willing to render you such assistance as may be in this connection.

The zamindari agents and the right wing followers tried their best to disrupt Sahajanand's tour of the districts. But the peasantry responded in large numbers and foiled their attempts. This incident was important for another reason. Sahajanand was a member of the Bihar PCC working committee but the lower level Congress committees had taken action against him with full support from right wingers. The PCC later on endorsed this action. The Kisan Sabha was given no opportunity to explain its stand. Sahajanand raised the issue of civil liberties,[110] but Prasad and Patel were determined to oppose the Kisan Sabha at all levels.

The Bihar PCC's action was to be discussed at the Bombay CWC meeting. Prasad knew that 'we should have to be in the position of accused persons' and 'we must be ready with our defence'.[111] He collected CID reports relating to the activities of the Kisan Sabha

[108] *Congress Socialist* II, December 1937, for details see Kapil Kumar, 'Congress–Peasant Relationship', p. 242.

[109] C.P. Singh to Prasad, 1 January 1938, RPP, F. No. III/1937, NAI.

[110] *The Hindustan Times*, 5 January 1938.

[111] Prasad to Sri Krisna Sinha, 22 December 1937, RPP, Roll 8.

leaders from the Premier of Bihar.[112] These were discussed with Gandhi by Patel, Prasad, Azad, Rajagopalachari, and Jamnalal Bajaj.[113] The Premier of Bihar had told Patel that 'if only the Working Committee will support them through thick and thin instead of censuring them at every step, they will manage Bihar well'.[114] At the same time the Premier assured the Governor of Bihar that 'he would get that support (from the CWC) so long as Mr. Gandhi was alive'.[115] The CWC supported the Bihar PCC's action without even asking the Kisan Sabha or its leadership to explain its stand.

Let us examine the 'enormous mischief' of which Swami Sahajanand was accused by the right wingers. In actual practice he was making the peasants aware of their rights; organizing them; urging them to join the Congress in large numbers and remind the ministers to implement the much propagated Faizpur agrarian programme; asking the Congress leaders to fulfil the promises made during the elections; preaching self-defensive measures against the violence perpetrated by the landlords, thus struggling not only against the British but also against their allies within the Indian society. This was termed as working against the Congress creed and breaking the Congress discipline.[116] The Kisan Sabha was also accused of sheltering disgruntled elements who were hostile to the Congress; but no specific names were ever cited in this regard. Another charge was that the Kisan Sabha preached violence and was creating an atmosphere of class-war.[117] Nowhere did the Kisan Sabha incite attacks on landlords. On the contrary, the peasants were advised to adopt collective self-defensive measures such as prostrating in the fields if forcefully evicted. In fact, for the right wing even Gandhian forms of struggle were tantamount to violence if adopted against

[112] Ibid.

[113] *Search Light*, 5 January 1938.

[114] Mahadev Desai to Birla, 22 December 1937, in G.D. Birla, op. cit., p. 127.

[115] Hallet to Linlithgow, 7 January 1938, LP No. 44.

[116] For the controversy between Sahajanand and the Bihar PCC, see Kapil Kumar, 'Congress–Peasant Relationship', pp. 242–3.

[117] *Harijan*, 22 January 1938.

the landlords. Working against the declared Congress policy of consulting the Kisan Sabha and negotiating with the landlords were not considered as acts of indiscipline by the right wing. But if the peasants as a protest against this deviation, peacefully marched to the councils demanding justice and implementation of Congress promises, that was 'indiscipline'.

We have earlier mentioned Patel's instructions to Prasad regarding the selection of AICC delegates for the Haripura session. During the election of delegates there was massive violence, intimidation and booth capturing in many regions of Bihar.[118] Incidentally we have the Report of the Violence Enquiry Committee (VEC) which reveals the methods adopted by all the anti-Left forces to crush the Kisan Sabha. The Report pointed out that there was a 'widespread desire to capture Congress organizations by all kinds of people so that the position of advantage might be used for securing patronage for themselves, their friends and relations, and for capturing, local bodies'.[119]

There was a planned attempt by the right wing and the zamindars to establish their firm hold over the Congress organization. We list here the methods adopted by them in this regard:[120]

1. Congress membership forms or receipt books were refused to peasants where as a large number of zamindari *amalas* (agents) were enrolled as Congress members.
2. Constituencies were carved in such a manner as to split the peasant or pro-peasant voters within the Congress.
3. Wherever it was possible, the Kisan Sabha members were not allowed to file nomination papers or their papers were rejected.
4. Propaganda against pro-Kisan Sabha Congressmen was carried on the lines that as socialists they were persons who did not believe in God or that they had been turned out of the Congress.[121]
5. Right wing loyalists or pro-zamindari persons were appointed as returning officers.[122]

[118] *Janta*, 5 January 1938.
[119] AICC Papers, P 6/1939–40.
[120] Ibid.
[121] *Sangharsh*, 7 January 1938.
[122] AICC Papers, P 6/1939–40.

6. Elections were manipulated. There were many cases where the election process remained incomplete and yet the returning officers declared the pro-zamindari candidates as winners. Later on the VEC questioned the basis of these declarations.
7. Where the Kisan Sabha candidates had won, their election was set aside by the DCC tribunals on one pretext or another.[123]
8. To cover up these manipulations kisan sabhaite Congressmen were implicated in cases of violence and criminal cases were instituted against them. This was done under instructions from the Bihar Premier and a jubilant Governor informed the Viceroy: 'My Prime Minister tells me that his followers are starting criminal cases'.[124] Pro-peasant Congressmen, while facing the violence of the zamindari and right wing sponsored candidates, did not approach the police owing to their fidelity to the Congress directive that 'in a dispute between Congressmen regarding Congress affairs the aid of civil authorities should not be invoked.[125] When the VEC toured the areas to look into the charges against the Kisan Sabha, it was the pro-zamindari and right wing loyalists who refused to cooperate with the Committee.[126] The VEC found no truth in the allegations against the Kisan Sabha. But its report, being an indictment of the right wing forces, was not made public.

The situation in other provinces was not much different as far as the tactics of the right wing were concerned. In UP a close watch was kept on pro-peasant Congressmen. The UP PCC's circular of 7 June 1938 asked the local committees to send regular reports regarding the activities of the Kisan Sabha. The following points were to be taken special care of in the reports:[127]

1. Is there any tension between the Kisan Sabha and the Congress?
2. No such person is active in the Kisan Sabha against whom disciplinary action was taken.

[123] Ibid.
[124] Hallet to Linlithgow, 7 January 1938, LP, No. 44.
[125] AICC Papers, P-6/1939-40; P-3 (I1)/1938–9.
[126] Ibid.
[127] Ibid.

3. Is the flag of the Kisan Sabha the tri-colour one or some other?
4. Are the Congress members hurt by the Kisan Sabha activities?
5. Whether the Kisan Sabha is affiliated to any provincial organization? Whether its accounts are managed or not? What influence does it carry with the people?

Mohanlal Saxena stressed in a confidential circular to the PCC members:[128]

At a time when the Congress had to meet the onslaughts from the Muslim League, the zamindars and taluqdars and the capitalists interests, for any section of the Congressmen to go about propagating that the Congress has betrayed the kisans and that they should not expect any good from it, is nothing short of, treason and needs being dealt with a strong hand.

He was prepared to accept taluqdari and capitalist attack on Congress, but he would not take the peasants' support against them. What a section of Congressmen was being accused of preaching was not true. In fact this section was opposing the increasing influence of the taluqdars in the Congress and urging the Congress to protect itself from opportunists who were bringing a bad name to it.

Baba Ram Chandra was one such Congressman for whom Gandhi was the only leader and Congress the supreme party. But his worry was that the capitalists and landlords were '*destroying our pious Congress*'.[129] Congressmen were, 'flowing in the stream of office acceptance', and landlords were joining the national body 'not to serve the people but in order to control the people through various legal provisions'. He admitted that by acquiring office the Congress had brought some light to the darker life of the peasants. But on the whole they remained entrapped by 'thugs, under whose influence the Congress forgets its real self and we have to face miseries'. He was afraid that even swaraj would not end the 'people's miseries if such people took over from the White sarkar'.[130] The Congress commitment to serve the people was being altered under

[128] Ibid.
[129] BRP. SF, No. 3.
[130] Ibid.

the influence of landlords:[131] 'By practising oppression efforts are being made to weaken the kisans and mazdurs and make them submissive. The kisans are every day sending evidences in this regard to the Congress office.'

So critical was he of the functioning of local level Congress leaders that he wrote:[132]

> After wearing khadi and being Congress leaders, with the help of police they assault the peasants. By this treachery they are ruining the Congress. . . . Congress dress, stick in hand, with police at their back, then why dust should not be thrown in the eyes of the ministers.

He asserted that like 'managers and agents had destroyed princes and landlords, some *khaddardharis* (those who wore *khaddar*) were destroying the Congress; the outcome was that instead of peace there was corruption'.

It was no coincidence that such voices were raised in other regions also. In Vishakhapatnam a Congress Vigilance Committee was formed to save the Congress from 'cunning calculating politicians who newly joined the Congress' and 'created a mercenary army amongst primary members . . . to fight election battles'. V. Anuntha Rao, the secretary of this committee, called for a 'cleanse the Congress campaign' in order to maintain the sanctity of the Congress organization.[133] The Partapgarh DCC, worried about the growing influence of peasants within the organization, suspended its elections. In Dehradun the demand for introducing secret ballot in organizational elections, made by the ordinary members (*prajavarg*), was consistently rejected by the DCC office bearers (*adhikarivarg*).[134] Villagers from Ballia also complained to Nehru about malpractices in delegates' elections.[135]

We may mention here the suspension of Markande Singh from the post of Secretary, Varanasi DCC. He was actively associated with an agitation against an oppressive zamindar. The District

[131] Ibid.
[132] Ibid.
[133] AICC Papers, F. No. P-3 (p-II)/1938-39.
[134] Ibid.
[135] Ibid.

Magistrate complained to the DCC about this, and the latter described it as a serious breach of Congress discipline. However, Markande Singh was debarred from holding office in DCC or Mandal CC for two years on the charge of financial irregularities that allegedly amounted to Rs. 5. The action taken against him, the DCC asserted, was on the milder side because 'it was greatly due to his efforts that Congress gained its strength in the district during the last year. His hard work and popularity went a long way in securing a thundering majority for the Congress during the last elections'.[136]

In Madras Rajagopalachari ridiculed Jagannathadas for arranging functions for Indulal Yagnik as 'the general impression among our friends in Bombay is that he is no more helpful to Congress and distinctly the opposite'.[137] Another example of his onslaught on the left was what he wrote to Pattabhi Sitaramayya:[138]

> Ignorance of the working of political institutions and actors on the political stage outside our province combined with incorrigible tendency to offer pooja to outsiders leads our municipal bodies and local organizations, to all sorts of irreconcilable positions and stupid resolutions. What is the meaning of Masulipatem Municipality to present address of welcome to Mr. Giri and Mr. M.N. Roy?

And soon a circular was issued to *taluq* and district Congress committees that they should, seek prior permission from the PCC for arranging such functions. David Arnold's study demonstrates that Rajagopalachari was inviting zamindars and capitalists to join the Congress so that they could protect their interests.[139]

An important episode of Rajagopalachari's premiership was the prosecution of S.S. Batliwala who used to come from Bombay to organize the peasants. In the Venkatagiri zamindari he delivered a speech on 3 September 1937, highlighting the sufferings of the

[136] Ibid.

[137] Rajagopalachari to Jagannathadas, 20 May 1937, *C. Rajagopalachari Papers* (CRP), Roll I, NMML.

[138] Rajagopalachari to Pattabhi, 7 June 1937, ibid.

[139] David Arnold, *The Congress in Tamilnad: Nationalist Politics in South India 1919–37* (New Delhi, 1977), pp. 167–8.

people and attributing them to exploitation by the Maharaja (a Justice Party member). The redressal of the grievances was to be sought by becoming members of the Congress, organizing themselves, and representing their grievances to the Congress ministers.[140] Rajagopalachari was 'very anxious' about his arrest before he could make any more speeches. Soon he was arrested. During, the prosecution Rajagopalachari 'took the trouble personally to go through the public prosecutor's arguments to the court and suggested amendments'.[141] Rajagopalachari was very keen that the 'attack on constituted government and incitement to violence should be stressed and as little as possible made of the attacks on Great Britain and British rule'.[142] Why such a course was advocated became clear as the case proceeded. Batliwala's defence was that as the official policy of the Congress party was the 'severance of the British connection, he cannot be punished for advocating the policy of the party in power'.[143] To justify his defence he asked for the presence of the Premier as a witness. This was refused by the judge. In spite of the assessors' verdict of not guilty, Batliwala was sentenced to six mohths' simple imprisonment. A jubilant Rajagopalachari commented that the 'prosecution had the desired results' as no 'such speeches were delivered in Madras after that'.[144]

In Bombay Congress MLAs went around warning the peasants not to join the kisan sabhas.[145] When Parulekar introduced certain amendments in the Small Landholders Relief Bill, the ministers felt that the Bill already went further than they liked. At the same time, they knew that their 'supporters would be unwilling' to vote against the amendments. The only course left for the ministers was to check the introduction of the amendments, and for this they approached the Governor of Bombay. The latter reported to the Viceroy.[146]

[140] LP, Roll 6S.
[141] Ibid.
[142] Ibid.
[143] Ibid.
[144] Ibid.
[145] *Congress Socialist*, 11 December 1937.
[146] Governor of Bombay to Viceroy, 25 January 1938, LP, No. 5.

They were, however, most reluctant to make the bill any wider than originally proposed and so he (Home Minister) hoped that I would come to their rescue by making use of my discretionary power to prevent the introduction of any widening amendments. I told him that in other words, he wanted the Governor rather than the minister to shoulder responsibility of turning down a popular proposal, and that I do not regard that as a proper course to adopt. . . . I am quite convinced that their attempt to make the Governor use his discretion to get ministers out of their parliamentary difficulties had to be resisted.

It may be noted that the use of discretionary powers by the governors was made an issue by the Congress at the time of office acceptance. Thus, Jayaprakash Narayan was not lying when he observed: 'While formerly they could see who their enemies were, at present the Gandhi cap and *khaddar kurta* stood between the people and their enemies, shielding the latter from the attacks of the former.'[147]

The Prime Minister of Orissa withdrew certain concessions which he was about to offer to the peasantry as a part of Congress policy on the instructions of Prasad.[148] Nand Kishore Das, Deputy Speaker of the Orissa Assembly, congratulated Prasad for taking a bold stand against the Kisan Sabha and thus showing the way to the Orissa PCC to deal with the peasants.[149] The peasants of Orissa had high hopes from the Congress ministry. They were stunned when the zamindar of Kalli Kote had lorry loads of Reserve Police paraded in his villages to warn them that even in Congress regime he was as powerful as ever.[150]

We are not going into the details of tenancy legislation in various Congress ruled provinces. But the overall picture which emerges indicates a pro-zamindari tilt on the part of Congress ministries.[151] In April 1938 the Viceroy reported back home:[152] 'The ministries

[147] *Times of India*, 26 January 1938.

[148] Premier of Orissa to Prasad, 7 December 1937, RPP, Roll 5, NMML.

[149] *Amrita Bazar Patrika*, 14 January 1938.

[150] N.G. Ranga to S.C. Bose, 11 January 1937, Indulal Yagnik Papers (IYP). Subject Files 14, NMML.

[151] All the provincial Governors expressed this opinion to the Viceroy on the tenancy bills.

[152] LP, No. 142.

deserve credit for meeting this threat with resolution. The policy of the Congress party towards the kisan organizations has been firm, and even repressive.'

In the same month Gandhi wrote in *Harijan*:[153]

My study of separate kisan organizations has led me definitely to the conclusion that they are not working for the interests of kisans but are organized only with a view to capturing the Congress organization. They can do even this by leading the kisans along the right channels, but I am afraid they are misleading them. If the kisans and their leaders will capture the Congress by doing nothing but authorized Congress work, there is no harm. But if they do so by making false registers, storming meetings and so on, it will be something like Fascism.

As always with Gandhi, it was the kisan, his organization and his leadership which were at fault, not the zamindars or the right wing leaders on whose information Gandhi's study of kisan organizations was based.

The onslaught on the Kisan Sabha was further encouraged by capitalists like G.D. Birla. Birla was a crucial link between the Congress leaders, Congress ministers and the British government.[154] A unique feature of the Indian transition towards capitalism is the support extended to feudalism by the capitalists. The latter left no stone unturned to see that the peasant movement was crushed. Birla himself owned a zamindari of eight lakhs in Bihar.[155] He 'very much disliked the peasants in Bihar marching to the Assembly house', and wrote to Mahadev Desai:[156]

I fear that in course of time indiscipline will grow more and more unless strict measures are taken. I only hope that the Congress authorities are fully alive to the situation and they will take all necessary measures.

Birla often acted as a messenger, to convey to the Viceroy the assurances given by the ministers, with regard to 'agrarian trouble':[157]

[153] *Harijan*, 23 April 1938.

[154] This observation is based on an examination of correspondence among Gandhi, Mahadev Desai, G.B. Pant, Rajagopalachari, Birla, etc.

[155] G.D. Birla, op. cit., p. 308.

[156] Ibid.

[157] Ibid.

Pantji sent back a very reassuring letter saying there was nothing to worry about agrarian trouble or Cawnpore (where the workers were fighting for their rights) and that he was keeping his fingers on the pulse. I conveyed this reassuring news to the Viceroy who was quite pleased.

Another good news for the Viceroy was that 'all big leaders of the Gandhi Seva Sangh were strenuously working to fight violence' in the countryside.[158]

Various controversies relating to the *danda* cult, flag issue or peasant marches to the councils have been dealt with elsewhere.[159] The imprisonment and prosecution of peasant leaders continued unabated under the Congress ministries (one can cite here the arrests of Rahul Sankrityayan, Jadunandan Sharma, etc.) Though the Congress stood for the release of political prisoners, the UP ministry assured the Governor that it would not press for the release of Chauri Chaura prisoners as they did not come under the category of political prisoners.[160] In Bihar those political prisoners who were on hunger strike for their release in the Hazari Bagh jail were told by a minister that more important than their release was the question of giving agrarian relief to the peasants;[161] whereas the peasants were told that more important was the release of political prisoners. When political prisoners were eventually released, both Gandhi and the right wing opposed their public welcome. Gandhi lamented:[162] 'If my reading of the Congress method is correct, the large public demonstration that took place on the discharge of Kakori prisoners was, to say the least; a political mistake.'

Contrary to the fears of the right wing, even Nehru shared the condemnation of this demonstration in UP.[163]

There was a big gap in Nehru's utterances and actions. On every occasion when it came to taking sides he backed out from supporting the Kisan Sabha and sided with the right wing.[164] At the

[158] Ibid.

[159] See Kapil Kumar, 'Congress–Peasants Relationship'.

[160] Haig to Linlithgow, 20 January 1938, HP, Roll 2, NMML.

[161] Krishanaballabh Sahay to Prasad, 13 October 1937, RPP, Roll 8, NMML.

[162] G.D. Birla, op. cit., p. 81.

[163] Ibid.

[164] See Kapil Kumar, 'Congress–Peasant Relationship', pp. 238, 248.

Haripura session he strongly defended the views expressed against the Kisan Sabha in the General Secretary's report.[165] Even after the Congress ministries had laid down office in 1939, he advised Shibban Lal Saxena to refrain from pro-peasant activities in Gorakhpur, and assured the Viceroy in this regard.[166] However, in public he maintained a pro-Left stance.

The Kisan Sabha, all through the 1930s, constantly supported the Congress. At no stage did it ever pose an alternative to the Congress or worked against it—even at the time when it faced direct action from the right wing. In spite of its anti-landlord ideology, the Kisan Sabha even compromised once the landlords had been taken in as Congress candidates during the elections. This was done as the Congress was considered as the supreme organization that the Kisan Sabha was bound to follow.[167] Though opposed to office acceptance, the Kisan Sabha stood by the Congress decision. It expected the ministries to bring relief to the peasants. But even when the right wing joined hands with the landlords, ignoring the Kisan Sabha, the kisan leaders organized the peasantry to remind the Congress of its pledges and promises to the peasantry, without ever opposing the Congress. As Sahajanand put it:[168]

> It is not understandable why the ministers are afraid of peasant demonstrations and meetings. . . . If we don't hold them now when will we hold them. . . . It is wrong to say that these are aimed at expressing no-confidence in the ministries.

The great 'mischief monger', as the rightists described him, always asserted.[169]

> I believe in the basic principles of the Congress. . . . I accept them not merely because they are the principles of the Congress but because under the peculiar conditions for the freedom of the country and emancipation of the kisans from oppression and exploitation no other line of work is possible.

[165] *Amrita Bazar Patrika*, 17 January 1935. See also, Kapil Kumar, 'Ideology, Congress and Peasants in 1930s: Class Adjustment or Submission?', *Social Scientist*, August–September 1986.

[166] Nehru to Linlithgow, 6 October 1939, J. Nehru Papers, Correspondence, Vol. 42, S. No. 2704, NMML.

[167] Sahajanand, op. cit., p. 481.

[168] *Sangharsh*, 10 January 1935.

[169] *Congress Socialist*, 12 March 1935.

Sahajanand tried his best to assure the right wing that whatever *shakti* (strength) he had would be devoted to strengthen the Congress as he had 'faith and confidence in the Congress'. The Kisan Sabhaites also, he pleaded, had the right 'to serve the Congress, the country and the mankind'.[170]

At a time when Vijay Lakshmi Pandit was advocating dictatorship within the Congress[171] and the right wing was virtually begging the government to distinguish between them and the left wing,[172] Sahajanand made it clear:[173]

> We all cling to the Congress not for its magic or mystery, but because it represents the nation, it has not taken any false step at critical junctures. . . . All our attempts are simply to strengthen its hands in taking opportune decisions at this most critical juncture of our national struggle for deliverance.

He declared times without number that none but a lunatic could think of weakening the Congress at the present phase of India's struggle for independence.[174] The Kisan Sabha wanted to transform the creed and mentality of the Congress from within. When N.G. Ranga, in Andhra Pradesh, wanted to come out from the Congress, it was P. Sundarayya who restrained him.[175] And this despite the fact that Sundarayya's nomination paper to contest for the AICC at the time of the Tripuri session had been rejected on the ground that he was a communist.[176] This was another clear case of ideological victimization within the Congress.

The peasants and their organizations were faced with the triple oppression of the British, landlords and the Congress right wing. Still they stood firmly behind the Congress in the struggle. Why was it so? We shall attempt to answer this question at two levels:

170 Ibid.

171 Haig to Linlithgow, 10 April 1939, HP, Roll I.

172 The secret, the confidential correspondence of various provincial governors with the Viceroy refers to, is this attitude of the Congress right wing during 1939–40, LP.

173 Speech on 4 October 1939, IYP, SF, No. 11.

174 Ibid.

175 Ranga to Yagnik, 23 October 1939, IYP, SF, No. 11.

176 AICC Papers, P-3(II)/1938–9.

looking at the stance of the kisan leadership and at the peasants in general. The kisan leadership stood for strengthening the freedom struggle. But it differed from the bourgeois Congress leadership with regard to the direction of the freedom struggle. The kisan leadership was not only for independence from the British rule but also worked for breaking the hegemony of the zamindars and capitalists. Its dilemma was: how to achieve this without weakening the freedom struggle? The policy it pursued was to mobilize the peasants behind the Kisan Sabha as well as the Congress; to strengthen the Congress from within; not to pose an alternative to the Congress and at the same time expose the vested interests in the Congress; go in for constructive criticism if the Congress leadership deviated from its declared policy in relation to the peasantry. At no stage did the kisan leadership ask the peasants to come out of the Congress or withdraw support. It had an altogether different perception of nationalism as understood and propagated by the right wing nationalists.

Right wing nationalism was aimed at achieving freedom from the British and sustaining the hegemony of the dominant social groups in the Indian society. The entire onslaught on the kisan sabhas was motivated by this class outlook. The propaganda that the kisan sabhas were opposed to the Congress was a handy cover to safeguard vested interests and check the growing influence of the Left. The divide between the Left and the Right was not on the issue of violence and non-violence[177] but on firm ideological positions regarding the nature of Indian society—present and future.

From the peasants' point of view certain explanations seem possible.

The peasants' perception of Gandhi and the Congress was that of a great helper of the oppressed. This perception gained currency due to the public posture and the pro-peasant propaganda of the Congress. The peasants interpreted the Congress message of nationalism in relation to their own economic and social grievances. The Con-

[177] A recent study has reduced the entire ideological struggle within the Congress and the freedom struggle to the issue of violence and non-violence, Bipan Chandra, op. cit.

gress kept handing a post-dated cheque to the peasantry which read 'when swaraj comes all your grievances would go'. As the issuing authority was held in great esteem, the peasants believed in cashing the cheque at a future date.

Moreover, besides supporting the Congress there was virtually no political choice before the peasants. They could not afford to support the Liberals, who had a pro-British image, or political parties like the National Agriculturist Party, which were political organizations of landlords. The upper strata of the peasantry did support the Proja Krishak Party in Bengal and the Unionist Party in the Punjab. But for this the pro-landlord stance of the provincial Congress was responsible to a great extent. The Communist Party, during this period, hardly functioned in an organized form. Still in its formative stage, it was subject to various limitations and hardships. It was in the 1940s that the communists organized and led the heroic struggles of Tebhaga and Telangana.

The peasants and their leadership even compromised their interests for the sake of nationalism whereas the Congress leaders used this for sustaining their hold not only over the freedom struggle but over the masses as well.

CHAPTER 8

Ideology, Congress and Peasants in 1930s: Class Adjustment or Submission?*

From the time the Indian National Congress entered the phase of mass politics and mass struggles till the coming of independence one crucial question which bothered the British was, what would be the attitude of Congress towards the agrarian issues—particularly the no-rent demand of the peasantry? The official literature reveals the concern over this issue for it was the peasantry which provided the bulk of manpower for the Congress in the course of the freedom struggle. To analyse the Congress attitude towards the peasants and vice versa we have to take into account the various roles of the Congress—as a platform, as an organized political party, in the course of mass movements and while in power (1937–9). This relationship in the light of the Indian National Movement (INM) has been studied by historians of various schools—Nationalist, Colonial, Marxist, Liberal, Subaltern, etc. The most recent analysis has been put forward by the Neo-Nationalist historians while discussing the 'long-term dynamics' of the Indian National Congress.[1] One can take issues with them on various aspects but I shall confine myself to the peasant question.

It has been argued by Bipan Chandra that the INM was basically the product of the 'central or primary contradiction' of colonial India, the contradiction between colonialism and Indian people.[2] Thus, according to him 'inner class contradictions had to be seen as secondary and therefore subordinated to the primary contradict-

*The paper was earlier published in *Social Scientist*, Vol. 14, Nos. 8/9 (August–September 1986), pp. 40–58.

[1] Bipan Chandra, 'The Long Term Dynamics of the Indian National Congress'. Presidential Address to the Indian History Congress, Amritsar, 1985.

[2] Ibid.

ion; they had to be seen as contradictions within the camp of the people and class struggles based on them had to be waged in a non-antagonistic fashion'. He asserts that the 'Congress, and in particular Gandhi, practised the strategy of class adjustment' and the INC had 'no class essence'. In his analysis the interests of the Indian people are projected as a whole against colonialism (one would like to know the attitude of princes and landlords *vis-à-vis* colonialism when independence was in sight); Nationalism as the sole ideology of the Congress which 'never laid down any ideological condition for joining it' 'Marxism found a ready welcome and no strong anti-Marxist intellectual current developed in the nationalist ranks till 1947, and 'at no stage did a break in the Congress occur over ideology'. His assumption is that the 'ideological openness' enhanced the possibility of transforming the Congress and the 'responsibility for the failure' to effect 'a basic transformation of the Congress ideology' lies not in 'the inevitability of the stranglehold of the right wing or Gandhi over it' but has to be 'basically located in the theories and practices of the left'. The right wing, he stresses, was 'willing to go quite far in accommodating the left so long as it remained within the parameters of class adjustment and peaceful change'. He has many more observations such as pro-poor orientation of the Congress; basing politics on the poor and the shift from PCP (Pressure-Compromise-Pressure) to STS (Struggle-Truce-Struggle).[3]

None among the 'Left'[4] in India ever undermined the historical necessity of fighting colonialism nor does any Marxist historian undermine it in his analyses. But at the same time what we believe is that any class or group of the Indian society which sided with colonialism was in itself a constituent of the 'primary contradiction' and would not agree to it being projected as an inner or secondary contradiction in the name of having a united front. Such a possibility could have been there only if the Indian landlords sided with the

[3] Ibid. All citations are from there.

[4] When I use the term Left for 1930s, I include Communists, Socialists, Kisan Sabhas and Trade Unions. We refuse to accept Jawaharlal Nehru in this category, for a leader has to be judged by his actions and not by his speeches alone.

INC but this was not the case.[5] It has, while fighting colonialism become fashionable to cite Mao on class adjustment.[6] What should be taken into account is that Mao advocated this at a time when Japanese imperialism was trying to make inroads in China and the landlords were not the active supporters of imperialism. Even then Mao adopted and advocated a cautious approach towards them and the aim of agrarian revolution was never forgotten. In India the INC never had agrarian revolution as its aim, either as a primary or a secondary goal. Moreover, imperialism was firmly entrenched here having the active support of the landlords—not only individually but also from their class organizations. If combating imperialism was the only issue, the sort of class adjustment being advocated had been in a way experienced by the Indian people way back in 1857 which ultimately resulted in the princes and landlords throwing in their lot with imperialism and further oppression of the peasantry.

It would not be a vague generalization to state that in rural India the British authority was known more so through the landlords than any other leverage of the Raj.[7] In the imperial language they were the forces of order, the loyal supporters and the 'bulwark against the disintegrating forces'.[8] They played a dominant role in strengthening the British authority and opposed any kind of anti-British activity. To quote the Nawab of Chattari (in 1939):[9] '. . . the greatest of all services the zamindars had rendered was the maintenance of law and order in the rural areas.'

Bipan Chandra acknowledges that 'the zamindars and landlords did not support the Congress except individually' they 'either supported . . . officially sponsored organizations or had . . . their own political parties'.[10] Yet, in his analysis they do not form a part of the 'primary contradiction'. Even in individual capacity, where

[5] For landlords' support to imperialism see also Kapil Kumar, *Peasants in Revolt* (New Delhi, 1985), pp. 177–8.

[6] Chandra, op. cit.

[7] Kumar, op. cit.

[8] Ibid.

[9] All India Landholders Conference, Lucknow, April 1939 in *India Annual Register*, 1939, Vol. I, p. 392.

[10] Chandra, op. cit.

they did support the Congress, was the support forthcoming due to nationalism? Was not any vested class interest also behind it? I have elsewhere shown that the landlords were never a constituent in the multi-class alliance against colonialism.[11] Though the Congress had always assured them about their status and privileges it was only during the ministry period that a formal direct relationship was established between the two. To sustain their dominant position, to pursue their class interests, the Congress victory in elections and the increasing influence of the left wing among the masses were the factors responsible for this direct relationship which the landlords and the Congress right wing sought with each other. The outcome was the Congress–Zamindar pact in Bihar and similar negotiations in other regions. The revealing feature of this pact and negotiations is that while questions related to landlords' rights and privileges, along with the tenants' position, were discussed and agreed upon there was no mention of landlords role in the INM, i.e. their role in the Congress's fight against colonialism. In the vast literature available on Congress–Zamindar negotiations (1937–9) we find that those negotiating on behalf of the Congress at no stage asked the landlords to support or side with the national movement. These leaders (Rajendra Prasad, Sardar Patel, Maulana Azad, etc.) were fully aware of the fact that they had acted against the declared policy (Lucknow and Faizpur resolutions) of the Congress and they took precautions to justify their actions. This is apparent from what Rajendra Prasad wrote to Ramdayalu Sinha:[12]

> . . . we had gone to the furthest length possible and had *done so even at the risk of being openly criticised* in the All India Congress Committee *of having gone against the Congress resolution.* I had *in anticipation brought* the Maulana so that if any question arose in the Working Committee or the AICC, I might *have a strong supporter by my side.*

Prasad had no doubts that he 'shall come in for a great deal of criticism from not only the Kisan Sabha but Congressmen in general

[11] Kapil Kumar, 'Peasants, Congress, and the Struggle for Freedom 1917–39', Kapil Kumar (ed.), *Congress and Classes* (Delhi, 1988).

[12] Rajendra Prasad to Ramdayalu Sinha, 7 December 1937. Rajendra Prasad Papers (RPP), Nehru Memorial Museum & Library (NMML), Roll 5 (emphasis added).

and even perhaps from our high command'.[13] Azad was assigned the task of taking Jawaharlal Nehru into confidence and he believed that the latter had 'an uncommon capacity for thought and to work in cooperation with others'. Azad gave the assurance that there will be no difficulty as far as Nehru was concerned.[14] The green signal from Nehru, to go against the declared Congress policy, came when Kriplani wrote on his behalf:[15] 'If you and Maulana Saheb were satisfied it was alright'.

What followed was the process for agreement during which Prasad pleaded with landlords that if the Congress proposals were 'unsatisfactory, the zamindars should be prepared to propose a better solution' and assured Mohd. Ismail that the 'Government will not fail to give it their utmost consideration'.[16] Here I am not going into the details of the agreement but worth mentioning is what Patel advised Prasad:[17]

> It is no use trying to improve it, if it has to be forced down the throats of unwilling landlords. We shall have to resist the excessive demands of the tenants who have been worked up and expect too much from the Congress ministries.

Who had worked up the peasants during this period? Precisely it was the Congress election propaganda in the countryside to muster peasants' support. The Faizpur agrarian programme, Nehru believed, was of 'great importance' for the rural voters and was prominently propagated during the election campaign.[18] Canvassing amid the Allahabad villagers he had stated:[19]

> There were only two parties in India—those fighting for the cause of people and the other against it. They (people) had no power to solve that problem of poverty. Only a handful of people were ruling over them . . . whether the rulers

[13] Rajendra Prasad to Maharaja Darbhanga, 20 April 1938, Rajéndra Prasad Papers (RPP), National Archives of India (NAI), FI/A-1938.

[14] Azad to Rajendra Prasad, 26 and 28 November 1937, ibid.

[15] Kripalani to Rajendra Prasad, 29 November 1937, F-1/1937, ibid.

[16] Rajendra Prasad to Mohd. Ismail, 12 October 1937, RPP, NMML, Roll 8.

[17] Patel to R. Prasad, 4 December 1937, ibid.

[18] *The Bombay Sentinel*, 4 January 1937.

[19] *Bombay Chronicle*, 26 January 1937.

were Indians or Englishmen they only knew how to further their ends. . . . The Congress was going to the Councils to keep out Khan Bahadurs, Raja Bahadurs and Nawabs who sided with government.

Patel had told the peasants that it was only the Congress candidate 'who will sooner or later help him out of the morass of poverty into which he is sunk'.[20] A growing feeling among the peasants was that the Congress Raj would replace the British Raj in two months time. The following example from UP is one out of many which indicates how and why the peasant expectations had gone up:[21]

Congress volunteers are going about with notebooks and asking tenants what their present rent was. The tenant says perhaps Rs. 2 a *bigha.* The Congress volunteer says: 'That's all right. If you vote for the Congress that will be put down to 4 annas'. He writes it down in his notebook and the unfortunate villager is duly impressed.

An interesting development of such propaganda in Bihar was that some of the voters regarded the ballot box as a letter box for Gandhi and 'smuggled in petitions addressed to him with their voting papers'.[22] Even during the interim ministry period peasant sentiments were utilized to embarrass the government. When the Nawab of Chattari formed his ministry in UP, the tenants were encouraged by the Congress not to pay rents as all arrears would be remitted when the Congress assumed office.[23] But once in office, the Congress advised them to pay rents immediately or else it will lead to evictions.[24] Thus, it was clear that the peasant had to be resisted—not the landlord, and the right wing had all the liberty to go back on

[20] Ibid. After the elections those peasants who supported the Congress had to further face oppression by zamindars, 19 February 1937, ibid.; *Sangharsh*, 19 September 1938.

[21] Haig to Linlithgow, 29 October 1936, Linlithgow Papers (hereafter LP), SN 112, NMML.

[22] James Sifton to Linlithgow, 9 February 1937, ibid. 55.

[23] Quarterly Survey of Political and Constitutional Position in British India, No. 1, LP, SN 142.

[24] Amrita Bazar Patrika, 2 January 1938; *Hindustan Times*, 6 January 1938; F. No. 18/1/38, Home Poll, NAI.

election promises and flout the Lucknow and Faizpur resolutions of the Congress in relation to peasantry.

The Maharaja of Darbhanga, after getting a negative reply in relation to the zamindars being protected as a minority by the British, sought the Bihar Governors' advise regarding their joining the Congress.[25] But this was found to be ultimately prejudicial to their interests. The answer was to have a strong zamindari organization and through it influence the Congress. This led to the formation of the All India Landholders Association (AILA) in April 1939. Throughout the ministry period the zamindars confidently declared that for their sake 'the kisan movement was being suppressed by the Congress' and it was in their interest to 'strengthen the hands of the government in counteracting the mischievous move of the leftist group in the Congress to make Russia of India'.[26] The Congress 'had no alternative but to compromise with the zamindars', the only 'question was whether the right wingers remained in office or not.'[27] Maharaja Darbhanga stressed in his presidential address to the AILA conference:[28]

> Most of those who are in power in the Congress organization which runs the government of seven provinces want adjustment and peace . . . we want adjustment because therein *lies our security.* We want peace because only then we *can develop our strength.* For a minority interest like ours it is only desperation that can drive us to fight and I have reasons to believe that *so long as the group following the directions of Mahatma Gandhi rules in the Congress and the Socialists and Communists are kept in check we shall not have to take the extreme step.*

It is evident that the landlords were duty bound to support and actively assist the right wing—which also looked upon them for this—in curbing the left, but had no obligation to support the same group in the fight against colonialism. The lone voice of Chandreshwar Prasad Singh (leader of the opposition in Bihar), raised reluctantly at the AILA conference, to fight for freedom found no response. But a resolution was passed to form a Committee of

[25] Hallet to Linlithgow, 17 August 1937, LP, SN 113.

[26] *Hindustan Times*, 6 January 1938.

[27] Ibid.

[28] *Indian Annual Register*, 1939, Vol. I, p. 396 (emphasis added).

Understanding for negotiating with the Congress and provincial governments regarding the problems of landlords and tenants.[29] In fact when it came to opposing the British, the landlords would not distinguish between the right and the left but treated the Congress as one. The point I intend to highlight is that the landlords were not a constituent in the multi-class alliance against the British, but at the same time were in alliance with the group within the Congress which stood for the suppression of the kisan movement.

Here I am not, even for a moment, negating the historical necessity of fighting colonialism but as mentioned earlier I treat landlordism as very much a part of what the Neo-Nationalists describe as the 'primary contradiction'. While projecting landlordism as secondary they advocate a policy of class adjustment which they believe was rightly pursued by the Congress and Gandhi in particular. This they stress should have been followed by the left and there is no mention in their analysis about the left taking guard against this 'inner contradiction'. They fail to acknowledge the fear of a takeover by the 'secondary contradiction' once the 'primary contradiction' has been dealt with—the fear which came true after 15 August 1947. Can a progressive theoretician or historian advocate such a historiography? I leave the question open.

Moreover, I suggest that what Gandhi and the right wing was preaching to the peasants was not 'class adjustment' or collaboration with the landlords but submission to them: 'You should bear a little if the zamindar torments you'; 'If the zamindar harass them I would ask my kisan brethren not to fight with them but adopt a conciliatory attitude'; 'Kisans must be advised scrupulously to abide by their agreement with the zamindar, whether such agreement is written or inferred from custom'.[30] One can go on adding such citations. The legitimate interests of the zamindars were described by Mahadev Desai as a 'commission for the use of their intelligence in wisely directing the energies of their tenants'.[31] Despite acknowledging the 'present terrible inequality' between them, Gandhi

[29] Ibid, p. 398.

[30] *Young India*, 26 January, 9 March and 18 May 1922.

[31] *Harijan*, 25 December 1937.

treated the two at par, for his logic was:[32] 'The man who supplies brains and metal is as much a tiller as the one who labours with his hands.'

Certainly Gandhi was not unaware of the exploitation of the peasants but his outcry was against peasant violence and he was silent about the violence practised by the landlords. It was the sole responsibility of the peasant to improve relations with the zamindar. And if the peasants were prepared to carry the struggle by adopting non-violent methods, still they were to be checked in the name of charkha, *khaddar* or the constructive programme.[33] The solution for high rents, forced labour, cesses, evictions, etc., was the constructive programme of Gandhi. It is interesting to cite 'a good example of class adjustment' by referring to Gandhi's manifesto to UP kisans in 1931 asking them to pay 75 or 50 per cent rent,[34] but equally important here is to cite that Nehru was sent there to restrain the peasants[35] and the kind of tactics he adopted. Kalka Prasad, who wanted to peacefully picket the house of a landlord demanding restoration of lands to the peasants evicted during the Civil Disobedience movement, was suspended from the Congress and Nehru assured the taluqdar:[36]

> I am sorry that Kalka Prasad should have behaved in this manner and put you to trouble. But I hope you realize that Congress has nothing to do with any such acts.
>
> You will appreciate that this is the fault of some misguided individuals. We propose to take action against them. . . . Meanwhile I shall be glad if you will inform me of any grievance that you might have against the local Congress workers in Rai Bareilly.

A similar action was taken against Markande Singh in 1938 at

[32] Ibid., 23 April 1938.

[33] *Young India*, 26 January 1922. See also Kapil Kumar, 'Peasants' Perception of Gandhi and his programme: Oudh 1920–1922', *Social Scientist*, February 1983.

[34] Bipan Chandra, op. cit.

[35] Gandhi to Mohan Lal Saxena, 15 June 1931. *Collected Works*, Vol. XLVI, 1931, p. 384.

[36] Nehru's Letters to Umanath Baksh Singh 26 and 28 July 1931 and to Sect. UPCC, 2 July 1931, AICC, G-59/1931, NMML.

Benares.[37] Gandhi regarded the agrarian unrest as a 'much greater danger' and the 'real danger' (in 1939) with the Congress having the responsibility to discipline it.[38] The disciplined peasants, in Gandhian terminology, were those who would not even non-violently oppose the zamindar's violence; would not stop services to the landlords; would pay rents; would not prevent the arrest of their leaders and abide by all government laws. All this was to be done in spite of landlords' hostility to the INM. Thus, the argument of class adjustment for maintaining unity in the name of nationalism fails to explain the situation in totality.

On many occasions the issue of national unity was set aside by the Congress. The picketing of landlords was checked in the name of unity whereas the picketing of a Muslim shop was encouraged[39] in the full knowledge that such an act would lead to communal disturbances. This leads us to conclude that issues which did not attack the class character of the Congress could be taken up at the cost of national unity but issues, where questions of class conflict were involved, were to be suppressed in the name of national unity. Mushirul Hasan has shown that even during 'the mass contact Muslim peasants and underprivileged groups in the countryside, the very sections supposed to be mobilized on a massive scale were largely ignored'.[40] His study shows how communal minded persons led the district Congress committees; Muslims associated with Congress were not allowed to contest PCC elections and how the right wingers worked for the defeat of those Congress candidates who happened to be Muslims.[41] Mobilization on economic lines, in order to combat communalism, was not to be taken up or was to be opposed by the right wingers. It is a cruel joke of history that the very leadership which would suppress economic issues in the

[37] P-20 (P2)/1938-39, ibid.

[38] G.D. Birla (ed.), *Bapu: A Unique Association* (*BAUA*), Vol. 3 (Bombay 1977), p. 267.

[39] See Gyanendra Pandey, *The Ascendancy of the Congress in Uttar Pradesh, 1926–35* (Delhi 1978), p. 130.

[40] Mushirul Hasan, 'The Muslim Mass Contact Campaign: An Attempt at Political Mobilization', Occasional Papers, No. XIV, NMML.

[41] Ibid.

name of violence and bloodshed could not avoid it though it came through a communal divide of the country. Let us examine the ideological openness of the Congress right wing but not only in the light of various radical resolutions (Karachi to Faizpur) adopted by the Congress but also in relation to the actual functioning of the party and in relation to their implementation. During the Calcutta AICC meeting in October 1937 it was strongly felt by the right wing that they should organize themselves and Jairamdas Doulatrams' suggestion that 'we should not sit down over the matter any more' was put into active operation.[42] Instructions were issued that all 'orthodox Programmewallas' would work in concerted manner or else there would be 'great difficulty' in future.[43] In clear language Patel wrote to Prasad:[44]

> Bapu is not at all happy. . . . Anyway we may have a fixed struggle at Haripura. . . . Please see that in selection of delegates, eliminate all anti-Gandhi elements. We must no more tolerate the forces of disorder in the name of united front. They have taken undue advantage of our toleration, but time has come for a definite stand.

Patel's belief, all throughout, had been that the Kisan Sabha 'will give much greater trouble in future'; that is why he had 'always been against its formation' and 'such rival organizations' were 'bound to destroy the Congress prestige'. He asserted:[45] 'They (peasant leaders) are waiting for a time when they could displace us. That is why I have given them no quarters.'

Prasad instructed his friends in Bihar to organize on the lines suggested by Patel. The right wing and the zamindars joined hands to crush the Kisan Sabha and establish their firm hold over the Congress organization. We list here the methods adopted for achieving this aim.[46]

[42] Rajendra Prasad to Sri Krishna Sinha, 2 December 1937. Rajendra Prasad Correspondence and Selected Writings (RPCS), Vol. I (Delhi, 1984), p. 131.

[43] Ibid.

[44] Patel to Prasad, 12 December 1937, ibid., p. 141, (emphasis added).

[45] Patel to Prasad, 2 October 1937, ibid., p. 103.

[46] AICC, F. No. P. 3 (11)/1930-39 and F. No. P. 6, 1939/40, NMML.

1. Congress membership forms were refused to peasants whereas a large number of zamindari *amalas* (agents) were enrolled as members.
2. Wherever it was possible, the Kisan Sabha members were not allowed to file nomination papers. In Andhra also the nomination of P. Sundarayya for Congress delegate's seat from Kovur Taluq, Nellore was rejected on the ground that he was a communist.[47] The propaganda against the pro-Kisan Sabha Congressmen was carried on the lines that as socialists they were irreligious persons who did not believe in God or that they had been turned out from the Congress.[48]
3. Pro-zamindari returning officers were appointed who manipulated elections against the peasant candidates.
4. Where the peasant delegates got elected there were appeals against them and the DCC election tribunals set aside their election on one pretext or the other.
5. To cover up these manipulations the pro-Kisan Sabha Congressmen were implicated in cases of violence and criminal cases were instituted against them. This resulted in convictions. This was done under the instructions of the Bihar Premier, for a happy Governor informed the Viceroy:[49] 'My Prime Minister tells me that his followers are starting criminal cases'.

The pro-peasant Congressmen while facing the violence of the zamindar and right wing sponsored candidates did not approach the police on account of their faith in the Congress creed that 'in a dispute between Congressmen regarding Congress affairs the aid of civil authorities should not be invoked'.[50]

Rajendra Prasad, in a letter to the Bihar PM, cited a long circular from Nehru to the members of the Working Committee:[51]

> He refers to the awakening among kisans, industrial labourers and students and points out that the Congress ministries have to deal with the situation

[47] Ibid.
[48] *Sangharsh*, 7 January 1938.
[49] Hallet to Linlithgow, 7 January 1938, LP, Roll 44.
[50] AICC, F. No. P. 3 (11), 1936–9.
[51] RPCS, Vol. I, p. 130.

tactfully. The use of repressive laws and coercive methods he naturally dislikes and opines that this can be restored to only in very exceptional cases.

Prasad asserted that Nehru's views were to be kept in mind while dealing with the situation. We have seen the tactics adopted during the organizational elections but there was more in store to deal with the Kisan Sabha. Instead of acting against the Kisan Sabha from the top, the right wing initiated the onslaught from the district level. The Champaran, Saran and Monghyr DCCs instructed Sahajanand Saraswati—a member of the Bihar PCC and president of the Bihar Kisan Sabha—not to visit the districts and local Congressmen were threatened with disciplinary action if they attended his meetings.[52] Though Sahajanand raised the issue of civil liberties[53] regarding the ban, Patel welcomed it:[54]

> Personally I feel that such action should have been taken long ago, but better late than never is a good thing. I hope it is not late to mend matters and prevent the enormous mischief that Swami was doing.

Let us also examine the 'enormous mischief' of the Swami during this period.[55] In actual practice he was making the peasants aware of their rights; organizing them; urging them to join the Congress in large numbers and reminding the ministers to implement the accepted agrarian programme and fulfil the promises made during the elections; preaching self-defensive measures against the violence practised by landlords and advocating a fight not only against imperialism but against its allies also. This was termed as working against the Congress creed and breaking the Congress discipline. One wonders what this discipline was for it was not applicable on the right wing or all the anti-left forces in the Congress even when their activities were openly against the publicly declared policy of the Congress. The Kisan Sabha was also accused of sheltering

[52] *Congress Socialist*, 11 December 1937.

[53] LP, S. No. 142; *Harijan*, 25 December 1937.

[54] Patel to Prasad, 16 December 1937, RPCS, Vol. I, p. 143.

[55] See also Kapil Kumar, 'Congress-Peasants Relationship in the Late 1930s' in D.N. Panigrahi (ed.), *Economy, Society and Politics in Modern India* (Delhi, 1985).

disgruntled elements or people who were hostile to the Congress but no specific names were ever cited in this regard. Another issue raised was that the Kisan Sabha preached violence and was creating an atmosphere of class war. Nowhere did the Kisan Sabha incite attacks on landlords, loot them or cause their physical annihilation. On the contrary the peasants were advised self-defensive measures like prostrating in the fields if forcefully evicted. In fact for the right wing if the peasants even adopted Gandhian forms of struggle against the landlords, it was violence and Nehru was also with the right wing as we have seen in the case of Kalka Prasad. Going against the Congress policy of consulting the Kisan Sabha and negotiating with zamindars was discipline but if the peasants, as a protest against this, peacefully marched to the councils demanding justice and implementation of Congress promises, that was indiscipline and 'rowdism'. On the contrary, the zamindars were given a free hand to parade lorry loads of reserve police in their villages so as to warn the peasants that even 'in Congress Raj' they were 'still as powerful as ever' and the peasants in spite of crop failure, should pay exorbitant rents.[56]

Beside the landlords, there were two other forces which took an active part in encouraging the right wing to take action against the Kisan Sabha. The first obviously was the colonial government. All official secret and confidential correspondence of this period refers to the agrarian danger. The Viceroy suggested to the Governor of Bihar to 'give a bed time story' to his ministers of how in the good old days the government 'used to stop nonsense of this sort'.[57] The ministers fully realized the danger and 'advocated that the kisan leaders correspondence should be intercepted'[58] and the government should have verbatim reports of the speeches delivered by the kisan leaders.[59] And by April 1938 the Viceroy was reporting home:[60] 'The ministries deserve credit for meeting this threat with resolution. The policy of the Congress party towards the kisan organizations has been firm, and even repressive.'

[56] N.G. Ranga to Subhas Bose, 11 January 1939, Indulal Yagnik Papers (IYP), SF No. 14, NMML.

[57] Linlithgow to Hallet, 26 December 1937, LP, SN 110.

[58] Hallet to Linlithgow, 5 December 1937, ibid.

[59] 9 November 1937, ibid.

[60] *Quarterly Survey*, ibid., SN 142.

The second was the personality of G.D. Birla, the capitalist—who served as a link between the Congress leaders, ministers and the British government during this period.[61] He 'very much disliked the peasants in Bihar marching to the Assembly house' and wrote to Mahadev Desai:[62]

> I fear that in course of time indiscipline will grow more and more unless strict measures are taken. I only hope that the Congress authorities are fully alive to the situation and they *will take all necessary measures.*

We have quite a few letters exchanged between Birla and Desai which urge for action against the Kisan Sabha:[63]

> Unless the Congress tells the peasants clearly that their position could be improved ultimately through their own hard work alone and not by any stroke of wand, I don't think this discontent will sub-side. . . . All the enthusiasm about the release of prisoners will begin to fade after some time. People will demand more bread and bread is not going to come out of the confiscation of zamindaris. . . . The question of discontent is just now linked with economics and unless steps are taken to make the peasants realize what is possible and what not, I fear the ferment will grow to such an extent that it will become impossible after a certain stage for the ministers to maintain discipline.

What we see is that the period between September and December 1937 saw hectic activity and exchange of views amongst the landlords, capitalists, British government and the right wing in relation to the peasant question, with all of them urging the ministers to take strong action.

The Premier of Bihar 'told Vallabhbhai that if only the Working Committee will support them through thick and thin instead of censuring them at every step, they will manage Bihar well'.[64] And the CWC came out in defence of the action taken by the Bihar PCC against the Kisan Sabha and its leadership. It is relevant to see how this whole process went through. Rajendra Prasad had collected, from the Bihar Premier, CID reports related to the

[61] These observations are based on examining the correspondence of Gandhi, Birla, Prasad, Patel, etc.

[62] *BAUA*, p. 76.

[63] Ibid., p. 106.

[64] Ibid., p. 127.

activities of kisan leaders. These were informally placed before the CWC members.[65] The Kisan Sabha was given no opportunity to explain or plead its position and the rightists emerged victorious. All along they had been sure about their success and the Bihar Premier had assured the Governor that 'he was confident that he would get their support so long as Mr. Gandhi was alive'.[66]

Sahajanand, as a protest, resigned from the Working Committee of the Bihar PCC.[67] This was welcomed by the right wing but still he was considered dangerous as he had not resigned from the Congress.[68] If he was really guilty of what he was accused of (violence, class war, indiscipline, hostility to ministers, etc.) why was he not prosecuted? The Congress ministry was 'very anxious' to do that but the difficulty felt was, firstly, he always kept himself 'just within the law'[69] and secondly, as the Governor felt, he had in his possession 'complete evidence of corruption involving the Prime Minister's son' and the PM (S.K. Sinha) feared that 'he would not hesitate to use it if attacked'.[70]

If in Bombay Congress MLAs were warning peasants against joining the Kisan Sabha,[71] in Madras Rajagopalachari was practising other methods. He ridiculed Jagannath Das for arranging functions for Indulal Yagnik as 'the general impression among our friends in Bombay is that he is not now helpful to Congress and distinctly the opposite'.[72] Another example of his onslaught on the left is what he wrote to Pattabhi:[73]

Ignorance of the working of political institutions and actors on the political stage outside our province combined with incorrigible tendency to offer pooja to outsiders leads our municipal bodies and local organizations to all sorts of irreconcilable positions and stupid resolutions. What is the meaning

[65] *Searchlight*, 5 January 1938.

[66] Hallet to Linlithgow, 7 January 1938, LP, Roll 44.

[67] *Hindustan Times*, 5 January 1938; see also Kapil Kumar, 'Congress-Peasant Relationship in late 1930s', op. cit.

[68] *Harijan*, 29 January 1938.

[69] Stewart to Linlithgow, 20 December 1937, LP, SN 113.

[70] Ibid., 24 January 1938, ibid., Roll 45.

[71] *Congress Socialist*, 11 December 1937.

[72] 20 May 1937, Rajagopalachari Papers, NMML, Roll 1.

[73] 7 June 1937, ibid.

of Masulipaten Municipality to present address of welcome to Mr. Giri and Mr. M.N. Roy?

And soon a circular was issued to taluk and district committees to seek prior permission for arranging such functions. This was followed by the Batliwala case in Madras.

S.S. Batliwala used to come to Madras from Bombay to preach among the peasants. In the Venkatagiri zamindari he discussed the peasant grievances; attributed them to the landlord; asked peasants to organize and become Congress members; represent their grievances to ministers.[74] Rajagopalachari was 'very anxious' about his arrest before he could make any more speeches. During his prosecution Rajagopalachari 'took the trouble personally to go through the public prosecutor's arguments to the court and suggested amendments'. He was very keen that the 'attack on constituted government and incitement to violence should be stressed and as little as possible made of the attacks on Great Britain and British rule'.[75] Why such a course was advocated became clear as the case proceeded. Batliwala's defence was that as the official policy of the Congress party, which is in power today, is the severance of the British connection, he 'cannot be punished for advocating the policy of the party in power'.[76] To justify this he asked for the presence of the PM as a witness which was obviously refused by the judge. In spite of the assessor's verdict of not guilty, the judge sentenced him for 5 months simple imprisonment. Rajagopalachari's comment was that the prosecution had the desired results as no such speeches were delivered in Madras after that.[77]

The Congress stood for the release of political prisoners but the release of Chauri Chaura prisoners was not to be stressed[78] and the prosecution and imprisonment of peasant leaders continued under the Congress ministries (one can cite here the arrests of Rahul Sankrityayan, Jadunandan Sharma, etc.). We would also like to cite

[74] L.P. Roll 65.

[75] Ibid.

[76] Ibid.

[77] Ibid.

[78] Haig to Linlithgow, 30 January 1938, Haig Papers, NMML, Roll 2.

here that when the political prisoners were on hunger strike in the Patna jail they were told by a minister that more important than their release was the question of giving agrarian relief to peasants[79] and the peasants were told that more important was the release of political prisoners. On the other hand, not only the right wing but Gandhi himself was opposed to the released prisoners being given public welcome or being carried in processions after their release:[80] 'If my reading of the Congress method is correct, the large public demonstration that took place on the discharge of Kakori prisoners, was to say the least, a political mistake.'

The right wing believed Nehru would resent this[81] but Desai was happy to tell Birla that Nehru 'fully appreciated it' and had personally refrained from taking part in demonstrations and receptions.[82] In Ahmedabad Nehru made a public statement disapproving them entirely.[83] Difference over methods could be one thing but using the colonial language while referring to the political prisoners was a common practice with the right wingers, as a letter from Desai to Birla indicates.[84]

> You know the Kakori dacoit prisoners who were convicted some years ago of the most violent and unpardonable crimes. Pantji released them all. . . . But the moment their release was announced, our idiotic Congress committee makes an announcement of taking those people out in procession. Poor Pantji was absolutely at sea. He was persuaded to be firm. He made it clear that if they persisted it would not be possible for him to do any similar thing in future. Jawaharlal, too, did not give any encouragement to the Congress enthusiasts. And so every thing ended well.

In UP a close eye was being kept on pro-kisan Congressmen. The UP PCC circular of 7 June 1938 asked the local committees to send regular reports regarding the activities of Kisan Sabha. The following points were to be taken special care of in the reports:[85]

[79] Krishnaballabh Sahay to Prasad, 13 October 1937, RPP, NMML, Roll 8.
[80] *BAUA*, Vol. 3, p. 81.
[81] Ibid., p. 22.
[82] Ibid., p. 91.
[83] Ibid., p. 95.
[84] Ibid., p. 68.
[85] AICC, F. No. P 20 (p 2)/1938-39, NMML.

1. Is there any tension between Kisan Sabha and the Congress?
2. No such person is active in Kisan Sabha against whom disciplinary action was taken.
3. The flag of the Kisan Sabha is tri-colour or some other one.
4. Are the Congress members hurt by the Kisan Sabha activities?
5. Whether the Kisan Sabha is affiliated to any provincial organization: whether its accounts are managed or not; what influence it carries with the people.

Mohanlal Sexena issued a confidential circular to PCC members stressing:[86]

At a time when the Congress has to meet the onslaughts from the Muslim League, the zamindars and taluqdars and the capitalist interests, for any section of the Congressmen to go about propagating that the Congress has betrayed the kisans and that they should not expect any good from it, is nothing short of treason and needs being dealt with a strong hand.

On the one hand, he was accepting taluqdari and capitalists attack on Congress but was not prepared to take peasants support against them. What a section of Congressmen was being accused of preaching was not true. In fact, this section was opposing the increasing influence of the taluqdars in the Congress and urging the Congress to protect itself from opportunists who were bringing a bad name to it. Baba Ram Chandra in UP was one such Congressman for whom Gandhi was the only leader and Congress the supreme party. His worry was that the capitalists and landlords were 'destroying our pious Congress'.[87] The Congressmen were 'flowing in the stream of office acceptance' and the landlords joined the national body 'not to serve the people but in order to control the people through various legal provisions'. He admitted that by acquiring office the Congress had brought some light to the darker life of peasants but on the whole they remained entrapped by 'thugs, under whose influence the Congress forgets its real self and we have to face miseries'. He was alarmed at this increasing influence and if unchecked, he believed, 'even swaraj would not end the

[86] AICC, 17/1939, ibid.

[87] Baba Ram Chandra Papers, Part I, SF No. 3, NMML.

people's miseries as these people will take over from the white Sarkar'.[88] The Congress commitment to serve the people was being altered under the influence of landlords:[89]

By practising oppression, efforts are being made to weaken the kisans and mazdurs and make them submissive. The kisans are every day sending evidences in this regard to Congress office.

So critical was he of the functioning of the local level Congress leaders that he wrote:[90]

After wearing khadi and being Congress leaders, with the help of police they assault the peasants. By this treachery they are ruining the Congress. . . . Congressi dress, stick in hand, with police at their back, then why dust should not be thrown in the eyes of the ministers.

He asserted that the way managers and agents had destroyed princes and landlords some *khaddardharies* were doing the same to the Congress; the outcome was that instead of peace there was corruption.[91] It was no coincidence that such voices were raised in other regions also. In Vishakhapatnam a Congress Vigilance Committee was formed to save the Congress from 'cunning, calculating politicians who newly joined the Congress' and 'created a mercenary army amongst primary members . . . to fight election battles'.[92] V. Anuntha Rao, the secretary of this committee, appealed to start 'cleanse the Congress campaign' to maintain the sanctity of the Congress organization.[93] Not less revealing was the Report of the Violence Enquiry Committee instituted by Bihar PCC. It was reported that there was 'a widespread desire to capture Congress organizations by all kinds of people to get the position of advantage for themselves, their friends and relations and for capturing local bodies'.[94] Office acceptance 'no doubt did bring some relief to the

[88] Ibid.
[89] Ibid.
[90] SF No. 2 A, ibid.
[91] Ibid.
[92] AICC, F. No. P. 3 (11)/1938-39, NMML.
[93] Ibid.
[94] Ibid.

people' but 'it also started attracting opportunists and political adventurers'. Even the old Congressmen 'felt that now was the time for reward for the services made by them in the past' and 'there was heart burning if in the distribution of spoils some went without a share'.[95] However the report was kept confidential as it was an indictment of the right wingers.

At the Haripura session, N.G. Ranga objected to the presentation of the General Secretary's report on Congress activities since the Faizpur session. The objection was in relation to the portions which dealt with the kisan activities. Pages 31 to 34 of the report gave the impression that 'on the whole the kisans and workers' were 'growing a sort of anti-Congress atmosphere in the country'.[96] The outgoing president Jawaharlal, while defending the report, argued that the statements were a fact with the exception that they 'cannot be made into a generalization'. He referred to the Congress constitution under which the General Secretary was required to submit a report and it was for the 'house to express its opinion over it'.[97] Sahajanand opined that though technically the report expressed the views of an individual but none the less they gave the impression that they were the views of the Congress. Ranga's motion was lost when put to vote.[98] Nehru had not only withdrawn support to the Kisan Sabha but had strongly defended the views expressed against the Kisan Sabha. This was an about turn from his earlier advice to Sahajanand in 1936 'to keep the Sabha separate from the Congress'.[99] He had advocated that the peasants should get organized; 'stand on their own legs and form kisan sabhas in every village'.[100] In 1937 also he had declared:[101] 'The outstanding problem of India is the peasant problem. All else is secondary.'

The coming of Congress ministries, he felt, had given new hope and new life to the peasants where as the big zamindars and taluq-

[95] Ibid.

[96] *Amrita Bazar Patrika*, 17 January 1938.

[97] Ibid.

[98] Ibid.

[99] Sahajanand Papers, Roll 1, NMML.

[100] *Bombay Chronicle*, 16 April 1936.

[101] AICC, F. No. P-9/1937.

dars were 'organising to resist their long deferred justice to the peasantry'.[102] How much of a leftist was Nehru or how much he stood for the peasants is best understood not just by taking into account his public utterances but by his actual operational politics. On each occasion whether it was the controversy over Andhra pledge, the *danda* cult, selection of candidates, tenancy legislation, kisan demonstrations, the ban on Kisan Sabha, etc., he not only sided with the right wing but put his weight against the Kisan Sabha.[103] He virtually kept himself aloof on the tenancy bills giving a free hand to the right wing to deal as they wished. He did not hesitate to condemn peasant demonstrations,[104] and as we have seen earlier, was directly responsible for the ouster of leaders like Kalka Prasad. He went to the extent of warning peasant leaders like Shibban Lal Saxena even after the resignation of ministries and assured the Viceroy in this regard.[105] In public, however, he maintained a socialist posture by criticizing the attempt to drive out the left from the Congress which would 'spread confusion in the mass mind, more especially the peasantry and thus weaken the Congress'.[106]

The Kisan Sabha, all through the 1930s constantly supported the Congress. At no stage did it ever pose an alternative to the Congress or work against it—even at the time when it faced direct action from the right wing. In spite of its anti-landlord ideology, the Kisan Sabha compromised once the landlords had been taken in as Congress candidates for some seats in Bihar during the elections. This was done as Congress was considered as the superior organization and the Kisan Sabha was bound to follow the Congress dictates.[107] It was opposed to the acceptance of office but once the Congress decided to go ahead the Kisan Sabha stood by the Congress decision. It looked up on the ministries to bring relief to the peasants

[102] Ibid.

[103] See Kumar, 'Congress–Peasant Relationship in late 1930s', op. cit.

[104] Ibid.

[105] Nehru to Linlithgow, 6 October 1939, J. Nehru Papers, correspondence Vol. 42, S. No. 2704, NMML.

[106] *Bombay Chronicle*, 17 February 1938.

[107] Sahajanand, *Mera Jivan Sangharsh* (Patna, 1952), p. 481.

and when the right wing joined hands with the landlords ignoring the Kisan Sabha, the kisan leaders organized the peasantry but not to oppose the Congress but to remind it of the pledges and promises made to the peasantry. As Sahajanand put it:[108]

It is not understandable why the ministers are afraid of peasant demonstrations and meetings. . . . If we don't hold them now when will we hold them. It is wrong to say that these are aimed at expressing no confidence in the ministries.

The great 'mischief monger' as the rightists described him always asserted:[109]

I believe in the basic principles of the Congress. . . . I accept them not merely because they are the principles of the Congress but because under the peculiar conditions for the freedom of the country and emancipation of the kisans from oppression and exploitation no other line of work is possible.

He tried his best to assure the right wing that whatever *shakti* (strength) he had he would devote to the strengthening of the Congress as he 'had faith and confidence in the Congress' and pleaded that the 'kisan sabhaites also claimed the right to serve the Congress, the country and the mankind'.[110]

Bipan Chandra has argued that Sahajanand 'would not give an iota of concession to or make any accommodation with the Congress ministry'[111]—an over simplification and baseless generalization with no evidence to cite for a period full of complexities.

At a time when Vijay Lakshmi Pandit was advocating dictatorship within the Congress organization to check growing indiscipline[112] and the right wing was virtually begging from the government to distinguish between them and the left wing[113] Sahajanand Saraswati was advocating (1939):[114]

[108] *Sangarsh*, 10 January 1938.

[109] *Congress Socialist*, 12 March 1938.

[110] Ibid.

[111] Bipan Chandra, op. cit.

[112] Haig to Linlithgow, 10 April 1939, Haig Papers, Roll 1.

[113] The papers of various Governors and the Viceroy contain lots of reporting in this regard during the period 1939–40.

[114] 4 October 1939, IYP, SF No. 11.

We all cling to the Congress not for its magic or mystery, but because it represents the nation, it has not taken any false step at critical junctures. . . . All our attempts are simply to strengthen its hands in taking opportune decisions at this most critical juncture in our national struggle for deliverance.

He had 'declared times without number that none but a lunatic could think of weakening the Congress at the present phase of the evolution of India's struggle for independence'.[115] The Kisan Sabha wanted to transform the creed and mentality of the Congress from within.[116] When N.G. Ranga, in Andhra, wanted to come out from Congress, it was Sundarayya who restrained him.[117]

The divide between the right and left in the Congress was not on the issue of violence and non-violence as argued by Bipan Chandra[118] but on firm ideological positions regarding the nature of Indian society. The entire onslaught on the Kisan Sabha or the left was motivated not due to their taking an alternative position but due to the class outlook of the rightist leadership which controlled the high command and local organizations. The Kisan Sabha faced the triple oppression (British, landlords and Congress right wing) during this period. Yet the Kisan Sabha supported the INC and the peasants stood firmly behind the Congress.

If the Congress had a definite strategy to fight imperialism it also pursued a strategy not only to check but also curb the left and the Kisan Sabha. The 'long-term dynamics' of the Congress (if there was any) has to be analysed by also taking into account these twin objectives of the Congress.

[115] SF No. 4, ibid.

[116] Ibid.

[117] Ranga to Yagnik, 23 October 1939, F. No. 14, ibid.

[118] Bipan Chandra, op. cit. The author is thankful to the Nehru Memorial Museum & Library, New Delhi for granting a fellowship which helped him in collecting material on 'Congress–Peasant Relation 1917–42'.

CHAPTER 9

Big Business and the Peasantry*

The struggle for India's freedom from the 1920s onwards was closely interlinked with the perceptions, hopes and aspirations of different social classes or interest groups. These were related not only to contemporary social reality but also to what place these classes or groups would have in an independent India. It was not merely a question of nationalism *vis-à-vis* the British but also nationalism in relation to class group interests—class perception of nationalism.[1]

It was this class perception which governed and determined the attitude of Indian capitalists towards the British, the Congress, Gandhi, the working class and the peasantry. In this attitude, at times, there appeared to be variations or ambiguities due to differing interpretations and projections but in the ultimate analysis, it was the class perception that guided the capitalist' reactions to events, institutions, and personalities. For example G.D. Birla would inform the British that he only financed the Gandhi Seva Sangh, All India Spinners Association or the Harijan Sewak Sangh and had nothing to do with the political activities of the Congress. He took pains to assure the Secretary of State for India Sir Samuel Hoare that he had never taken part or financed the Civil Disobedience movement; he had only been and was a 'severe critic of the financial policy of the government'.[2] And his closeness to Gandhi was because of his belief that 'men of his [Gandhi's] type are not

*This paper was presented at a seminar at Indian Institute of Management, Ahmedabad and published in Dwijendra Tripathi (ed.), *Business and Politics* (New Delhi, 1989).

[1] See Kapil Kumar (ed.), *Congress and Classes* (New Delhi, 1988), Introduction.

[2] G.D. Birla to Samuel Hoare, 14 March 1932; G.D. Birla, *Bapu : A Unique Association* (Bombay, 1977), Vol. 1, p. 181.

only friends of India *but also of Great Britain*' (emphasis added).[3] He further stressed that the government 'will find us always ready to work for the economic interest, leaving aside sentiments and politics'.[4] Note the words *sentiments* and *politics*.

Birla was not an exception to this brand of nationalism pursued by capitalists. Lala Shri Ram was worried in 1940 about the troops being posted at the frontiers, which might give an impression to the people that the government did not have adequate force to control the interior. Hence he pleaded with Purshotamdas Thakurdas, another leading capitalist, that

> we could ask the Viceroy . . . that the government should every now and then *pass some troops with tanks, cars, lorries, guns etc. near or through different towns, so that people may not think that there are no troops left in the country*, or that they are all concentrated either at frontier or at port towns.[5] (emphasis added)

The Lala's suggestion obviously was to demoralize people from taking recourse to any kind of agitation or revolt against the government. Almost at the same time Birla wrote to Thakurdas: 'In the name of war industrialization, we should not allow government to do anything to put up new industries under the control of British interests'.[6]

Similarly, during the Quit India movement a delegation of the Federation of Indian Chambers of Commerce and Industry (FICCI) requested the Viceroy to release Gandhi immediately as he alone could check attacks on government property. Members of the delegation felt that if these attacks were not stopped, very soon there would be attacks on private property. And their plea for Gandhi's release was not motivated by nationalism but was due to the 'long-term interests of the British in the country.'[7] Referring to Chur-

[3] Ibid. In the same letter Birla also wrote that 'Gandhiji is the greatest force on the side of peace and order. He alone is responsible for keeping the left wing in India under check'.

[4] Ibid.

[5] Shri Ram to Purshotamdas, 6 June 1940, Purshotamdas Thakurdas Papers, hereinafter PT Papers, File No. 239/I, Nehru Memorial Museum & Library, New Delhi.

[6] G.D. Birla to Purshotamdas, 25 June 1940, ibid.

[7] Ibid., File No. 239/V.

chill's assertion that he had not become 'the King's First Minister to preside over the liquidation of the British Empire', Thakurdas said at a meeting of the East India Cotton Association in 1942:

> If it was a warning given to the people of India, I think it necessary to say on behalf of the Indian commercial community that *the various demands put forward by the commercial community did not and could not aim at the liquidation of British Empire.* In fact, that is the *last thing* that any commercial man in the British commonwealth would desire.[8] [emphasis added]

The plea for the growth of native industry in a colony was no doubt against the imperialist interests but the prime concern of the Indian capitalists was to safeguard their own interests not only during the national movement but in a free India as well. How were these interests to the guarded? By deriving more and more concessions from the colonial state; by mustering support from nationalist leadership and parties in the name of establishing and encouraging indigenous industry; by increasing the number of their friends and sympathizers within the Congress, and by seeking the umbrella of both nationalists' right wing and the colonial government to crust peasants and working-class movements.

A number of works analysing the capitalist development and the political attitude of Indian capitalists have come out in recent years. Their attitude to the peasantry and peasant organizations has, however, received less scholarly attention than it deserves. A balanced understanding demands a proper enquiry into this aspect, and this is what this paper intends to do. It must, however, be admitted at the outset that the theme is too vast to be explored in a short paper and what is being presented here is only a tentative effort.

I

Before going further into the subject, it is necessary to note that many leading capitalists had landed interests. One may cite here the zamindaris of the Tatas and the Birlas.[9] Many big businessmen

[8] Ibid.

[9] Birla has purchased a big estate in Chotanagpur for Rs. 8 lakh. G.D. Birla to Mirabehn, 7 July 1939, Birla, op. cit. Vol. 3, p. 343.

not only gave donations and contribution to Gandhi and his various *sanghas* and associations; they also indulged in moneylending on a large scale and loaned vast sums to political leaders. C. Rajagopalachari used to get *hundis* of huge amounts from the Birlas[10] but the most telling case is that of Rajendra Prasad. In July 1936, Chiranjilal Bardjatia, manager of the Bachraj Jamnalal firm at Wardha and a founder pillar of the Bharat Jain Mahamandal, on a query from Jamnalal Bajaj regarding Rajendra Prasad's estate and accounts, informed him:

> Birlaji gave Rs. 45,000 to Rajendra Babu and in lieu of this on Birlaji's instructions mortage possession of the estate was taken in your name. He will return the money in 9 years. If it is not returned in 9 years the estate will be ours. Since we have mortgage possession, the interest will keep coming from estate's income every year. If we don't get the money in future, there will be no need to file a suit because the entire estate is in our control due to mortgage possession. We have given Rs. 27,000 and have got the pronote signed in the name of our shop.[11]

In another letter Bardjatia wrote:

> After coming from Chapra I had a talk with Birlaji which was as follows: (A) Some land is to be settled. If the settlement takes place 15000 to 20000 rupees can come soon. (B) The sum invested by Babuji [Rajendra Prasad] in Electricity company is being settled with Bihar Bank. If the settlement comes through we get shares on debentures and our invested money won't suffer (would be safe.) We have written to Rajendra Prasad a number of times about settling the estate but he could find no time out of Congress work; hence no sale.[12]

It is to be noted here that Rajendra Prasad was to be the prime architect of the Congress–Zamindar pact in Bihar in opposition to the Kisan Sabha in 1937.[13]

If the capitalists were owning land or indulging in moneylending

[10] There are references to this in C. Rajgopalachari Papers available in Nehru Memorial Museum & Library, New Delhi.

[11] Jamnalal Bajaj, *Patravyavahar* (New Delhi, 1969), Vol. VII, pp. 131–2.

[12] Ibid., p. 132.

[13] See Kapil Kumar, 'Congress–Peasant Relationship in the late 1930s', in D.N. Panigrahi (ed.), *Aspects of Economy, Society and Politics in Modern India* (New Delhi, 1984), p. 242.

many political leaders bought shares and debentures in their companies. For example, Indira Gandhi (then Indu, 23 years old) after consulting her father asked Jamnalal Bajaj to buy shares on their behalf: 'I have heard there is great profit in Tatas shares these days', she added.[14] Although our evidence on politicians' corporate investments is scanty at the moment, there is no doubt that this reflects on the mental attitude of the nationalist leadership towards the capitalists and that the financial interests of both were interlinked to a large extent.

The capitalist reaction to the Bardoli Satyagraha must be viewed in this light. When Thakurdas and Birla acted as intermediaries between the government and Vallabhbhai Patel to bring about a settlement, Thakurdas wrote to Patel: 'I had no doubt that you will always be prepared to settle this question *without humiliation to government* [emphasis added] and at the same time without humiliation to the people whose cause you have espoused'.[15] Thakurdas believed that Patel's leadership and firm stand had 'been successful in so far as it has attracted public notice all over India'.[16] On the other hand, Birla strongly argued with Gandhi in favour of a settlement saying '. . . if the only issue be the question of deposit of revenues, I for one would favour the ideas of some independent individual making the necessary deposits. This will help the government save face and will also keep Vallabhbhai free from the tangle'.[17] Birla told Gandhi that the government would 'assume an aggressive posture' and symptoms were wholly favourable for an agreement. Though well aware that the Bardoli struggle was likely to be of great help in 'our work relating to the Simon Commission', Birla urged Gandhi that 'the struggle should be kept apart from the wider issue of political struggle'.[18] The question here is why did Birla want it so? Nothing is spelt out clearly but the inference is clear, i.e. the economic interest of the peasantry was to be kept apart from national issues and the peasantry movement was not to

[14] Indu to Jamnalal Bajaj, 30 October 1941, Jamnalal Bajaj, *Patravyavahar* (New Delhi, 1958), Vol. I, p. 13.

[15] Thakurdas to Patel, 14 June 1928, PT Papers, File No. 74/II.

[16] Ibid.

[17] Birla to Gandhi, 25 July 1928, Birla, op. cit., Vol. 1, p. 103.

[18] Ibid.

be allowed to go beyond a point. After the settlement, however, Birla was glad that the Bardoli affairs were 'after all settled and the triumph has been for the people'. He regarded this 'as an eye opener to all the concerned' which would 'put new life into the dwindling forces of nationalism'.[19]

It would be useful for our analysis here to have some idea about Birla's understanding of the peasants' condition. In a letter of W.D. Croft in 1932 he wrote: 'In connection with my business, I had recently to travel in a number of villages and I found that although there was a great economic distress, the agriculturist so far has been able to maintain nearly the same standard of living.'[20] Birla had concluded this on the basis of information received by him that in most cases the zamindars were not getting more than 50 per cent rent, the moneylenders were not receiving interest on loans advanced, and the peasants were selling gold. He felt that the agriculturist was not left with 'much surplus gold' and in case prices did not rise, there would be a total 'refusal to pay rent and interest'.[21] Three months later he averred that 'stabilization of prices at a higher level can undoubtedly reduce the burden of agriculturist, as he is a debtor and has to pay a fixed revenue for his land'.[22] This he wrote to Gandhi, but the accent in his argument to Lord Lothian was slightly different:

> A rise in price of food stuff alone will help the cultivator only partially, as the cultivator is both a producer as well as a substantial consumer. The cultivator can, therefore, largely gain only if there is a rise in the prices of those articles which are exported, and jute and cotton stand first in the list of such produce.[23]

In these arguments taken together, Birla's concerns are clear. He was worried about the exports of cotton and jute in which he himself traded, and he lamented the loss of rent and interest by zamindars and moneylenders. His reference to the gold stocks to the peasants

[19] Birla to Thakurdas, 7 August 1928, PT Papers, File No. 74/I.

[20] Birla to Croft, 30 April 1932, Birla, op. cit., Vol. 1, pp. 181-2.

[21] Ibid.

[22] Birla to Gandhi, 22 July 1932, ibid., p. 201.

[23] Birla to Lothian, 4 August 1932, ibid., p. 213.

betrayed his ignorance of the ground realities, and he seems to have overlooked the fact that the rise in prices helped the middlemen and not the cultivator, except in extremely limited cases.

During the period the Congress ministers were in power in most of the provinces, Birla played a crucial role in guiding the Congress right wing and determining its attitude towards working-class and peasant struggles. This was a period when the peasant movement was gaining strength all over the country and the kisan sabhas faced a lot of problems with the Congress right wing. I have discussed these issues elsewhere.[24] Here I would attempt to establish the links between the actions of the colonial government, Congress ministers, Congress right wing and Birla in relation to the Kisan Sabha's activities.

In August 1937 the Bihar Kisan Sabha organized a peasants' march to the assembly. The aim was to remind the Congress ministry of the promises made to the peasantry during the election campaigns. The Viceroy believed that this was a movement which 'needed careful watching'[25] whereas the Governor of Bihar considered it a 'harmless demonstration'—the peasants 'were well-behaved and good humoured . . . rather like a body of tourists on a sight seeing tour'. The Viceroy, fearing that in future 'such demonstrations might degenerate into assemblies which might be rather a menace to the public peace',[26] advised the Congress premier of the province to take stern action.

Birla at this time was in England and was being regularly informed about events in India. Feeling that 'indiscipline as getting rampant' he wrote to Mahadev Desai:

> I very much disliked the peasants in Bihar marching to the Assembly house and occupying all the seats of the Assembly and refusing to vacate them and told them all sorts of sweet things without telling them that they were wrong in occupying the Assembly seats and refusing to vacate them.[27]

[24] See Kumar (ed.), *Congress and Classes*, pp. 238–51.

[25] Linlithgow, 25 August 1937, Linlithgow Papers (LP), S. No. 113, NMML, New Delhi.

[26] Hallet to Linlithgow, 3 September 1937, ibid.

[27] Birla to Desai, 4 September 1937, Birla, op. cit., Vol. 3, pp. 76–7.

Birla feared that 'in course of time indiscipline will grow more and more unless strict measures are taken'. He hoped that the 'Congress authorities are fully alive to the situation and they will take all necessary measures'. The rank and file, according to him, was 'confusing freedom with indiscipline'.[28] He also discussed at great length with the Viceroy the growing peasant movement in Bihar and the United Provinces (UP, now Uttar Pradesh). The Viceroy asked him to 'convey it to proper quarters that it would be very bad for the ministers, if the Governor had to use his own responsibility for maintenance of law and order'.[29] Birla assured the Viceroy that 'Pant [Govind Ballabh, the Prime Minister of UP] was fully conscious of his responsibility'. He told him that 'all big leaders of the Gandhi Sewa Sangh were strenuously working to fight out violence'. The Viceroy 'was very happy to hear this'. Nevertheless, Birla made it clear to Mahadev Desai that his own fear was that the Congress ministries in these two provinces had not fully realized the 'seriousness of the growing danger to non-violence'.[30]

Birla was of the view that 'perhaps for the next few months the most important task of the ministers would be to suppress all incitement to violence'. But this was to be done 'partly through prosecution and partly through redressing the grievances of the people'. The root cause of the troubles, according to him, was the 'exaggerated expectations'.[31] Birla believed that the discontent would not subside 'unless the Congress tells the peasants clearly that their position could be improved ultimately through their own hard work alone and not by any stroke of wand'.[32] In his opinion, abolishing the zamindari or nationalization of accumulated wealth would 'hardly add much to the existing income of the masses'.[33] 'Bread is not going to come out of confiscation of zamindaris', he wrote. 'Our ministers', he further added, 'will have to decide from this

[28] Ibid.

[29] Birla to Desai, 4 December 1937, ibid., pp. 105–6.

[30] Ibid.

[31] For details of these expectations, see Kumar (ed.) *Congress and Classes*, pp. 235–6.

[32] Birla to Desai, 4 December 1937, Birla, op. cit., Vol. 3, p. 106.

[33] Ibid.

very moment as to what they are going to do for ameliorating the condition of the people. If they think that the amelioration depends on the confiscation of the properties, then I think they are deceiving themselves'.[34] And then he presented a frightening scenario:

> The question of discontent just now is linked up with economics and unless steps are taken to make the peasants realize what is possible and what is not, I fear the ferment will grow to such an extent that it will become impossible after a certain stage for the ministers to maintain discipline. And as Bapu has said so many time, inviting the help of the Military will be the death knell of the provincial government.[35]

Thus, what Birla was basically demanding here was total check on peasant's actions; strict measures by ministers and an end to the talk of confiscation of zamindaris or private property. Here was a case of direct support to zamindars by a capitalist.

Barely six days after Birla had written the above letter to Mahadev Desai, the Congress leadership put a ban on the Bihar Kisan Sabha on 10 December 1937. This was later ratified by the Congress Working Committee. The speeches of kisan leader were reported by the Central Intelligence Department and their mail intercepted. It was during this period that the Congress under the guidance of Rajendra Prasad, Patel and Maulana Abul Kalam Azad entered into an agreement with the landlords in Bihar, and kisan workers were prosecuted.[36] When all this was going on Mahadev Desai informed Birla that the 'situation has decidedly improved in Bihar'.[37] Similarly, Pant send a 'very reassuring' letter to Birla saying that 'there was nothing to worry about agrarian trouble and he was keeping his fingers on the pulse'. The Viceroy hearing this reassuring news from Birla was 'quite pleased'.[38] But both Birla and Desai were quite upset over Rafi Ahmed Kidwai's declaration at a kisan meeting at Partapgarh on 20 December that 'the Congress government would either be forced to adopt coercive measures or get out of office if the

[34] Ibid.

[35] Ibid.

[36] See Kumar (ed.), *Congress and Classes*, pp. 242–3.

[37] Desai to Birla, 22 December 1937 Birla, op. cit., Vol. 3, p. 127.

[38] Birla to Desai, 21 December 1937, ibid., p. 124.

peasants did not abide by the laws in force today'.[39] Kidwai was a Congress minister in UP but instead of changing the tenancy laws enacted by an alien government, he was asking the peasants to follow them. But the British, Birla and Desai felt that 'a responsible minister cannot run away from his responsibility by offering to resign'.[40] Gandhi agreed with Birla that 'anarchical tendencies are striking roots in the Congress' and assured him that 'I have been exerting my utmost to check this development'.[41] He was not referring to the peasants or workers alone. During this period, any kind of mass action, including innocent public welcome of released political prisoners, was condemned by Gandhi, the right wing and Birla.[42]

II

An important development from 1936 onwards was the coming closer of the All-India Trade Union Congress (AITUS) and the All-India Kisan Sabha (AIKS). The latter appealed to peasants to celebrate May Day and cooperate with city workers in their struggles against capitalists. As a prominent kisan leader Sahajanand Saraswati pointed out:

> Till recently it [May Day] had been the international day of only factory workers throughout the world and agrarian workers and peasantry had very little, if at all, realized its significance. Gradually came the turn of the European and American peasants and they began to observe it and thus showed their solidarity with factory comrades. Only last year, the Kisans throughout our country observed the Kisan day on 1 May and thus expressed their solidarity with the workers all over the world.[43]

All affiliates of the AIKS celebrated May Day and by 1938 the slogan '*Kisan mazdur raj Kayam ho*' (Let the worker-peasant regime emerge) had gained momentum. The AIKS was attempting to make the peasants aware of their responsibility towards other exploited

[39] *Modern Review*, LXII (1938), p. 119.
[40] Birla, op. cit., Vol. 3, pp. 132, 141.
[41] Gandhi to Birla, 26 August 1938, ibid., p. 187.
[42] See Kumar (ed.), *Congress and Classes*, p. 249.
[43] *All India Kisan Bulletin* (*AIKB*), 16 April 1937.

classes.[44] It also organized the sweepers in Gaya who went on strike for higher wages. In certain pockets united actions were taken. For example, in December 1937 the Textile Workers Union of Nagpur organized a march to the assembly in association with kisan, demanding that the Congress ministry should outline its labour policy and give immediate relief from wage cuts to textile workers.[45]

When the Congress imposed a ban on the Bihar Kisan Sabha in December 1937, an AITUC session held in January 1938 condemned it in strong language and assured the AIKS of its full support in the fight against landlordism and vested interests. The session also passed resolutions favouring abolition of zamindars and all other intermediaries.[46] The Bihar Kisan Sabha expressed its gratitude to the AITUC for supporting the peasants' cause.[47] In the speeches of virtually all AIKS leaders as well as the peasant leaders operating at local levels, feudalism and capitalism were mentioned together and the zamindars and capitalists as synonyms of peasant exploitation.[48] In November 1938, the Kanpur factory workers expressed solidarity with peasants and denounced the pro-landlord attitude of the Congress ministry in relation to the Tenancy Bill.[49] Sahajanand believed that the entire socio-economic problem revolved around the peasant. This was because a significant proportion of the urban proletariat consisted of those who migrated in search of some relief from suffering confronted in rural areas, and kept alternating between fields and mills.[50] Interestingly, this rural–urban link was described by Birla to Churchill: 'No townsman is a pure townsman in India. Everyone maintains touch with the villages.'[51] Gandhi was conscious

[44] Ibid., 22 April 1938.

[45] Ibid., 10 December 1937.

[46] Ibid., 14 January 1938.

[47] Ibid., 4 February 1938.

[48] During the late 1930s, Baba Ram Chandra was very critical of capitalist domination. Baba Ram Chandra Papers, SF No. 3, NMML, New Delhi. For his work amongst peasants, see Kapil Kumar, *Peasants in Revolt*, New Delhi, 1984.

[49] *AIKB*, 11 November 1938.

[50] *Congress Socialist*, 26 December 1936.

[51] Birla to Churchill, August 1935, Birla, op. cit., Vol. 2, p. 141.

of the growing unrest among the peasants as he admitted in a letter to Guy Wint in 1939:

The agrarian unrest is a much greater danger, but if the Congress retains non-violence it is bound to be disciplined. We who believe in non-violence are trying to cope with it, but we may fail. And yet we are not going the way of China. In China peasants can be soldiers at will but not here in India. In India we cannot make soldiers so easily. But I agree that you have spotted the real danger. However, it will cease if the Congress can produce real type of workers for the villages.[52]

The Mahatma 'did not dread' the labour unrest much 'for factory labourers were not more than 20 lakhs 'who lived 'only in artificial cities'. Discarding the 'psychological importance' of labour unrest and confident that 'those bent on mischief cannot spread red ruin in the villages' Gandhi advised Wint to 'hook his mind to the villages and not the towns'.[53]

A number of Gandhi Sewa Sangh volunteers were moved into Bihar villages to counter the Kisan Sabha propaganda. Significantly enough, what these volunteers preached was not class adjustment or class collaborations but class submission.[54] And we must take note of the fact that the Sangh was financed by G.D. Birla. The coming together of the working class and the peasants was alarming for the Congress right wing and capitalists who worked hand in hand. For example Ramkrishna Dalmia, an emerging industrialist, had financed the Congress in Bihar during the elections of 1937.[55] The same year Rajendra Prasad advocated the candidature of Dalmia for a by-election to the central assembly as an independent candidate, supported by the Congress. He wrote to Patel:

As I told you Dalmia would like to have the seat *but on account of his many business connections he does not* like to take the Congress ticket. As you know he

[52] Ibid., Vol. 3, p. 224.

[53] Ibid.

[54] See Kapil Kumar, 'Ideology Congress and Peasants in 1930s: Class Adjustment or Submission?', *Social Scientist*, XIV-89 (August–September 1986), pp. 40–55.

[55] There are many letters exchanged between Dalmia, Bajaj and Rejendra Prasad in this regard.

has been always helpful and there is a feeling in some of our workers that it is worthwhile leaving this seat uncontested. Personally I have confidence that he will support the Congress in most matters [emphasis added].[56]

Prasad also brought to Patel's notice that 'there may be some among Congressman particularly those connected with Kisan Sabha who may disapprove of this action'.[57] In the earlier election Dalmia had lost to the Congress candidate supported by the Kisan Sabha. Patel turned down Prasad's proposal perhaps because of his fears that support to Dalmia would further aggravate the political challenge to the right wing leadership and its alliance with the capitalist, but this does not detract from the significance of Prasad's suggestion.

The growing unity of the peasants and the working class served them well as several agitations succeeded only because of their mutual support. In this regard the labour strike at the sugar mill in Bihta in Bihar is noteworthy. Promoted by Dalmia in 1932 the mill had been established in response to the protection granted to the sugar industry[58] which encouraged virtually all leading capitalists to invest in this industry. To establish his mill Dalmia sought the help of Rajendra Prasad and Swami Sahajanand Saraswati who, though working for the peasants, was during this phase a staunch Gandhian. The Swami would later regret his association with Dalmia but conceded:

It was only through this mill that how shrewdly the rich selfish capitalists exploit the people. How big leaders and the Mahatma entrapped in their grip, help them in this and are unable to realize for people's welfare. But in reality it is the capitalist who used them to exploit the poor.[59]

Dalmia faced problems with zamindars of Bihta in buying land for the mill. The vice-chairman of the Danapur local board approached Sahajanand and sought to assure him: 'He should not be

[56] Rajendra Prasad to Patel, 5 May 1937, Rajendra Prasad Papers, NMML, New Delhi.

[57] Ibid.

[58] See Sanjay Baru, 'State and Industrialization: The Political Economy of Sugar Policy, 1932–47', in Panigrahi (ed.), op. cit., p. 105.

[59] Sahajanand Saraswati, *Mera Jiwan Sangharsh* (Patna, 1952), p. 455.

worried about donations for his Ashram. Once he helps the *milwalas* in getting land, money would be no problem.'[60] Sahajanand took strong exception to this offer saying: I piss on such money as it will enslave me to the *millwalas*'.[61] Yet he did help Dalmia in acquiring land because he thought, to quote his own words, 'that since a tax of Rs. 6 and 5 annas has been imposed on imported sugar, sugar mills will open in this region. So instead of a foreigner opening it this Dalmia would be much better because he wears a Gandhi cap and calls himself a Congressman. People also consider him so.'[62]

Soon the industrialist's family started visiting the Swami's ashram. Dalmia proposed that his sister's son be allowed to stay in the ashram. The young man's mother and grandmother also supported this request. They wanted to construct a house for their ward in the ashram but Sahajanand refused to go along, saying that he could not break the rules and no servants could be provided in the ashram. The family continued its visits and on various pretexts, like *puja, birthday*, etc., would leave small amounts of money during these visits for sweets to be distributed among the ashramites. Sahajanand put a stop to this also, realizing that Dalmia's generous gestures might tie his hands if he decided to stand up against the mill management to espouse the peasant cause in future. To quote his own picturesque language: 'It is said when a thief goes to commit burglary he takes some jaggery for the dogs. When they bark, it is fed to them and this stops their barking. The same is done by the capitalist. Knowing that we are going to bark, they offer us jaggery in advance.'[63]

Significantly, Rajendra Prasad was included as a director of the mill and Madan Mohan Malviya was to come for its inauguration. On the occasion of the opening of the mill, a number of promise were made. The workers were promised model houses for themselves and schools for their children; and the peasants were assured high prices for cane. It was stated that an existing rival company in the

[60] Ibid.
[61] Ibid.
[62] Ibid.
[63] Ibid., p. 456.

vicinity, the Sutherland Mills owned by Englishmen, incurred a great deal of avoidable expenditure because of which it paid lower wages to the worker and less price to the grower for his cane. The Dalmia factory would husband its resources carefully; hence the peasants would get high prices for cane, and workers higher wages. And yet the sugar produced here would be cheaper than in the English company.[64] It is quite clear that the management wished to take full advantage of the rising swadeshi sentiments.

But what actually happened in relation to peasants and workers was worse that what was happening in the English mill. The price offered by the Dalmias for cane was 3 annas per maund as against 6 annas by the Sutherland Mills. When this was brought to the promoter's notice by Sahajanand, Dalmia's reply was that 'he has to see the principle of demand and supply'. Now the tug of war started. Sahajanand warned the peasants not to give up jaggery-making or else they would become the slaves of the mill. The mill management wanted the peasants to stop producing jaggery to ensure supply of raw material to the mill. Dalmia even accused Sahajanand of opposing the mill out of grudge because the latter had asked Dalmia for Rs. 2,000, which had been refused. But it did not carry any weight with the peasants and the mill was ultimately forced to abide by its promises and pay 7 to 8 annas per maund about 1 anna more than paid by other mills.[65] Sahajanand informed Nehru of Dalmia's promises and what he was doing now. He believed that Dalmia had trapped Rajendra Prasad into accepting the directorship of the mill. At this time Prasad was imprisoned and Sahajanand believed that Prasad 'realizes everything . . . and is ready to resign from the directorship of the Mills . . . only his confinement is a great obstacle'.[66] But Sahajanand was not aware of the actual relationship between Prasad and Dalmia to which we have referred earlier.

The cane growers were not fully satisfied with the value they

[64] Ibid.

[65] Ibid.

[66] Sahajanand to J. Nehru, 2 November 1933, J. Nehru Papers, Vol. 91, NMML, New Delhi.

received for their produce and the worker's discontent in the meantime was also mounting. The result was Dalmia mill witnessed as many as three strikes within a brief period of two years between 1936 and 1938. The first strike was in 1936, the issue being sugar cane prices. For months the peasants stopped the supply of sugar cane to the factory. The mill procured it from different places at 12 to 14 annas per maund but was not prepared to offer the same prices to local cultivators. The peasants picketed the bullock-carts that carried cane to the mill and many were arrested. Though the mill suffered heavy losses the strike failed.[67] Yet the success lay elsewhere. The peasants had learnt their first lesson in strike against a capitalist and were better prepared next time.

In January 1937 the mill-workers went on strike for higher wages. In support of workers the peasants stopped supplying sugar cane to the mill. This forced the mill to accept the workers' demands within forty-eight hours of the commencement of the strike. Towards the end of 1938, the workers again went on strike on the ground of non-implementation of the agreement. But only 250 workers could hold on due to threats and repression by the management. Again the peasants came to their rescue and refused to supply cane. About 250 of them were jailed within a brief span of two days. This time the management approached Sahajanand with a lump sum donation of Rs. 10,200 per month for the ashram. The emissary who came with this offer had to flee the ashram for his life and ultimately the mill had to concede the demands.[68]

The peasant-worker joint action perturbed the capitalist and alarmed the sugar syndicate. Besides Dalmia, Birla, Shri Ram and Jamnalal Bajaj owned sugar factories in UP and Bihar.[69] The Congress depended on the sugar lobby for funds. As Pant wrote to Bajaj: 'There are many sugar factories in Gorakhpur. In case you can take pains to go there, I firmly believe, you will be able to get a good amount of money. . . . It will create inconvenience to you but . . . it is for

[67] Sahajanand Saraswati, op. cit., p. 459.

[68] Ibid. Such struggles continued in future also against retrenchment of workers.

[69] Sanjay Baru, op. cit., p. 108.

you to save us from financial difficulties.'[70] This perhaps explains why even Jawaharlal Nehru chose to silence Shibbanlal Saxena in Gorakhpur. Saxena was mobilizing the sugar cane growers and other peasants in the 1930s. The sugar lobby complained against him to the Viceroy and Gandhi. Jawaharlal wrote the Viceroy: 'I must confess he [Saxena] is crude of speech and occasionally his tongue runs away with him when he discusses the plight of the peasantry. *We have warned him privately several times* and our advice has had effect on him'[71] (emphasis added).

These instances demonstrate that by the late 1930s the kisan sabhas and the pro-peasant leadership were not only advocating the peasants' cause but also opposing both the zamindars and the capitalist. This stance is reflected not only in their position on economic demands but the way these demands were related to the political struggle against the British. All this added to the coming closer of the right wing Congressmen and the capitalist. The capitalist left no stone unturned to guide and strengthen the right wing in checking not only the working class but the awakening among the peasants also. Birla's condemnation of peasant marches and stress on discipline is one amongst the many cases that can be cited in this context. The friendly relationship of the capitalist with the British on the one hand and their growing influence in the Congress on the other remained a constant factor in the freedom struggle. A unique feature of the Indian transition towards capitalism has been not the conflict between capitalism and feudalism, but their mutual cooperation, support and a policy of accommodating each other. Devising methods to crush the peasants struggle was a part of this mutual understanding duly supported by the Congress right wing.

[70] Bajaj, op. cit., p. 42.

[71] Nehru to Viceroy, 6 October 1939, J. Nehru Papers, Vol. 42.

PART 3

COMMUNALISM?

CHAPTER 10

Dominant-Grassroots Dichotomy in Hindu–Muslim Relations: A Study of Political Mobilization in Colonial and Post-Colonial India*

No religion preaches violence or killing of human beings. However, the irony is that, historically speaking, the amounts of killings that have taken place in the name of religion surpass even the killings in wars or by any other reason. This is because the way religious ideologies have been usurped by the dominant vested interests to make use of religion for carrying forward their own agendas at the cost of common people, i.e. the grassroots of human society. There has always been a dichotomy in relation to the usage of religion by the dominant groups and the commoners in practically every society. Very often the worship of same gods has been invoked by divergent social groups even within the same community to carry forward or fight for their own group interests. In fact, the peasant wars in Germany are the classic illustrations of these two facets of the religion.[1] The Indian society has witnessed all kinds of usage of religion, i.e. from its immensely conservative social implications to social reforms; from serving the dominant groups to challenging this dominance by the commoners; from inter-community conflict to harmony; for political mobilization in the freedom struggle and

* This paper was presented at a UNESCO sponsored Conference on Inter-community relations at the University of South Australia, Adelaide, September 2008. It is not possible to deal with all the aspects in a paper. However, I have picked up instances that represent the arguments I am trying to build.

[1] Frederick Engels, *The Peasant War in Germany* (Moscow, 1974). There was also a time in England when the monarchy, the rising bourgeoisie and the commoners, each had their own god fighting the others.

Partition and in modern India for vote bank politics.[2] It is in this context that one must analyse the usage of religion by different groups in order to have a better understanding of inter-community relationships so as to enable in establishing a peaceful and harmonious society.

Hindu–Muslim relations have been subjected to research by scholars from different disciplines with divergent ideological frameworks and the ongoing research has created a huge corpus of literature.[3] However, most of the researches in this area have a stereotype conclusion that the two communities have always been at crossroads; there is a great divide between the two, and the Partition of India was a logical outcome of this religious divide that was supported by all Muslims in India. Based on official records, newspaper reports and private papers of the leaders and political parties, such history writing only reflects the perceptions and attitudes of the dominant and elite groupings within these communities and distances itself from the grassroots' social reality. It knowingly avoids researching the relationship among the common people where the communities stood together, fought together, had a strong process of cultural assimilation and so on. This kind of history often ignores or suppresses such research which proves the harmonious and cordial relations among the communities. The personal vested interests, spiced with ideological covers, are so dominant among the scholars that they interpret, cite or use the sources twisting them as per the occasion which suites their own politics and career. For example we have a historian, who, while lecturing in UK universities stresses that the British were not responsible for the Partition of India. In Pakistan he absolves the Muslim League from this responsibility. In Delhi, he does not hold the Congress responsible for Partition and when he lectures in Kolkata, he puts the responsibility on imperialism. After all he has been seeking benefits from all and has

[2] Also see, Kapil Kumar, *Peasants in Revolt: Tenants, Landlords, Congress and the Raj in Oudh: 1886–1922* (New Delhi, 1984), pp. 221–3.

[3] It is difficult to review all the literature on this theme and also to cite the vast research along with the sources. This paper presents an alternate view which is based on official and non-official sources and for post-colonial period on the field experiences of the author.

been rewarded with fellowships, visits and high positions. He can be secular as well as a spokesperson for the minority, depending on the audience or the occasion, as the case may be.[4]

I

All shades of literature that post-mortems the Partition of India and the creation of Pakistan—irrespective of ideological thrusts—highlights and stresses upon religious divide as its cause, genocide, violence, barbarianism and forced migration as an outcome and so on. This, I consider to be a one-sided view which represents the biased, negative and dark aspects of human history. Thus, what have been transmitted to the next generations are the hatred, divide and antagonism between the Hindus and the Muslims along with the gory memories of Partition, often under-playing or ignoring the role of the British. Such a portrait can only be a hurdle in improving inter-community relations and very often it leads to increased communal tensions contributing to riots. This is because generations of youth are fed with this information, thus, closing the doors for re-conciliation and cooperation amongst the two communities in regions where misconceptions exist or are created for vote politics in contemporary India. Agreed, such violent incidents and events did take place and are history. At the same time we must remember that along the side of these events some thing else also happened in history. In the midst of Partition violence there were also cases where the neighbours belonging to one community saved the lives or gave shelter to those of the other community risking their own lives;[5] where the common people opposed the idea of Partition;[6]

[4] I am holding the name of the scholar for reasons of privacy but the assumption is based on my discussions with a number of scholars and historians like Prof. Jayanto Ray from Kolkata and I take full responsibility for this.

[5] As a child I have heard of many such incidents from my maternal grandparents, uncles and aunts who migrated from Lahore in 1947. I am sure there are still many people alive who passed through such experiences and it is for the researchers to locate them and record their memoirs.

[6] It must be remembered that it was a fraction of the population with voting rights based on property qualifications that voted in favour of Pakistan and not

where the people in spite of communal rioting in some areas were still carrying joint struggles against the British.[7] Do the history textbooks contain such cases? Or how many scholars have researched this? Is it not the job of the historian to research and transmit such history (how so ever meagre these incidents might have been) to the next generations and of course with a judgement that this was humanism, this was rationality, this was peace and brotherhood that needs to be practised in the modern world. This is the way for a historian to play a positive role in bridging the gap between communities and make use of history to strengthen inter-community relations and contribute towards societal development. Unfortunately, the historians have miserably failed in this as they safeguard their personal interests only and have willy-nilly contributed to widen the divide. However, in this context the creative writers have done a much better job. One only has to look at Rahi Masoom Reza's novel *Adha Gaon* (Half Village) or Khushwant Singh's *A Train to Pakistan*, besides many other novels to prove this point. As peace is the need of the day then the history of peace, history of harmonious relationships, history of cultural assimilation and development of multi-cultural societies or emergence of new cultures has to be researched, taught and preached. And I emphasize preached to all. You can't establish a peaceful world by teaching the history of violence and hatred and that too based on biased perceptions, religious fanaticism, terrorism or ideological cover-ups.

We have had enough of these models of researching riots, causes

---

the common people. The 'lower castes' and lower classes had no voting rights and could not voice their views. 'It is the upper class Muslims who voted for it', Asghar Ali Engineer, *South Asian Voice*, April 1998. Engineer also is of the opinion that 'the Pakistan movement was not led by religious divines'. Ibid. Similarly, Yasmin Khan has also exposed 'the obliviousness of the small elite driving division' in the most recent publication on the Partition of India, Yasmin Khan, *The Great Partition: The Making of India and Pakistan* (New Delhi, 2007).

[7] The Royal Naval Mutiny, Movement against the INA trials, the Postal Workers Strike, etc., are some examples that have been elaborately cited by Sumit Sarkar, 'Popular Movements and National Leadership, 1945–7', *Economic and Political Weekly*, April 1982.

of hatred, etc., and in some cases even if actions have been initiated with all honesty on the basis of the findings of such research, the results are hardly positive or encouraging because all such studies land up in a blame game or are confined to refereed journals. What *I am arguing is the reverse model based on empirical evidences that communal rioting and community division is a sporadic phenomenon and not a continuous ongoing lifestyle of the people.* Incase there is communal rioting in ten cities one must also take into account that another three thousand cities and thousands of small towns and villages are peaceful with people leading a normal life. Hence, in the reverse model what *I suggest is to study and analyse the causes of: harmonious and peaceful co-existence, the brotherly relations and mutual cooperation along with the factors that provide sustainability to such relationships: the living examples of cultural assimilation where ever it exists and apply those situations in the riot driven or riot sensitive areas. In this model there are no blames or charges and counter charges but appreciation and praise for peaceful co-existence and harmony with an appeal to replicate that model.* For example, the metro city of Mumbai had laughed at Bhiwandi communal riots. But when Mumbai was in flames, the whole of Bhiwandi was on the streets. The priests and the moulvis, the old and young from both the communities patrolled the streets to ensure that no mischief-monger starts a riot. Why not learn from this and replicate it?

Another aspect to be accounted for in this reverse model is to understand that religion is a social reality which should not be misused for vote bank politics or appeasement by political parties in a modern democratic state. It is not just the 'opium of the masses' but also the 'heart of the heartless society' and the state has to ensure equal opportunities and rights for all its citizens irrespective of the religions they belong to or follow. On the other hand, it is for the citizens also to ensure that their religion is not hijacked by fanatics or terrorists for their own vested interests.

The all mighty Soviet State could not uproot religion from the psyche of the people and the left in India has been using religion as per its convenience. The CPI supported the Pakistan resolution, i.e. the division of the country by an imperialist power based on religion. Today also, the left in India follows a policy towards religion that is full of hypocrisy and contradictions. It condemns religion as a social reality and at the same time uses the Durga Puja as a front to increase its cadres in Bengal.[8] They beat the drum of secularism and at the same time ask Taslima Nasreen, the exiled Bangladeshi author to leave Bengal so as to appease the Muslim vote bank as *fatwas*[9] have been issued by the imams for the head of Taslima with no action against them from the democratic government at the centre in India or the left government in Bengal and the Congress government in Andhra Pradesh. The left parties have no hesitation in tying up with communal political parties like the Muslim League in Kerala[10] yet they condemn the Hindu communal parties. They fail to realize that communalism is communalism, irrespective of any religion—minority or majority. If it exists amongst anyone of them it will lead to its emergence amongst the other. One has to remember the difference between religion and communalism and work for the eradication of the later among both—the majority as well as the minority. The left government in Bengal invited the Muslim riot victims of Gujarat to settle in Bengal.[11] This appeared to be a very good gesture but this gesture becomes negative and smells of vote bank politics. Had it been a humanitarian gesture based on the principles of secularism then the same invitation

[8] Durga Puja is the most popular of the Hindu festivals in Bengal where Goddess Durga is worshipped. It is deep-rooted in the Bengali culture and the left parties have not only accepted it but make good use of it for political purposes.

[9] *Fresh Fatwa Against Taslima*, Kolkata Newsline, cited in expressindia.com, Saturday, 18 August 2007. It is important to note that whereas the Deoband Muftis criticized the *fatwa* against Taslima which had a prize of Rs.1,00,000 (US $2,500 at that time) for anyone eliminating her if she did not leave the country in a month's time, the left government in 2008 ordered her to leave Bengal (kafila.org; taslimanasrin.com). This demonstrates the hypocrisy of the left parties in relation to secularism as they are more worried about the orthodox Muslim vote banks.

[10] Since 1967, the left parties have formed an alliance with the Muslim League in Kerala, see *Political Background*, official website of Kerala government—www.kerala.gov.in.

[11] *Times of India*, 10 August 2003, timesofindia.indiatimes.com.

should have been extended to the Kashmir's Hindu migrants as more than half million Hindus have been thrown out of Kashmir by the militants—a big blow to the cultural assimilation and co-existence for centuries of the two communities in Kashmir. Here again, it is not the common people but the politics of the dominant groups that has created such a situation, very often with support from the military junta from across the borders where democratic forces are still struggling to have a hold.

This is vote bank opportunism in the name of secularism and that too one-sided, which is devoid of ideological principles. And here too, there is a dichotomy evident between the cadres and the politbureau dictates. Many among the cadres are, by and large, genuinely secular and also question the appeasement decisions. But the party has no democratic functioning, hence no answers but dictates only in the name of tactics, strategy and survival of the party in a bourgeoisie set-up, i.e. a policy of opportunism.[12] The reason I am being critical of the left is that it is the only political party in India that claims to be following a scientific and rational ideology based on principles. However, there is a great hiatus between what is claimed, preached and actually practised by both—the CPI and the CPM.

II

Let me go a little further to highlight certain facts related to the Partition of India—the most controversial and sensitive issue in the history of South Asia whose memories are used by dominant interests to mar inter-community relations today also. I am not citing any new sources but attempting to reiterate, once again, what has been intentionally discarded or kept away from the people. 'Our national organization had taken a decision in favour of Partition but the entire people grieved over Partition'[13] were the words of

[12] The author was a member of the CPI(M) till 1996 and witness to many such questions raised by the cadres and suppressed by the leadership.

[13] Maulana Abul Kalam Azad, *India Wins Freedom* (Hyderabad, 1988), p. 226.

Maulana Azad as compared to Jawaharlal Nehru who admitted that they were a 'tired people', not prepared to go to the gallows once again for the sake of the country.[14] And Mahatma Gandhi who had declared that 'Partition would be over my dead body' did not feel like breaking his 'silence day' even while meeting Mountbatten on 2 June 1947 on this issue that affected the millions and wrote on a piece of paper 'have I said one word against you in my speeches? If you admit that I have not, your warning is superfluous.'[15] This was considered by Mountbatten as 'a document of historic importance'.[16] Yet, The Mahatma broke his *maunvrata* (silence) when the Pakistan resolution was moved in the Congress session by G.B. Pant and it appeared that in case there was to be a vote, it might be defeated. Gandhi's speech to the delegates was an emotional blackmail that he often practised in his politics. No doubt, that by now he had become redundant for those very leaders whom he only had created or promoted within the Congress as he himself confessed that today there were fellow monarchs in the Congress if he still considered himself to be one. In fact, Gandhi made contradictory statements on Pakistan at different occasions but the hard fact is that in spite of his earlier vehement opposition, he ultimately approved of the idea. It is a well recorded fact of history that during his last meeting with Abdul Gaffar Khan, the Gandhi of North-West Frontier Provinces who wanted to merge with India or have autonomy for Baluchistan, Mahatma Gandhi pleaded that he should accept Pakistani as a reality and work for it really being a Pakistan.

Another fact, worth mentioning here, is the correspondence between Aruna Asaf Ali and Gandhi during this period cited by Sumit Sarkar.[17] She wrote to Gandhi to come out and lead a movement against the Partition and cited Hindu–Muslim unity that was well

[14] Interview (1960) cited in Leonard Mosley, *The Last Days of the British Raj* (Bombay, 1971), p. 285.

[15] *Collected Works of Mahatma Gandhi*, Vol. 95, 30 April–6 July 1947, p. 191.

[16] Ibid.

[17] Sarkar, *Popular Movements and National Leadership*, op. cit., p. 862. Also see *Collected Works of Mahatma Gandhi*, Vol. 90, p. 5.

demonstrated recently during the INA trials, Royal Naval Mutiny at Indian ports, the Postal strikes and so on. Gandhi rejected this unity as they had joined hands on barricades and talked of the divide between the communities. In fact, the great leader of the masses who has been lauded by scholars and politicians as one who knew the pulse of the masses either did not want to read the pulse at that hour or found himself too weak to lead the common men and women. A frustrated Aruna Asaf Ali wrote back that they can join hands at barricades only. I would like to stress that Gandhi was not only a political philosopher but also an active politician. Hence, any analysis of him will be appropriate only if it takes into account both, his real polity in action as well as his thoughts and writings. The thrust of the Gandhi led national movement was on non-violence. The revolutionaries, peasants, workers and the left wing were all condemned for violence by the Congress. Yet, violence came because of communalism and the acceptance of partition decision by the Congress. Can we isolate the genocide and violence that followed the stamping of partition decision from the non-violent struggle for India's independence that left behind a legacy of communal rioting and now terrorism? The responsibility for the genocide has to be owned more by the British than any one else as they remained moot spectators in spite of having all the resources still at their disposal to implement a peaceful transfer of power.[18] The British government had wanted to leave India by 1948. However, Lord Mountbatten had shortened this time to August 1947. Perhaps, Mountbatten was too much in a haste to be back in England with his lady than leaving her more in the company of *the would-be* Indian Prime Minister.[19] Whatever might have been the situation

[18] Also see Stanley Wolpert, *Shameful Flight: The Last Years of the British Empire in India* (New York, 2006).

[19] Starting from Maulana Abul Kalam Azad (op. cit., p. 198), who believed that it was the influence of Lady Mountbatten that Nehru agreed for Partition of India many works have come out on this relationship. I personally believe that no one should comment on the personal relationship of two adults unless that has a bearing on public life and in the case of Partition, I fear, this relationship did have a bearing. Some scholars believe that 'Mountbatten was impatient to get back to England and build his naval career'.

and whatever be the mental state and agony of the leaders, it is clear that they too have to share the responsibility of the violence and further, that the common people of both communities at the grassroots were not a party to the Partition of India that had been demanded or agreed upon by the dominant leadership. In fact, *India was divided not because of religion but in the name of religion.* The division of Pakistan leading to the creation of Bangladesh some 25 years later in 1971 further provides testimony to the argument being presented.

Advani's comment in Pakistan, during his goodwill visit in May 2005 that Jinnah was secular drew a lot of criticism within his own party not to say of the other political parties. This was a criticism based on the polity and communal perceptions of the dominant political elite of the day to be used as an emotional weapon for votes in a secular democracy. Or else how does one explain the following well-known facts?

- Jinnah never supported the Khilafat movement for the restoration of Khalifa in Turkey after the First World War as it had nothing to do with India, where as Gandhi and the Congress championed the Khilafat cause.
- Jinnah remained a staunch supporter of Tilak in Indian politics whereas Tilak is regarded as a staunch Hindu revivalist.
- Jinnah discarded as impractical and childish the map of Pakistan drawn by Rahamat Ali at Oxford.
- Jinnah rejected Iqbal's idea of Pakistan as a poets' dream—not reality.

Then why did the same Jinnah, who would not even follow or observe some of the essentials of Islamic religion demanded Pakistan as a separate State for Muslims in 1940? Yet, why he gave a trial to interim government experiment in 1946? Why he ultimately he went for a direct action day and got Pakistan created with the blessings of the British and connivance of the Congress leadership? Someone will also have to explain that why such regions went to Pakistan, with the exception of Sindh that had never been under the dominance of the Muslim League in spite of having a sizeable Muslim population? NWFP remained under the dominance of

Badshah Abdul Gaffar Khan and his Khudai Khidmatgars. Punjab had remained under the Unionist Party and Bengal, under the Proja Krishak Party. And if Pakistan was created for Muslims why was it that a large number of Muslims decided to stay back in India? The answer is clear that it was the Muslim dominant elite that wanted Pakistan and not the common people. The elections of 1937 had been a disaster for the former but the backtracking by the Congress in United Provinces[20] from its pre-election stance of offering ministerial berths to Muslim League even in the case of Congress victory provided a handy situation for religion being used as an effective tool in the power politics game leading to the celebration of Deliverance Day by the League in 1939 on the resignation of Congress ministries and ultimately the passing of Pakistan Resolution in 1940. Jinnah's fading image in politics got a boost when Gandhi started addressing him as *Quaid-e-Azam*[21] and he was back in the saddle in the early 1940s.

III

The medieval times in India had witnessed all kinds of situations when it comes to Hindu–Muslim relations. One has to measure the period in the context of the polity that existed in those times and not by the context of today. No doubt the invaders indulged in ghastly acts, demolished temples, killed Hindus and looted cities. Yet, some of them invaded at the invitation of the Hindu kings who had a score to settle with their neighbours as that was the political reality of that period. There is no justification for this kind of barbarianism in any human society of any age but the question is how long can we carry it forward while building a contemporary society wherein humanism, human rights, civil rights, respect for all religions and co-existence of all religions have emerged as modern values after an age of colonialism, imperialism and communism.

In the pre-colonial Indian context, it must be noted that the

[20] See Salil Mishra, *A Narrative of Communal Politics: Uttar Pradesh 1937–9* (New Delhi, 2001), pp. 323–5.

[21] Even a cursory look at the CWMG volumes for this period demonstrates this.

entire Mughal empire stood on the support of orthodox Hindu Rajputs. The power politics of the day was based on brothers killing brothers to capture the throne and belonging to the same community or religion was no consideration. Similarly, the princes of Jaipur and Jodhpur led Aurangzeb's forces against Shivaji where as the *Gardis* managed the Maratha guns. One can cite numerous examples in this regard as that was the politics of the day. But there also emerged some beautiful things through social interaction and assimilation of cultures once the invaders had settled themselves on the Indian soil. The Indian society from the ancient times did follow the concept of *Sarv Dharm Sambhav* (let all religions flourish) and has a tradition of assimilation of cultures. Whether it was the Greeks, the Huns, the Kushans, Arabs, Turks and so on, the cultural traditions got assimilated in the Indian society. It was this elasticity in the socio-religious life of India that Sufism emerged as a way of life. There were scholars like Amir Khusro or Dara Shikoh to cite only a few that studied the classical Sanskrit texts and many were translated into Persian. As an interaction of Persian and Devanagari, scripts and dialects, Urdu came up as a language of the common people. A new architecture that saw the confluence of both styles led to the construction of huge monuments like the Taj Mahal and so on. One can go on citing such examples of assimilation of cultures between the Hindus and the Muslims in different fields of life. Why not transmit these aspects of history to the present generation? It is this, the history of cultural assimilation, mutual cooperation and respect amongst the communities that will lead to the creation of a harmonious and peaceful society in the modern times.

IV

Coming to what has been termed as the modern period in Indian history, I consider the *sannyasi* and the *fakir* rebellion[22] as the first mighty challenge that the British faced in India and it took them almost thirty-five years to uproot it. Spread from Bengal to eastern UP this was an uprising of the peasantry wherein the Hindu *sannyasis*

[22] J.M. Ghosh, *Sanyasi and Fakir Raiders* (Calcutta, 1930); William R. Pinch, *Warrior Ascetics and Indian Empires* (Cambridge, 2006).

and the Muslim *fakirs* provided an ideological impetus to the peasants. And the same Hindu–Muslim unity was to be witnessed during 1857. A Mughal emperor, whose authority had been confined to a few lanes of Chandni Chowk in Delhi was not only once again proclaimed the *Badshah* (Emperor) of India but the most orthodox of the Hindu princes and leaders of 1857 like Nana Saheb, Kunwar Singh, Rani Laxmi Bai and a host of others, the common men and women, the Hindu and Muslim *sipahis* jointly not only accepted him as their emperor but fought the British under his banner. The call to the people was *Dilli chalo* (let's go to Delhi) the capital of the Mughal empire and not Calcutta—the capital of the British in India. In fact, it was the communal unity of this period that shaped the future British policies towards India and no doubt that the revolts of the peasants like the Moplahs were painted into communal colours by the British. The memories of 1857 always haunted the British who would go to any extent to ensure that the two communities do not unite against them, hence, a policy of divide and rule. Yet, religion, in the absence of modern ideologies remained an impetus for the Indians to oppose the British. In every peasant uprising we find a *baba* or a *sadhu* or a *faqir* making use of religious literature or symbols of both Hindus and Muslims for political mobilization at the grassroots levels. However, this mobilization encouraged communal harmony and joint struggles against the British and the landlords. This usage was contrary to the use of religion by the dominant groups and political parties.[23] A few examples of such usage are cited below:

1. In December 1920 a Kisan Sabha[24] meeting was organized at Ajodhya and about 80,000 peasants attended it in spite of the strong efforts of the British and the taluqdars to stop it. The doors

[23] See Kapil Kumar, 'The *Ramcharitmanas* as a Radical Text: Baba Ram Chandra in Oudh, 1920–50' in Sudhir Chandra (ed.), *Social Transformation and Creative Imagination* (Delhi, 1984), pp. 311–13. Also see Kapil Kumar, 'Peasants, Congress and the Struggle for Freedom: 1917–39', in Kapil Kumar (ed.), *The Congress and Classes: Peasants, Workers and Nationalism* (New Delhi), 1988, p. 227.

[24] Baba Ram Chandra Papers, Part I, SF Nos. 1 and 2A, NMML, New Delhi. Also see Kapil Kumar, *Peasants in Revolt*, op. cit., pp. 115–17.

of mosques and temples were thrown open to all. The leader of this movement was Baba Ram Chandra, a Maharashtrian brahmin who made extensive use of the verses of *Ramcharitmanas* to mobilize the peasants, define British rule and their exploitation by the taluqdars. The slogan of '*Jai Sita Ram*' became the war cry shouted by all peasants whether a Hindu or a Muslim.[25] The Baba moved around with *Ramayana* in one hand and Koran in the other. Here, was a use of religious literature and symbols for unity and mobilization of peasants against the exploiters which became more extensive when the revolt started.

2. In January 1921, when the peasants revolted, the call was that a person from each house should participate. In case a house failed to provide one, the family would incur the sin of killing four cows if Hindu or eating four pigs, if a Muslim.[26] This was a unity that brought back the memories of 1857 as Oudh had been its main centre.
3. During the Aika movement in Oudh in 1922, Madari Pasi mobilized the peasants through the recitation of *Katha Sat Narayan* and *Milad Sharief.* Hindus and Muslims in thousands attended the meetings where a hole would be dug into the ground and after pouring water into it, this would be taken to represent the holy Ganga River on which everyone would take a vow to be united.[27]
4. A similar unity was seen during the 1930s in practically all the movements launched under the All India Kisan Sabha in different parts of the country. The most striking feature is to cite the Commilla session of the AIKS in 1938. Commilla was predominantly populated by Muslim peasants and Bengal had a coalition government of Proja Krishak Party and Muslim League. Efforts were made by these parties to check the participation of Muslim peasants in the session. Writings from the holy Koran on pieces of papers were kept on the way to the venue with the belief that

[25] Ibid., p. 84.

[26] For strong unity amongst the Hindus and Muslim peasants see ibid., pp. 124–55.

[27] See ibid., pp. 191, 193, 199.

> the Muslims would not walk over them. The Muslim peasants came in large numbers, picked up these papers and kissed them, touched them with their foreheads and walked to the session.[28] Swami Sahajanand Saraswati, the president of the AIKS delivered a strong speech advocating that bread is greater than God. He stressed that only human beings worship God so his existence depends on the existence of human beings. For the existence of human beings you need bread and hence bread is greater than God. He accused God of taking care of those only who place costly offerings to him which the peasants can't do. So God is for the rich landlords and capitalists only and he should change himself.[29]

One can go on citing such examples of unity and joint struggles at different occasions during the freedom movement. The Revolutionary stream threw up revolutionaries from all communities and it was no coincidence that *halal* and *jhatka* mutton were cooked together at the meetings of the *Naujavan Bharat Sabha*—the student wing of the revolutionaries.[30] The formation and the operations carried out by the Indian National Army under the leadership of Rashbehari Bose and Subhas Chandra Bose is another unique example of Hindu–Muslim unity where the Indians settled in South-East Asia rendered all possible support to the INA. This unity was put to test again when after the war the British put on trial the INA prisoners intentionally picking Dhillon—a Sikh, Sehgal—a Hindu and Shah Nawaz—a Muslim. The entire country stood behind them, once again demonstrating communal unity which the leadership

[28] M.A. Rasool, *History of All India Kisan Sabha* (Calcutta, 1974), p. 38, *India Annual Register*, Vol. 1, 1938, p. 349. Also see Kapil Kumar, 'Congress–Peasant Relationship in the Late 1930s', in D.N. Panigrahi (ed.), *Economy, Society and Politics in Modern India* (New Delhi, 1985), p. 247.

[29] Swami Sahajanand Saraswati, *Mera Jeevan Sangharsh* (Patna, 1952), pp. 5–8.

[30] See Yashpal, Sinhvalocan, *Bharat Mein Sashastra Kranti Ki Kahani*, Part One, Allahabad, 1st edn. 1951, 6th edn. 1978, p. 96. Cited in S. Irfan Habib, *To Make the Deaf Hear, Ideology and Programme of Bhagat Singh and His Comrades* (New Delhi, 2007), p. 46.

failed to utilize in opposing the partition demand. The Royal Naval Mutiny in 1946 at Indian ports again sent a message of Hindu–Muslim unity to fight out the British and again the champions of non-violent struggle ignored it. Obviously, the leaders' were 'a tired people'.[31]

V

Under the shadows of partition and the barbarous communal riots, the post-colonial independent India (a secular democratic republic) has witnessed different facets of relationships between the two communities in different parts of the country. However, communal riots have generally been an urban phenomenon with a very few exceptions. Mostly, they kept occurring in the industrial and semi-industrial cities, largely because of vote bank politics and in some cases for economic or criminal rivalries that are fought in the garb of a religious divide. Practically, every political party has made use of religion to increase its vote bank and accordingly distributed tickets to their cadres for contesting elections, with each claiming that the minorities will be safe or will flourish under their government. Similarly, their attitude towards the minorities is governed by political interests which at times takes the shape of appeasement and at others of a stick and carrot policy. In the midst of this the real voices that stand for communal harmony are lost or weakened. On the one hand, we have come out of that stage when one used to have a separate Hindu *pani* (drinking water) or Muslim *pani* at railway stations to a stage where people belonging to all communities share their festivals and other aspects of social and cultural life. On the other hand, there is communal rioting and suspicion wherein the sufferers are the common people of either community. It has been argued that the Muslim minority consciousness was shaken by the demolition of Babri Masjid at Ajodhya in 1992. Partially, this may be correct but one should not forget the riots of

[31] In fact, Sumit Sarkar has given a graphic account of the popular movements of this period. See Sarkar, 'Popular Movements and Leaderships, 1945–7', op. cit., pp. 677–89.

1984 when the Sikhs were massacred in the streets of Delhi leading one to question that if this can happen to the Sikhs under a Congress government then what could be the fate of other minorities? And yet credit must go to the common men and women of India that it is they who have maintained and contributed in strengthening the secular fabric of Indian society. Let me recall here some of my personal experiences in this regard among the common people.

In January 1971, immediately after the riots in Ahmedabad we were there for inter-state athletics and four of us went for dinner to a small restaurant. A small boy came running to us only to tell that this was a Muslim eating joint and Hindus don't eat there. By this time the owner had also joined him. I told him that we have come to eat and would you serve us or not? After knowing that we take non-vegetarian he did not take any order and pleaded that the menu should be left to him. We ate a delicious meal and when asked for the bill, it would not be given. When I insisted the answer was; 'Hindus have eaten for the first time in my place so how can I charge you?' I was emotionally touched, yet, told him that we are here for four days and would like to eat here every day, but if you won't charge us we would not come again. For two minutes this man thought and then said 'in that case I won't charge any profit from you' and asked us for a nominal amount. This is also a facet of the relationship, not to mention that many others must have had similar experiences with the common people.

How many people know that there is a village in Mathura where the first child born in a family is made a Muslim and the second a Hindu? Among the Moola jats (the jats who converted to Islam) no marriage is considered to have solemnized unless the couple has taken a round of the holy Tulsi plant. Thousands of *mazars* spread all over the country are visited by millions of Hindus every day. On the temple–masjid issue in Ajodhya a poor rickshaw puller suggested that 'why don't they open a post office there? All will come to buy the postcards', whereas the suggestion of a barber was 'to open a hospital there where the poor can be treated and this would be a service which both the Gods will approve'. Solutions very different from what the educated elite and the dominant people offer, sticking to their fanatic positions. Lack of space constrains me from citing more such experiences. On the other hand, among the dominant groups moneylending and gambling further aggravated the situation in places like my hometown Meerut—notorious for communal rioting. The big local businessmen take huge loans from the banks only to lend that money on higher interest rates to others. There are particular dates for paying the instalments and in case the banks are closed the dates are extended and they seek a rebate on interest for the closure period. However, this rebate they do not give to those who have borrowed from them. Hence engineering a communal riot by hiring criminals to do the job is a common thing for them to get the markets closed. Thirty kilometres away is the town of Hapur—the second largest grain market in north India. Gambling is the pass time for the grain merchants who often make heavy bets as to whether there will be a riot or not. This also leads to engineering of communal rioting. This demonstrates the inhuman and barbaric actions of the dominant social groups, *vis-à-vis* the lives of the common people. The ruling governments, both in the states and as well at the Centre, irrespective of which political party is ruling, are aware of such situations but fail to act or are reluctant to act because of vote banks.

Education and literacy have both failed to eradicate the menace of communal divide and rioting. On the contrary, the more the educated, the more communal people become among the dominant social groups 'of either community'. And this kind of lobbying is done not only on the lines of communities but also in the name of caste or region. Though no one will openly accept this, it is a hard fact that even the Indian bureaucracy and police have been no exceptions to this kind of ghettoization wherein groupings are formed on the basis of community, caste and region. At the same time, the biggest threat to secularism and harmonious inter-community relations in India emerges from the criminalization of politics. The Indian polity, over the years, has seen an increase of criminals entering the political life for whom human life has no value. In many cases, in league with the politicians, the criminals ignite communal riots. Erosion of values in social life has been another contributory factor. Gone are the days when respected elders within the communities would come together and resolve the differences, if any. Now, it is free for all with the politicians and criminals in the lead. Unless the common people realize this and stand against it, the situation is only going to worsen.

In fact, it is for the common people to resolve the problems at their own levels rather than always looking up to the government or outsiders to find solutions for them. For example, women have a major role to play in this as they are the first sufferers of communal disharmony or a riot. If the women take a firm stand, I doubt whether the men will have the guts to indulge in violence. Even if a few families take such an initiative in a colony it can emerge as a full movement at the local grassroots level that could be a lesson for the Indian leadership and politicians.

Unfortunately, the diaspora perceptions[32] about inter-community relations in India are founded on media reporting or interaction with the educated elite, dominant social groups—the sources available to them. They are not based on the actions and thoughts of the common people.

Today's media is more governed by the market economy with intense competition among the electronic channels to break the news first to report or for exclusive coverage of events. There is little sense of socially responsible marketing in advertisements[33] and in many cases immature, inexperienced and untrained reporters report from the field on highly sensitive issues that have a bearing on social harmony and community relations. I am all for the freedom of the media but then the media too has to develop its own ethics or code of conduct on social responsibility.

For the last twenty years another dimension that has affected the relationship is terrorism. Fortunately, this has not led to communal riots that the terrorists aimed for but it has created waves of

[32] For a recent study in this regard see Papiya Ghosh, *Partition and The South Asian Diaspora: Extending the Subcontinent* (New Delhi, 2007).

[33] The author has done a study on advertising in electronic media in relation to social values. See Kapil Kumar, *Advertising in Electronic Media: The Death of Socially Responsible Marketing*, Press Council of India, Seminar Proceedings, 16 November 2006, pp. 38–41.

anger. What is needed is an extremely sincere effort on the part of the state to ensure that religious harmony is not disturbed; an equally effective effort has to be from the side of religious leadership to ensure that their religions are not hijacked by the terrorists.[34] Unfortunately, the state has failed to initiate action against all those few who preach hatred among different communities irrespective of their religion, region or caste.

Fanatics, who threaten of another Pakistan or lay a price on Taslima's head, those who preach that Muslims have no place in India or those who rake regional or communal hatred have to be dealt with as per the law of the land. Instead, the state has a policy of appeasement for both because of vote politics. Such tendencies ought to be nipped in the bud.

The state has to ensure that all the resources for development are equally available to all citizens rather then making statements that the minorities have the first right to these resources. Such political statements only vitiate the atmosphere rather than doing any good for the minorities. Let all be treated as equal citizens with equal rights and responsibilities and initiate methods that the people move forward rather than going back to outdated medieval ideologies as a solution to their problems.

There have been quite a few post-riot studies but the findings don't get reflected in policy formation. Such studies get submerged in the seminar rooms or academic journals, rather than going to the people or get lost in the blame game. Most of the NGOs too appear on the scene after the riots though the need is to work all the time in sensitive areas which are mostly known and identified in India. Moreover, it is for the people to fight fanaticism within their own communities' right at the colony or village level rather than always looking for solutions from above. It is time that we come out of stereotype theoretical models to understand the empirical reality and urge upon the dominant groups to follow the

[34] The recent united opposition to terrorism by the followers of all religions in India after 26 November 2008 Mumbai attacks is not only laudable but is an eye-opener to those who intend to create a wedge among the communities or those who support terrorists.

feelings of the common people. With a paradigm shift, let us teach, propagate, showcase and apply the reverse models of studying peace and harmony to help re-conciliation amongst the communities and build a peaceful society not only in relation to inter-community relations based on religions but also based on castes/regions keeping in view the Indian context and internationally, the ethinicity, nationalities and religions. More and more scholars have to come forward to research the instances and events of harmony, adaptation and assimilation and their findings should reach the common people—not just confined as referred research papers to a few academics or libraries and seminar rooms.

In fact, the researchers would do a great service in the context of inter-community relations in India by researching how the Indian Diaspora in Trinidad and Tobago, Mauritius and other countries has marginalized the caste within the Indian community and developed harmonious relations with other communities. Here, you meet a family whose members follow and respect three different religions. I would like to end this paper by citing my experience at the University of West Indies in Trinidad. I have a student whose name is Rehana Madhu. I asked her whether she knew that the first name is Muslim and the second a Hindu? She answered in affirmative and added that she was a Christian and her husband a Hindu. Here is a society where Asha Mahbeer, Nafisa Ali and Daniel are first cousins-respecting, participating in and celebrating each others religious festivals. Indians, back home need to learn and follow such harmonious relationships, rather than felling prey to the political interests of all shades.

Index